FROM WOUNDED HEARTS

From Wounded Hearts: Faith Stories of Lesbian, Gay, Bisexual, and Transgendered People and Those Who Love Them

Copyright © 1998 by Roberta Showalter Kreider.

All rights reserved. No part of this publication may be reproduced, stored in a retrieval system, or transmitted in any form or by any means, electronic, mechanical, photocopy, recording, or otherwise, without the written permission of **Chi Rho Press, Inc.** For information, address Chi Rho Press, Inc., P.O. Box 7864, Gaithersburg, MD 20898-7864, USA.

Printed in the United States of America.

ISBN 1-888493-15-1

The cover art was designed by Bonita Kreider Nussbaum, the youngest daughter of Roberta and Harold Kreider. Ms. Nussbaum lives in Eugene, Oregon, with her husband Dean, and two sons, Ben (13) and Zak (10). She teaches adult education classes for high school dropouts at Lane Community College. Her interests include quilting, gardening, and reading. Bonita and her family like to travel, camp, hike, and enjoy participating in various sports.

Chi Rho Press, Inc.
P.O. Box 7864
Gaithersburg, MD 20898, USA
301/926-1208 phone/fax
ChiRhoPrss@aol.com e-mail

FROM WOUNDED HEARTS

Faith Stories of Lesbian, Gay, Bisexual, and Transgendered People and Those Who Love Them

Compiled and Edited by
Roberta Showalter Kreider

Chi Rho Press, Inc.
Gaithersburg, Maryland, USA

With Appreciation to Our Investors

Ten individuals, couples, and organizations had such faith in this project that they invested in promissory notes to make the publication of *From Wounded Hearts* possible. The editor and the publisher wish to thank the following people for their love and support:

Edmund Good III

James L. Helmuth

Lois and Clif Kenagy

Jo A. Longenecker and Laurinda Beckstead

J.R. Burkholder

Peggy Campolo

Brethren/Mennonite Parents

and three others who wish their

contribution to remain anonymous.

We thank them for making this book possible.

To Harold,
my faithful husband, lover, and friend
for over 50 years,
with love and appreciation
for the beautiful person YOU are.

and

To the memory of my brother Ray,
whose wounded heart
gave me the impetus to begin
this journey.

Table of Contents

vii

Acknowledgments

I want to express appreciation and gratitude,

— To God, the Creator and Lover of us all,

◆ for the increasing joy that has been mine as I have searched for the truth that is setting me free;

◆ for all the beautiful, caring people God has brought into my life as I have worked with these stories;

◆ for choosing me to be the instrument by which these stories could be told. I love books, but never dreamed that I would ever have a book published. As it became clear to me that God was asking me to bring these stories to the world, I wondered if I would really have the ability to do it. When I said, "yes," and set myself to the task, it was truly amazing how God was ahead of me every step of the way. Through it all my prayer has been, "Oh, God, please help me to be all that **you** sent me into the world to be — nothing more and nothing less." The strength and wisdom for *From Wounded Hearts* has truly been a gift from God;

◆ for providing a computer and giving me the skills I needed to use it much faster than I thought could be possible. Every time I encountered an obstacle, there was always some friend I could turn to for help. I remember one night during the early stages when I was terribly tired and frustrated and nobody seemed to know the answer to my question. I prayed, "Oh, God, please show me what to do." Then once again I clicked my mouse on format and searched for options. Suddenly, I saw "auto format." I timidly clicked it, and presto, that problem was solved for that particular story and I went to bed with gratitude.

♦ for all the surprises and affirmations God brought to me when I needed them the most.

— To my husband, Harold Kreider, for his constant encouragement, for believing I could really put a book together, for freeing me from many household chores, for often doing my share of our weekly church meetinghouse cleaning, for proofreading the stories and giving helpful suggestions, and for supporting me every step of the way.

— To all the authors for their inspiring stories, for their many hours of work, and for trusting me with this intimate part of their lives. The joy that many of them expressed for the opportunity to tell their stories has been a great incentive to me.

— To Rose Moyer, an answer to a prayer I never fully prayed. One morning in November 1997, I felt overwhelmed by the mountains of correspondence and the needed time to get the typing and editing done. As I headed toward my computer, I said, "Oh, God, how am I ever going to do it all? I could use a secretary, but I know we can not afford one." I felt assured again that God would give me the needed strength and wisdom and I sat down to begin the day's work. Two or three hours later, this young woman from our church called, "Roberta," she said, "I feel so badly about what has happened to Germantown.[1] As I was thinking about what I could do to help, I thought of you and your book. I think that book is very important and I want to help you." Rose is an excellent typist and an expert in computer skills. She offered to type the stories for me and put them on diskettes for my computer so I could edit them. She saved me many hours of work. She also shared her computer expertise with me and carefully worked out some computer glitches.

— To our daughter, Bonnie Kreider Nussbaum, for her encouragement and for taking time from her busy schedule to design the cover. She designed and redesigned it until we could both feel good about it.

---

[1] Gay and lesbian people living in committed relationships are members of Germantown (Pennsylvania) Mennonite Church. In October of 1997, a majority of the delegates from the Franconia Mennonite Conference voted to expel the Germantown congregation from the conference body.

— To Mary Lou Clemens and Rob Yoder who gave me editorial and publishing advice and encouragement. Rob also reviewed the terms of my contract with the publisher and gave helpful suggestions.

— To Darwin Zehr, another computer genius, for giving me an entire evening of training and to Ed Meyers for responding cheerfully to my telephone calls for help.

— To Howard Cohen, proprietor of Computer Station in Lansdale, Pennsylvania, who *did not just sell me a computer and forget about me,* but invited me to call him whenever I needed help. He walked me through many problems and gave me encouragement to make me feel that, even at my age, I could learn how to use this challenging modern tool. I appreciate his time and patience with me.

— To Judy Hartheimer, a journalist friend, who gave me valuable help and suggestions for seeking a publisher and for connecting me with Rabbi Alpert.

— To our friend Peggy Campolo, who has been an inspiration to me in my journey of faith. It is not an easy path for those of us who choose to walk with our lesbian, gay, bisexual, and transgendered sisters and brothers and their families. In seeking justice for the oppressed, as modeled by Jesus, we are thankful for Peggy's companionship along the way. I am honored to have her write the foreword for this book.

— To all our PFLAG (Parents, Families, and Friends of Lesbians and Gays) friends for their suggestions and excitement about the book.

— To all the gay people, parents, and friends who felt this book important enough to make a financial investment to assure an early publication.

— To R. Adam DeBaugh, my editor and publisher at Chi Rho Press. The very first time I contacted him, he was excited about the book. He has worked with me as a team player, not as a boss. I appreciate his sensitivity to my concern that every story be valued and edited with care. He has given the rare privilege to the authors and me to have the *final* word on how each story is presented. I have found Adam to be a very sensitive and caring person. It is my joy to count him as my friend and brother in the family of God.

— To Peggy Cramer, Grace Marie Gerber, and Hilda Landis who gave valuable assistance in the final proofreading of the book.

I hope I have not forgotten anyone, but if I have, please feel included as I say to **every one** who prayed for me, encouraged me, shared in postage expenses, or helped in any other way, "from the depth of my heart, **thank you!**"

Roberta Showalter Kreider

Publisher's Note

How *From Wounded Hearts* has come to be in your hands is a remarkable story. In February of this year (1998), I received a phone call from a very sweet sounding woman which began something like this: "My name is Roberta Kreider. I am a 72-year-old Mennonite heterosexual woman in rural Pennsylvania. My husband is a retired minister in the Mennonite Church. I have a book I hope you will be interested in publishing."

Now, my usual line to friends is that if I had a ten dollar sale for every page of unsolicited manuscript that crossed my desk Chi Rho Press would be as large as Random House by now. So I am understandably reluctant to encourage just anybody who wants to tell me about their book. Besides knowing the very high percentage of people who believe they have a book in them, as well as what I know about the position the Mennonite Church takes on homosexuality made me very skeptical. But one thing I learned early on as a publisher is never to reject any potential author out of hand — you never know where your next best seller is going to come from and God does work in mysterious ways, after all.

I thought it might be useful to point out to Mrs. Kreider that Chi Rho Press is a Christian publishing house serving (and largely publishing works by) the lesbian, gay, bisexual, and transgendered community. (After years of exclusively producing the work of LGBT authors, our first non-gay book and non-gay author, *My Memory Book: A Journal for Grieving Children* by Gretchen Gaines-Lane, published in 1995, has turned out to be a very important book and a best seller for Chi Rho Press.)

Of course, that did not faze Roberta Kreider a bit and she told me her book was by gay people and their families telling their faith stories. She explained that she had changed her mind about homosexuality as a result of getting to know gay people of faith and hearing the stories of their faith journeys (you will find her story of how God changed her mind in Chapter 50 of this volume). Since the publication in 1995 of *Called OUT! The Voices and Gifts of Lesbian, Gay, Bisexual, and Transgendered Presbyterians* (another best seller for Chi Rho Press), I have been fascinated by anthologies of LGBT people telling the stories of their spiritual journeys. I was immediately interested.

Roberta explained that she believed God would work on changing the hearts and minds of people of faith if they could only hear the stories of sexual minority people. She recalled how touched she and her husband Harold have been by the very personal, intimate, and often startling stories with which gay people have entrusted them. The lasting impression of these powerful tales, Roberta explained, was the genesis of this present volume.

By this time in our conversation I was not only intrigued by the idea, but totally captivated by Roberta herself! She is a woman of great strength, strong opinions, and deep, abiding faith. She is also persistent and strong willed, insistent and thoroughly delightful! We started talking seriously about Chi Rho Press publishing *From Wounded Hearts*. Roberta asked how soon it could be published. I replied, honestly, that a book can sometimes take up to three years. We are a small publishing house and move at an all too stately pace with most projects. I also told her that we had two other books in the pipeline which needed to be published before we could get to her book. Roberta astounded me by responding, with the perfect assurance that comes to people of great faith, that a lot of people want the book to be published by the beginning of July. I patiently tried to explain how difficult that would be, but Roberta cut right to the chase — "What would it take to get this book published by the beginning of July?"

The honest answer that I gave her was one word, "money." If we had cash in hand, either through sales or loans, the book could move speedily ahead. Without batting an eye this remarkable woman responded with supreme confidence that she was quite certain that her friends would come forward to raise whatever we needed. Roberta was as good as her word.

Ten individuals and couples have made loans to enable this book to be published. Not only has Roberta's vision of the importance of this collection of stories captured my imagination and commitment, but her enthusiasm and conviction is contagious. Many others have caught the excitement. *From Wounded Hearts* has had the highest advance sales of any book ever published by Chi Rho Press.

We are pleased and proud to bring *From Wounded Hearts: Faith Stories of Lesbian, Gay, Bisexual, and Transgendered People and Those Who Love Them* to you. In this volume you will find stories that charm you and anger you, inspire you to fear, pity, and joy, and perhaps, just perhaps, if you have doubts about the place of God's sexual minority children in the scheme of things, this book might help change your mind.

The 49 people whose stories you read here comprise a cross section of spiritual life in North America. They are from the United States of America and Canada. They come from many different religious backgrounds. Many of the writers here share the Anabaptist background of Roberta and Harold Kreider, Mennonites, Brethren, and Brethren in Christ. However, there are also folks from the American Baptist, Assemblies of God, Eastern Orthodox, Episcopalian, Lutheran, Methodist, Metropolitan Community Churches, Nazarene, Pentecostal, Presbyterian, Roman Catholic, Quaker, Southern Baptist, and United Church of Christ traditions, as well as a Jewish rabbi. The first section is by lesbian, gay, bisexual, and transgendered people. The second section contains articles written by "those who love them," parents, spouses, children, other family members, and friends.

In addition to all the people whom Roberta thanks in her Acknowledgments, I want to recognize the gifts and commitment of Kevin Stone Fries, the assistant editor at Chi Rho Press, for his long hours of painstaking work on this manuscript — often under a pressing deadline. The strength of Kevin's professionalism and commitment to our work is indicated by the fact that he is already at work on the next manuscript we hope to publish! I am extremely grateful for the skill and expertise he brings to this work.

We have edited the articles in this anthology rather lightly in order to preserve the authentic voice of each person. These are their words, their faith stories. While keeping in mind that many of the authors are not professional writers, we tried to balance the expectations of the general reader and the individual histories of the contributors. The first priority of Mrs. Kreider and Chi Rho Press is to maintain the integrity and authenticity of the contributors' faith journeys. It is our hope that the variety of perspective and style presented will only add to your enjoyment of *From Wounded Hearts*.

The articles in this book are characterized by sometimes jarring honesty, frankness, and vulnerability. Some of the articles are filled with pain as a result of how the writer or the writer's family member has been treated by the church. Some of the stories are triumphant. Some of the stories are sad. Some of our 49 authors have had to remain anonymous for various reasons. There are four parent-child pairings, with a chapter in the first section written by a gay person and one in the second section written by that person's parent or, in one case, daughter. Reading this book will certainly give you some understanding of the great diversity of the lesbian, gay, bisexual, and transgendered community and our families.

Ultimately, this book is not only a tribute to the amazing woman who pulled it all together. This book is also a tribute to the faith and struggle of every person who had a hand in its creation. The courage and commitment of these people has been a source of encouragement, joy, and inspiration to us here at Chi Rho Press. I hope it will be so for you. I gladly commend *From Wounded Hearts* to you with pride.

R. Adam DeBaugh
Director, Chi Rho Press, Inc.
6 July 1998

Foreword

For more than ten years now, my heart and my life's work have been with God's lesbian, gay, bisexual, and transgendered children. Coming to the realization that God wanted me to do this has been an integral part of my walk with Jesus Christ and my endeavor to follow the leading of the Holy Spirit. There has been much joy in my journey.

Sometimes, however, I feel as though I do not really belong anywhere. There are those of my lesbian, gay, bisexual, and transgendered friends who think that my strong belief in the Bible and in Jesus Christ makes me far too fundamental and narrow for them. On the other hand, because I believe that LGBT people are entitled to all of the rights that I, as a heterosexual person, enjoy — including the right to be married under the law of the land and with the blessing of the Church, many in the evangelical church think I am too liberal. My own dear husband's understanding of Scripture keeps him from being in complete agreement with me, even though we share a common commitment to justice for LGBT people.

Evangelicals Concerned is one group with which I feel at home and I am always looking for others. Several years ago, I found such a place when I spoke to a Brethren-Mennonite group called Connecting Families. This is a gathering of persons who are dealing with homosexuality — their own or that of a loved one. They gain strength, insight, and courage from coming together to share their stories.

The people I met at Connecting Families sang the old hymns with which I, the daughter of an American Baptist pastor, had grown up. They carried Bibles, too — many of them big Bibles. But the difference between them and some of the other people I had met who carried big Bibles was that these folks knew what the Bible really says. They were a living testimony to what the Bible has to say about unconditional love and the grace of God.

I was the speaker that weekend, but for me it was far more important that I was a listener.

Roberta Kreider was one of those to whom I listened. She and her husband Harold walked up to the front of the room together, and it was the strength of both of them that had found the courage to tell the story, even though it was told in Roberta's voice. Like everyone else in that room, I sat spellbound as she talked. Roberta is a good storyteller.

She told of her childhood with three older brothers and the baby brother who was such a delight to her. She called him Baby Ray. I will not repeat all of Roberta's story, because she tells it so well herself. [**Publisher's Note:** Roberta's story is found in Chapters 49 and 50 of this volume.] Suffice it to say here that nothing in Roberta's life prepared her for the time when she learned that her beloved brother Ray was, not only a gay man, but about to die of AIDS.

However, prepared or not, Roberta was ready. She had the kind of faith in God that allowed her to listen and to see clearly. Slowly she pushed aside the curtain of those things she had always thought and been told all of her life, and allowed the Holy Spirit to guide her in a wonderful new direction. She read and she studied. She talked to people, seeking out those who would be unlikely to cross her path. At times she herself could hardly believe how much her attitudes and opinions were changing, but Roberta had the courage to trust in God's leading and in what her own loving heart was telling her she had to do.

In the beginning, Roberta did not know much about homosexuality except that she had always been certain that it was a bad thing — a sin. Her journey from that place to being the editor of this book is the old, old story of what God can do with a life surrendered to God's will and purpose.

Today Roberta is a friend, an educator, and an advocate for those lesbian, gay, bisexual, and transgendered persons too often overlooked or scorned by church people. As their friend, she is a caring listener to many who must carefully pick and choose those with whom they can safely share their truth. That Roberta has given a lot of herself to listen to people is clearly demonstrated by the number and variety of stories she has gathered for this book.

As an educator, Roberta has read and studied to learn the answers to many difficult questions. She keeps a library of material that she is always ready and willing to share, including books and articles that explain how the Bible has been misused to shut out some of God's children.

I am impressed by her willingness to learn and by her ability to consider and accept truths that are far different from some of those she previously believed. I am equally impressed by the tenacity and certainty with which Roberta clings to those truths that are eternal. I admire the way she uses her fine mind to think through each new idea. Roberta does not accept or reject either ideas or people in whole groups, but gives thoughtful consideration to each one.

An important part of the educating this lady does is that she and Harold invite individuals and small groups into their home to view and discuss video tapes. She is always delighted to receive an enlightening or inspiring video and usually knows right away to whom she would like to show it. Hearts and minds are changed in her home.

Roberta is an untiring advocate for the cause of justice for LGBT people. I believe that she is able to keep going because she does not see her work simply as being for a cause. For Roberta, what she does is always for people — always something she does in God's name for God's children. God used the tragic loss of her brother Ray to touch her heart, and Roberta's heart was big enough to include the others she saw to be suffering as Ray had suffered.

Whenever anyone steps forward to carry the burdens of others, they also accept the hurts of those others, and Roberta has known pain in her journey. Some of that pain has come from having her beliefs questioned and her motives misunderstood by those she loves. But to know Roberta is to know that the joy in her life far outweighs the pain.

I have never visited the grave of Ray Showalter, but in the work of his sister, I have seen the finest living memorial that any Christian could ever hope to have.

I am blessed to be able to call Roberta Kreider my friend.

Peggy Campolo
PO Box 565
Wayne, PA 19087

Peggy Campolo is a writer and editor. She is a graduate of Eastern College and taught first grade prior to spending a number of years as a full-time wife and mother.

Mrs. Campolo has worked in real estate and public relations, and actively supports the ministry and work of her husband, Dr. Tony Campolo. She is a working member of Evangelicals Concerned, and serves on the Council of the Association of Welcoming and Affirming Baptists and the Board of Directors of the Philadelphia Baptist Association. She has spoken at churches, colleges, and conferences throughout the United States.

Mrs. Campolo and her husband live in St. Davids, Pennsylvania. They are the parents of two grown children and have three grandchildren.

Introduction

Homosexuality is a word I seldom heard until I was almost 60 years old. I had only a dim concept of what AIDS was until one day in July 1984 when I entered my brother's hospital room for one last visit before he died two weeks later. What a shock it was to learn that my brother, the father of three of my nieces and a nephew, was gay!

Now, fourteen years later, homosexuality is a much debated topic in most, if not all, of the mainline Christian churches. This debate is also present in Jewish culture and in other religions of the world. Differences of opinion are causing painful divisions in churches and families. I have come to believe that sharing the faith stories of people of diverse sexual orientations can lead us to common ground and help us to better understand one another.

I have a deep concern for all the young people in our world today who have not come to terms with their sexual orientation. Far too often, the Church is not a safe place for them. They have no role models to whom they can turn. Their homes are not safe havens in which to grow and learn of God's love. They need to know that God loves them just the way they have been created. The Rev. Michael S. Piazza, senior pastor of the world's largest gay and lesbian church (Cathedral of Hope Metropolitan Community Church, Dallas, Texas), opens a window for us to see the damage that is done by well-meaning counselors:

> Over the past twenty years as a pastor, I have counseled hundreds of people who had given up all hope of living happy, healthy, and holy lives because of the lies some homophobic pastor, priest, parent, or teacher told them. For those of us who grew up in evangelical or conservative Christian homes, wrestling

with faith and sexuality is difficult enough. For many lesbian and gay people, the struggle for too long resulted in only two options: One could sacrifice one's sexual integrity or give up one's faith. Hundreds, perhaps thousands, of men and women, young and old, have told me of their tortured journey as they tried to give up being gay but could not. They believed their only option was to give up being Christian. One young man said in all honesty, "Hey, if I am going to hell anyway, I may as well enjoy the trip." I never could convince him he had an alternative. That young man is dead now, the victim of a drug overdose.

The homo-hatred of the religious right has driven so many beautifully-gifted women and men into the arms of suicide, alcoholism, promiscuity, and self-destruction. It is impossible to overstate the damage done in human lives when they are made to believe they cannot be children of the God who created them.[1]

I am also very concerned about the many people who are driven into unnatural and unhappy marriages because most churches insist that there can be no other union than that between a man and a woman. I am distressed to hear of the damage done by organizations that claim to help people change their sexual orientation. Rev. Piazza shares from his experiences:

Over the years many people have claimed that God has transformed their sexual orientation. They said God removed or healed their homosexuality, but of the hundreds of people I know personally who went through such changes, every one of them eventually came to realize that all the "transformations" removed was their integrity. Out of more than three thousand people who attend our church, several hundred of them were once "ex-gays." Their stories are even more tragic due to the fact that under their religious delusion of being "delivered," they often married and, in many cases, had children. Often their spouses and children

---

[1] Reprinted by permission from *Holy Homosexuals: The Truth About Being Gay or Lesbian and Christian* by Michael S. Piazza. Dallas, TX: Sources of Hope Publishing House, 2nd ed., 1995, pp. 4 and 5.

also became victims of the religious right that forced innocent women and men to live a lie while trying to save their souls.[2]

All of us know gay or lesbian people. We have known them all of our lives. We are just not aware that they are gay. They work with us, they are doctors, nurses, lawyers, dentists, ministers, professors, artists, authors, cooks, entrepreneurs, and more. They sit with us in the church pews on Sunday morning. They teach our Christian Education classes and they serve on church committees. We value their friendship and opinions **until** — they can no longer live with themselves if they continue to hide who they are. It is so sad that they must live a lie in order to make people feel comfortable with them.

It is easy to judge and condemn someone whom we do not know. It is especially easy to judge a group of people whom we think do not measure up to our interpretation of what the Bible says. However, when we take time to learn to know gay people as individuals, our perception of them changes. This is why it is so important to tell our faith stories to one another. As the issue of homosexuality is debated in our churches we seldom ask the people we are calling sinners to tell us about their own personal experience of relationship with God. My own life and attitude has been profoundly changed by listening to the stories of lesbian, gay, bisexual, and transgendered people and their families. My conviction became very strong that in some way a forum must be provided for us to tell our stories. Finally, I realized that God was asking me to make it possible for some of these stories to be heard.

I pray that all who read this book can know that I truly am seeking to follow God in the way Jesus modeled. I want every reader to know that even if you do not agree with me, I trust that you also are sincerely seeking to follow God's way. None of us has *all* the right answers. My hope is that we can keep searching for the truth together and trusting that God will guide us all.

I am slowly learning to listen with love and care to the stories of *all* people God brings into my life. I am discovering

---

[2] Ibid. p. 9.

that I can rejoice in the beauty and integrity of each one's search for God. As we share our understanding of our Creator, we can inspire each other to walk more intimately with God.

I am neither called to judge nor coerce others to my viewpoint, but to allow each person to be where they are in their journey with God. I still have a long way to go because it does not come naturally to me. I grew up believing that it was my God-given duty to evangelize the world. To evangelize did not mean to tell the good news that in Jesus Christ we are all free to become what God wills us to be. Rather it meant to present the good news in such a way that people would feel guilty if they did not agree with my viewpoint. It is so liberating to know that my task is not to judge and condemn, but to love. "There is no fear in love, but perfect love casts out fear, for fear has to do with punishment, and whoever fears has not reached perfection in love" (1 John 4:8, New Revised Standard Version). Fear and judgmental attitudes cast out love, and create distance between me and others. These attitudes do not draw people to know and to love God.

In this book, people of different backgrounds have shared their stories of faith. The authors of these stories have grown up in various denominations and synagogues in the United States and Canada. Readers may find here a faith story of someone you love and admire. The stories reflect a wide variety of belief. Some stories may be threatening to the reader. Some may seem to you to lack faith entirely. Some experiences are similar, but each one is unique. The rich diversity of God's creation is evident. I invite you to read each story with love and care. If these journeys of faith help you to personally know individuals of different sexual orientations and enable you to hear what they are saying, this book will accomplish its purpose.

Roberta Showalter Kreider

E-mail address: Kreiders@juno.com

FROM WOUNDED HEARTS

Faith Stories of Lesbian, Gay, Bisexual, and Transgendered People and Those Who Love Them

Part One

Faith Stories of Lesbian, Gay, Bisexual, and Transgendered People

1

Rejected By The Church — Chosen By God

Martin R. Rock

I am the infamous Martin Rock from Washington, D.C. I am the Martin Rock that people have been trying to shut up for over 20 years! Conference moderators, conference officers, local churches, and Church of the Brethren pastors want to silence me. Most of my relatives and church leadership would probably be glad if I would just disappear from the public arena.

I was raised in a conservative family and church. The church said we could not have a television and only certain clothing was appropriate for church. We could not go bowling, play pool, or play card games. Smoking and drinking were not allowed. I was taught to stay away from Jews, Catholics, Mormons, and African-Americans (a different word was used then and it was not "black"). Also, I was to avoid homosexuals.

In my younger days, I worked briefly for the U.S. Government in Washington, D.C. I met all kinds of people. Coworkers were self-identified as Brown-skinned, Black, or Negroes. Others had yellow and red skin, most had white skin. They were Catholic, Jewish, Mormon, and Baptist. I was in trouble with my parents! But, I started to know people as people and as Christians. Wonderful people! I worked with these people in an office of the State Department that tried to refuse passports to American communists! My real education was beginning to happen.

During this time I was quite involved in the Washington City Church of the Brethren. I also visited people in their homes who were newcomers to the worship services. I told them about my faith and what the church and Christ meant to me.

From the time I was a kid, I heard pastors say things like, "I was called by God to the ministry." I always thought to myself, "Sure! God came down from Heaven and told you to be a pastor the rest of your life. Sure God did!" Until one morning during the worship service, *it happened to me.* It was a very physical and emotional experience. It was clear: God called me to work for the church for the rest of my life, but not in the pastorate. My pastor, of course, thought the calling was for me to be in the pastoral ministry. I told him that it was very clear what God told me. So, we decided that I should go into Brethren Volunteer Service (BVS).

At that time, BVS volunteers did not have too much to say about where they were assigned. I was called to work as an assistant to the director of BVS at the Church of the Brethren headquarters. I was upset when they announced I was going to Elgin, Illinois, instead of mental health work. That night I prayed about it and it became very clear to me that God wanted me to go to Elgin to work for the church. I was to go where the church needed me. Working at Elgin was quite an education. I met all kinds of people from all over the world. I worked there for about two and one-half years.

After BVS and a few interim months at the National Interreligious Service Board for Conscientious Objectors, I went to work for a church agency in Pennsylvania. I worked at the headquarters for about three years. Then I was asked to go to Vietnam. Again, it was a very clear calling. Within a month I was working for Vietnam Christian Service as a representative of my church agency.

I loved Vietnam and I loved my job! As part of my administrative duties in Saigon, I traveled a lot around the country to see our over 200 Vietnamese and foreign workers at our projects. I was in some very dangerous situations. I was caught in cross fire and rocket attacks, near strafing, escaped crazy soldiers, and flew in a plane being hit by gunfire. Once I was strapped to the outside of a helicopter because there was no room inside. Fortunately, they flew at least a mile off the ground to avoid possible gunfire. In thinking back, I believe I handled those experiences better than I cope with the way the Church treats me today. While I was in Asia, my agency also sent me to Japan, Hong Kong, India, and Indonesia to see what God was doing through the agency in those countries.

After about three years in Vietnam I was ready to ask for an extension of my term, but I received a cable asking me to return to work in the Africa Department at the headquarters in Pennsylvania. God's calling to continue to work for the church was very clear. I worked in that department for five years. I handled the day-to-day operations of the Africa programs with a multimillion dollar yearly budget plus other millions in relief funds to dip into for disasters. I traveled to Africa and Europe and throughout the U.S. on speaking engagements. On one trip I brought back $100,000 in contributions for our work. It was too bad I did not work on commission! One year I received the second largest raise in salary in the agency. They liked me for 11 years as a dedicated coworker, good friend, and committed Christian — *until* —

One day I was asked by my boss and the personnel director if I was gay. I did not lie. They asked for my resignation. I refused. Proceedings were then put into motion to fire me. Proper personnel procedures were not used. Rumors were circulated around the office building and across the country by staff members. When they started to receive letters and phone calls from prominent pastors, the president of a seminary, a prominent theologian, Executive Committee members, etc., they had to rethink what they were about to do.

I was told that when it went to the Executive Committee, I would be allowed to give my viewpoint, but that was a lie. Late one evening, after the staff was excused, the Executive Committee went into closed session and talked about me for an hour. This committee almost always rubber-stamped everything and hardly ever talked about an issue longer than 15 to 30 minutes.

The next day my boss and the personnel director each told me different versions of what happened at the committee meeting. I contacted a friend on the Executive Committee who told me that they gave the issue back to the staff to work out, and that firing was the last resort. So, the staff had to dialogue with me. This necessitated their going to the agency's lawyer and to the State Assistant Attorney General. They checked with a local mental health facility. They started their own education!

I was the first gay person to fight back. In the agency's overseas program, each time a heterosexual man was caught having an affair, his hand was slapped and he was told not to do it again. If it was a heterosexual woman, she was transferred to another country. If it was a gay man, he was on the next plane home and whatever lie he made up about leaving his project early would be perpetuated by headquarters. I had fought for many other causes during my time with that agency. They knew that I would fight for this one also.

I lost several good friends. Some staff members told me they disagreed with homosexuality, but they thought it was terrible that I was being kicked out. A few friends stuck by me. I had six months left on my contract. The final decision was to allow me to finish, but the contract would not be renewed.

I was blacklisted for six months by my immediate supervisor. He felt it was necessary to tell future employers of my sexual orientation if they contacted him for a reference. The executive director of the agency was not aware of this blacklisting until I confronted him with my suspicion that he was also part of it. He told me that, hereafter, I should use his name as the reference.

My supervisor felt I was no longer qualified to do my job. All incoming mail went to him and he decided who would handle it. So, I got very little mail except what he did not like to handle. He even responded to mail that I would normally have turned over to our secretary. During this time, I thought perhaps God was changing my calling. Perhaps I was to do another type of work. I was not ready to believe that. It seemed that God was not answering my prayers. Through it all God taught me patience and better listening skills.

Nine months later I found a job in Washington, D.C., with an interfaith agency working on development, hunger, and family farm issues. They had a nondiscrimination policy for gay people. I served nine years with this agency. Then the female executive director left and we discovered that the new male director was a bigot. Of course, I was the first to go. He asked me what stipulations I wanted in order for me to leave the job as soon as possible. They did not agree to my terms and hired a $200-an-hour lawyer for many hours. I engaged a lawyer for $75 for one hour. They became very upset because I hired a lawyer! In the end, I received more money and benefits than I originally requested. The agency paid a high price to get rid of me!

God's presence was very real to me during the next nine months as I searched for another job. The job market in Washington, D.C., was not very good during that time. In spite of that, one Sunday afternoon I received a phone call from an ecumenical organization with offices in the same building where I had previously worked. It became very clear to me that this was where God wanted me to continue my witness. That was twelve years ago and I still am serving in this agency.

In 1976, while the church was trying to strip me of my employment, the agency staff was telling a lot of people across the country about my sexual orientation. So, I thought I had better tell my mother and stepfather this information myself rather than to have them hear it inaccurately from a third party. They listened and that seemed to be the extent of it. Three weeks later I received a letter telling me never to come home again. I also found out that my mother wrote to the whole family, including cousins, telling them of my gayness and instructing them to not allow a visit. If I did visit unannounced, I was to be kept away from the children. As do a lot of people, she confused gay people with pedophiles.

At first my mother would respond to my letters with a lot of Bible verses. Her letters became increasingly worse, so I wrote that I would respond only to letters that showed respect. I occasionally sent her birthday and Christmas cards. The last couple of years I received Christmas cards from her.

My brother and his wife were very accepting of me. After my brother was diagnosed with terminal cancer, I traveled from my home in Washington, D.C. to western Pennsylvania as many weekends as I could for the next two years. Since there was a ten-year difference in our ages, we did not know each other very well before his illness. I am glad that I got to know him as a friend before he died.

In 1978, two years after he had told me, my mother was informed of my brother's terminal illness. My brother felt that she needed to know since he had only about six months of life left. At that time I received the worst letter I have ever received in my life. I have received some horrible letters over the years from supposed Christians, but this was the most painful. My mother wrote that my brother was dying because God was punishing the family as a consequence for my not repenting my gayness. The last time I saw my mother was at my brother's funeral. During the viewing, my mother told all the relatives and friends that all her children were now dead. It was very sad because I was constantly beside my sister-in-law and everyone knew I was there.

My mother died in 1992. I am the only survivor of my immediate family. Within hours after her death, I started receiving phone calls from relatives I had not seen or heard from since my brother's funeral in 1978. They would bring me up to date on the happenings in their lives and then ask, "What did your mother's will say?" I did not know and was very glad to refer them to the executor. I was not encouraged to attend her funeral so I was not there. I was not in her will. Her furniture and personal belongings were divided by relatives and I received nothing. All I asked for were a few photographs of my father since I had only one, but that request was denied.

My father and my sister had died quite a number of years ago. My sister's husband and children have not kept in contact with me. My brother's wife and one of their children keep in touch. As always, I continue to pray for my family. Over the years I have helped various members of the family financially when they needed it. I gave advice when asked. I even did some amateur marriage counseling — and it worked!

I worked for the church and was regarded almost as a pastor — and as a missionary when I worked in Vietnam. In those days, I was placed on a pedestal. When I returned from Vietnam, I attended our family reunion with over 200 people.

As the returning missionary I was asked to give grace at the mealtime. A distant cousin's son, who was not out of high school yet, sat beside me to talk about church work because he was being encouraged to think about the possibility of seminary. However, my pedestal was pulled out from under me very quickly when the family learned I was gay.

Because I am gay, part of my journey has been very painful, yet, through it all I have felt God's presence sustaining me. Jesus Christ is my Savior. It is as simple as this: **I love God and God loves me.**

In 1976, **Martin R. Rock** founded the Brethren/Mennonite Council for Lesbian and Gay Concerns, a caucus for Brethren and Mennonite denominations (P.O. Box 6300, Minneapolis, MN 55406-0300. Phone: (612)722-6906.
E-mail: BMCouncil@aol.com).

Martin is single, a member of the Church of the Brethren, and resides in Washington, D.C.

2

At Least I Am Not Dying

Sherry E. Franklin

In December of 1956, I was born to a young married couple who lived in the suburbs of Philadelphia, Pennsylvania. My father was raised as a Christian Scientist and my mother as a Methodist. Once married, they both were practicing Methodists. Three years after I was born, my brother was born and completed our family.

We attended the Methodist Church Mom grew up in as a family until I went to junior high school. Then we transferred our membership to a church closer to our home. Shortly afterwards, my parents and brother stopped going to church. Despite being alone in doing so, I continued to attend church, joining the choir and youth group.

As I grew up, I somehow knew that I was different. Though my friends and I had boyfriends, I did not feel the same towards boys as the other girls did. Even though I loved having guys in my life, I developed crushes on my female friends with whom I could identify.

I met the Lord before I realized that I am a lesbian. My earliest recollection of meeting God was in high school. I attended a church with a close friend of mine, and while listening to the preacher, realized that I had been missing something, and that something was a relationship with Jesus Christ. From that point on, I have counted on the Lord's strength to see me through some trying times in my life. God has never left my side, even when I have put God on the back burner.

As a young adult, I struggled with the apparent conflict between my sexuality and my spirituality. I did not feel as if I could be a Christian and a homosexual. I was led to believe, through teachings and my own reading of the Bible, that I had to choose between the two.

I attended West Chester University after graduating from high school in 1974. During these years, I met several Christian friends and joined the Fellowship of Christian Athletes and Campus Crusade for Christ. There were several churches in the area that I attended, however, none with regularity. I knew about my desire to be with women, but chose to identify with Christians for fear of not being accepted by my family and friends. Any gay activities that I attended, such as dances or parties, were done quietly and privately. Meanwhile, along with several of my friends, I continued to struggle with the dilemma of my sexual orientation and my Christian faith. As much as I wanted and needed to be both a lesbian and a Christian, the 70's were still not a period of social acceptance. I remained in the closet until the late 70's, when I was a college junior and senior. I drifted away from the Christian groups and spent much of my time with gay friends. I still believed that the two realities did not meet in common territory. I had limited fellowship with other Christians, with the exception of a small Bible study group with several women who had no knowledge of my sexual orientation. This group continued past my graduation in 1978, and into graduate school.

My coming out to my parents, although one of the most difficult times, is also one of the funniest stories of my life. During this period, I was in a very difficult relationship. I was obviously upset most of the time, and chose not to share my problem with my family. I happened to visit my parents during a "not-so-strong" day. Mom and Dad were there waiting for me. "Sit," said my father in his "worried" tone of voice. "Your mother and I know that you are going through something, and we are concerned about you." Of course, I was not ready at that time to share my lesbianism with them. I explained to them that I was not prepared to talk to them about my problem. My father did not accept this answer at all. "If I guess, will you be honest with us?" he asked. I felt cornered, and told him that indeed, I would be honest. He just came out with "You are gay, aren't you?" I was shocked. Somehow they knew. I said, "Yes, Dad, I am." With that, my mother broke down in hysterical sobbing. I was devastated. What might be acceptance had become a hysterical moment. Mom began to say, "Oh, thank God, thank God."

"Thank God?" I asked myself. "What is she talking about?" "Thank God," she went on. "We thought you had cancer." My parents were relieved that I was only gay and not dying of a terminal illness!

Since my coming out they have been largely accepting and supportive of me. They sometimes struggle with the idea of my not giving them grandchildren. At times they admit to wishing that I lived a different life, but at no time do I doubt their love for me despite my sexual orientation. I have been truly blessed by a family that does love me for who I am.

I have had the opportunity to be out personally and professionally, both in my career and serving on the Board of Directors for a local nonprofit agency that serves children.

As I begin my 40s, I find myself still without a home church. I have attended several welcoming and accepting churches, however, none exist in my local area. Should I find one, I would love to attend on a regular basis. It is a lifelong dream to be able to work with young adults who struggle with their sexual orientation and spiritual walk.

One of my most valuable and cherished relationships, however, is with a close group of Christian women whom I have known since college. The five of us are as different as night and day in lifestyle, interests, professions, opinions, political affiliation, and hobbies. Two of us are lesbian, the others are married and have children. All of us know the Lord, and it is God who has kept us together. What a blessing to know that my sisters will always be there when life takes its toll and I need to share my burden!

I have come to believe that I **can** be a lesbian **and** a Christian. Jesus commands us to "Love the Lord your God with all your heart, and with all your soul, and with all your mind" (Matthew 22:37). I find it difficult to believe that one who lived a life of love and sacrifice would ask us to love only people with certain labels. It is my prayer that in my life I see the walls crumble down between persons of different faith, color, sexual orientation, and political opinion. I believe that is what my Lord and Savior wants for all of us.

Sherry E. Franklin works as the Director of Community Based Services for a Human Services agency serving people with disabilities. As of this date, she still does not have a home church, but continues to be grateful for her spiritual friends and family who love and support her without condemnation. It is good to be alive!

3

A Preacher's Kid

Fred Bean

When you are a preacher's kid, you face a lot of expectations. My father was a minister, first in the Evangelical Congregation, and later in the Church of the Brethren. Church members expect you to set an example for other kids. Of course they would not be surprised if you were a brat — preacher's kids have that reputation too. But, would a preacher's kid grow up to be gay? Maybe the brats could, but I was one of the good kids. My three sisters and I were far from perfect, but often church members would compliment our parents on how well behaved we were. Many of those members were like a part of my family. I never wanted to disappoint my parents or my church family.

I am not sure when I first became aware I was gay. I was curious about men and men's bodies even before I reached the age of puberty. By the time I reached my teens, I started to notice all of the muscular guys at school but I always admired them from a distance. I convinced myself they just possessed qualities I wanted in myself. They were athletic, I was not. I was sure I wanted to be like them — not with them. I had friends who were girls, and a few times I went out on dates. But I never considered having sex with anyone. I was a good kid, and as my parents and my church had told me, good kids saved themselves for marriage.

I did have sexual urges. Masturbation was something my family had never talked about. I was not sure if it was a sin, and the first few times I did it, I was not even sure what I was doing.

Eventually I realized what it was and I read a few things that convinced me that, even if some people thought it was a sin, it was really perfectly natural. So what if it was images of men that aroused me? I was sure that would eventually change. I would meet a woman I loved and settle down and be married.

At age 13, the same time I was coming of age, my father died. I was no longer a preacher's kid. I was now the kid of a preacher's widow, still a member of the same Church of the Brethren congregation, and still living up to many of the same expectations. Now though, there were new pastors in the pulpit. I had grown up listening to my father's sermons. He was not the "fire and brimstone" type. I remember him as being more of a consensus builder, trying to bring people together. Now I sat in the pew every Sunday and listened to warnings about the wickedness of the end times in which we were living. Occasionally there would be a warning against the sin of homosexuality. But I thought I was not a homosexual. I had never had sex with anyone. I was eventually going to marry a woman — sometime in the distant future.

I went off to college and tried to push any sexual confusion aside. I did not want to do anything that my male roommates would find threatening. I had good friends, male and female. They became a family away from home for me. I also attended a church (a combination of Church of the Brethren and United Church of Christ) that became my third family. My college church was small and many of the members were fairly liberal — not much fire and brimstone here. It was warm and welcoming. I dated a little, a few girls from college and a girl from the church. But I never let the relationships get too serious. I still did not have any desire to have sex with women, and I was starting to accept that I never would. I had good friends, so who needed a sexual relationship? I could probably remain celibate the rest of my life. And if I could not? That was a problem that could be dealt with later.

As I started to accept my gay orientation I began to look for any information that I could read discreetly. I was not about to check out a book from the library or go to a gay bar — someone might see me. But, if it was a story in *Time* or *Newsweek* or the topic on "Donahue," it was safe. Those discussions in mainstream media began to convince me that being gay was okay — at least for those other people — if not for me. After all, I am a good kid, and good kids do not do that sort of thing.

I had no full-time job after I graduated from college so I moved back home with my mother, stepfather, and younger sister. I missed my college family. I got a part-time job and made some new friends. There was a group of about six of us, young men and women, who were good friends. But now I felt I had to be careful. I could not get too close to the women in the group. They might expect it to lead to something more and I was sure it would not. I could not get too close to the men in the group. They might suspect I was gay and I feared that would destroy any friendship.

I was back at my home church and back to those fire and brimstone sermons. It was different now, though. When the minister would preach against homosexuals, I would get a knot in my stomach. I knew he was talking about me, and I became increasingly convinced he was wrong. As I grew up, going to church on Sunday was automatic. There was no question, it was something I had to do. Now my mom had a new message for me: it was up to me. She knew I did not like a lot of what I was hearing in Sunday sermons (although I am not sure how she knew). So she was leaving it up to me if I wanted to continue attending. I took advantage of this new option and stopped going to church. I felt guilty and I missed some of my longtime church friends. But that knot in my stomach was gone, and my self-acceptance was growing.

At the same time I was feeling more and more isolated. I knew that I was a gay man. I knew of one or two other people who I suspected were gay, but I did not really know anyone who was gay. My group of post-college friends were starting to drift apart, and some were getting married. I decided I could either go through life feeling very lonely, or I could start trying to find other gay men. But where should I start? I lived in a small town. There were no gay support services or gay bars. A friend at work mentioned picking up a Pittsburgh alternative weekly paper that had a lot of unusual personal ads in the back. On my next trip to Pittsburgh, I found that weekly and answered one of the ads. That led to a few nervous dates that really went nowhere. It also led to a decision. I needed to get out of my parents' house and on my own. My job was in Johnstown, about 40 miles away, and I decided it was time to move closer to work. I was also secretly hoping that living in a larger town would lead to more opportunities to meet someone. My expectations of living life alone were giving way to hopes of meeting Mr. Right. Of course, I had not told this to my family or friends. I had confided to one female friend that I did not think I was straight because I feared our relationship was getting too close, but we never discussed it after that.

After a few months of house hunting, I became a home owner and out on my own in the big city of Johnstown. So where should a timid gay man go to meet other gay men? I was fairly certain there were no gay bars in town. The only gay bar I had ever heard mentioned had closed a couple of years earlier. I would not have been comfortable in a bar anyway. My family had considered drinking a sin. I did drink a little while in college and went to a few bars, but to this day, it is not a setting where I really feel comfortable. I was working out at a gym regularly, and I thought I might just meet someone by chance. I became friends with one of the guys at the gym. Bill was in his mid-30s and single. I wondered if he could be gay. But I was afraid to ask. We gradually got to know each other better. Finally, one night, the two of us were alone at his house, and he said, "There is something I want to ask you, but I am not sure if I should. Do you know what that question is?" I knew, and for the first time, I sat nervously talking about my sexuality with another gay man! I found out that Bill already had a lover. I had not found a boyfriend, but I had found a friend, a gay friend. It was wonderful!

Bill led a rather closeted life, and he was not prepared to play matchmaker for me. He and his partner did take me to a few out-of-town bars. But I am not a bar person, and I think bars are a terrible place to try to meet someone. When that did not work, I tried a personal ad. One local paper rejected my ad as inappropriate. The other published the ad and I met a couple guys. One seemed more timid than I. Another expected sex on the third date telling me I did not have to be in love to have sex. That was the wrong thing to say to this preacher's kid. I was not looking for sex — I was looking for love — a best friend with whom to spend my life.

My trips to out-of-town bars had introduced me to something new, the monthly Pittsburgh gay newspaper. I decided to give personal ads another try. I placed a detailed ad and opened a post office box to handle replies. I got several very nice letters. I met a few of the people who replied, went on a couple of dates and then I met Ed. I was instantly attracted to him. We had many of the same interests and could talk for hours. We soon became best friends, and lovers, even though we lived 60 miles apart.

That was seven years ago. Ed is still my best friend and lover. We still live apart, spending weekends and vacations together, but I am hoping we will soon be under one roof, as I look for a new career in Ed's hometown of Pittsburgh.

During seven years of coming out, I have found a new family — my family of gay friends. I came out to my immediate family within months of meeting Ed. There was no way I would have a significant other person in my life without telling my family. When I was alone, my sexuality was simply a matter I had no need to disclose. Now hiding it would require lying. Some Christians may disagree on whether homosexuality is wrong, but there was never any question in my mind that lying would be wrong.

My family never talked much about matters like this, and still does not. However, they greeted my news with love and support. Some of my family surprised me with how welcoming they were to my news and to Ed. One sister still has doubts about my decision to have a relationship. I think she would be more comfortable if I had chosen to remain celibate. From a Christian perspective, that appears to be the safe thing to do. But, did Jesus always do the safe thing? Does God really want me to spend my life alone, without a satisfying, intimate relationship? Is being gay some kind of unique test that God gives to a small but significant portion of people as some kind of gauge of willpower or faith? I have concluded the answer to these questions is "no." But I do not want to do battle with people in the church who disagree.

I do not currently have a church family, even though I know there are welcoming churches out there. I still believe in God, and I still think basic Christian principles provide a good framework for life. However, my own personal struggle has led me to question much of what many organized religions are teaching. Churches need to set standards for people to live by, but they should be standards that bring people together, not tear communities apart.

At age 36, I am still a preacher's kid. I still try to live up to other people's expectations. Some may be surprised when they find out that I am gay, but I am still the same person they always knew — just someone who is trying to be a good kid.

Fred Bean grew up as a "Preacher's Kid," with his late father, William Bean, serving as a minister in the Evangelical Congregation Church, and later in the Church of the Brethren. Fred was born and raised in Pennsylvania, and considers Somerset to be his hometown. He has a B.A. in Communications from Gannon University and worked for 15 years as a TV news producer and director. He is now pursuing a career as a computer service technician. He lives in Pittsburgh with his partner of eight years.

4

God, Gayness, and Me: My Personal Journey of Spiritual and Sexual Wholeness

Paul Deeming

I knew I was different as early as age five. I did not have a word for it and would not have even known what the word "homosexual" meant. However, I knew the feelings that I had were somehow different and something to be kept hidden and secret. No one ever said anything directly about it — my parents, family, society — but I knew my secret made me different and for anyone to find out about it would mean trouble. Robbie, my best friend from childhood, and I "played" with each other for years, but we never thought of it as anything sexual. We simply enjoyed touching each other, holding each other, and making up fantasy games. I suppose you might attribute this to normal childhood play, however, in later childhood years I had a girl best friend, and we never played those games!

My biological parents, who died before I came out, never really discussed sexuality with me. I remember my mom giving me the book, *Everything You Wanted to Know About Sex But Were Afraid to Ask*, when I was a junior in high school. She told me to read it, and if I had any questions to ask my dad. I did read it, but I could not tell her that I already knew most of what it talked about. I never talked to my dad about it either. This superficial level of communication was common in our household. We never addressed issues of sexuality, especially mine, until my freshman year of college. I was away for the weekend and my parents decided to paint my bedroom. This would have been all right except I had a stash of pornographic magazines, both gay and straight, under my dresser. When I returned, I realized they had to move all the furniture to enable them to paint. The house was like ice for two weeks as we all avoided the subject. Finally one day, as Mom and I were in the car together, she suddenly blurted out, "You aren't turning gay on us, are you?" Being in deep denial of the truth, I panicked and replied, "No, I am holding them for a friend." At the time, I thought it was a pretty good answer, and it seemed to satisfy Mom since she did not ask any more questions. Now that I look back, I do not think Mom was that gullible. I wish we could have talked about it and been able to develop an honest relationship. I think I would have found that they would have been very accepting after the initial shock. They always said to us kids, "We just want you to be happy." I feel certain they knew, but we just never acknowledged it. I wonder how it would have affected my development and shortened my life in the closet if they had been able to express their feelings so I could express mine. But, would I have been able to get through the fear and denial within me in order to allow myself to talk about it with them? I doubt it.

I became acutely aware of other boys in seventh grade. There were a couple of fellows in gym class who, even as I think back today, seemed more like adults physically than 12, 13, and 14 year old kids. It was my first experience with crushes! However, I still knew that these feelings and yearnings must remain silent and deeply hidden. Little did I realize then that they would stay that way for the next two decades.

I have always described my mid-teen years as my blossoming time. Those years were a time of experimenting, uncertainty, and frustration. Unfortunately, I had no guidance or role models to assure me that being gay was all right. My feelings, self-image, and self-esteem were deeply buried. I was beginning to know myself as a sexual being, but one who was different from the majority of people. Yet, I was still far from admitting to myself that I was a gay man.

Religion and spirituality really did not come into the picture until my high school and post-college years. My parents had taken us to the Episcopalian Church as kids because they felt it was their parental duty. They were not strongly religious people. In fact, my dad and his mother fought most of his life over the issue: she believed one must go to church every Sunday and he did not. When we arrived at an age where they felt we could make our own decisions about church, roughly around high school age, our parents did not push us any further.

I began attending a Methodist Church in the small Oklahoma town where we were living. I had been invited to a taco dinner with the youth group and I liked the dynamics of the group: acceptance, commonality, a cause (saving the world in Jesus' name), and fun. I became very active, and even began working in the Lay Witness Missions program, a team of adults and youth who led weekend retreats for churches that needed help to deal with issues or revitalize their congregations. Here I was, Super Christian, yet, still holding my deep, dark secrets inside. I went through years of internal torture, trying to be the best Christian I could while having these supposedly evil and forbidden feelings. Sometimes the thoughts became actions. I had no way of reconciling the two parts of my life and could not divorce myself from either one. I felt trapped and extremely guilty. I was constantly waging war within myself, sometimes the Christian side of me winning, and other times the sexual and human side winning. I would succumb to the pleasure I felt of fantasy and masturbation, then immediately drown in a sea of guilt over it. I would immediately plead for forgiveness from God as I thought was right to do, yet felt unworthy of even asking for it.

During college, I thought that if I just tried harder, I could lead a better life and be more pleasing to God. I would just pray harder, read the Bible more, and keep a closer watch on my "dirty" thoughts. I imagined I had an angel of sorts sitting on my shoulder who would "bonk" me on the head the instant I had a dirty thought. I scrutinized myself so closely during this time that I believe I came dangerously close to pushing myself over the edge mentally and emotionally. Finally, I just gave up and said to myself, "Well, if this is what it takes to please God, then forget about even trying! I just can not do it." I was sure I could never measure up. Contrary to the fact that no one had ever said anything negative directly to me about homosexuality, I felt like a complete failure and a horrible, evil person. I, as many young gay and lesbian people do, received indirect and subliminal kinds of messages from society and the media around me. I knew this was not a subject that I could share with anyone without great reprisals. I pretty much dropped the religious part of my life. I gave up. I knew I could not measure up to God and I was tired of trying. I did not attend any church for the rest of college nor for several years afterwards. I had always been a "doubting Thomas" type, and this surely did not help strengthen the very little faith I had, either in myself or in God.

In the summers of 1985 and 1986, I got a job stage managing for a summer stock theatre in Clinton, Iowa. During these two summers, I met a family that I credit with bringing me back to the Lord. Pat, whom I refer to as "Mom," would gently invite me to church with them even though I constantly made up excuses not to go. By this time, I felt I had no use for church and figured God and I just did not make good company. After the life I had led, I felt convinced that I did not fit in with all those good people. However, her persistence paid off and I came back to the Lord, rededicating my life to Christ. Yet I still dealt with the problem that I had not shaken my homosexuality and the tug of war within me resumed. I became so very close to this family that they became a true family to me. Mom finally figured out that I was gay about six years into our relationship. I shared with her where I had been and how I had struggled, and they loved me just the same. You see, even though I was gay, in a sense that was all right, because I was "fighting it, praying against it, and God would eventually make me straight." I tried very hard to believe that premise and live it. Looking back, I can certainly say that I tried my best to fit. I prayed many prayers, cried many tears, and did everything I knew to do so that God would finally take pity on me and "zap!" make me straight. I could not figure out why this was not happening when I felt I could do no more.

My coming out process was the turning point of my life. I did not plan it and did not expect it. It just began to happen on its own as life was starting to cave in on me. At that point I just could not handle it anymore, and there was no more avoiding it either. Evading issues, lying, covering my tracks, making up stories as to where I had been or who I had been with, and not being able to share anything of my life with my family for fear of being found out was taking too much energy. At the same time, I had a coming out of sorts with my spiritual beliefs. I could not address my sexuality without addressing the conflicting information I had received from my belief system. I also came to the realization that I really did not know who I was. I had spent all my life trying to please others, people as well as God, and had lost complete sense of who I was. I had to deal with all three issues simultaneously. It was complex and difficult to say the least! I retreated from everything in my life except work, which I had to do, and spent the better part of a year coming to terms with myself. How? I do not know (many people in the closet ask me what the steps are). I know it took a lot of thinking, exploring, and soul searching. The hardest thing to do was to face these issues and admit things in my life that I did not want to face, especially in my belief system.

I think that is the issue with our religious communities: willingness to face the possibility that their current interpretation of the Bible could be wrong in regard to gay and lesbian people. That might force them to question their whole belief system. If their interpretation of the Bible about gays and lesbians is wrong, then how many other errors might they find? This possibility scares them to death! The fear that their whole belief system may crumble around them is too much for them to bear, so they continue to hold on to a set of erroneous beliefs. I think this is the key to our struggle to convince our religious families not to believe in a system that would condemn us.

It has been over five years since I chose to be honest about who I am. I have never regretted my decision to come out. It was not an overnight process, and in some respects it continues on to this very day, but it has enabled me to be a much better person. I had previously been extremely passive because I avoided anything that would draw attention to me, namely, conflicts and dispute. To this day I hate conflicts of any type. Now I am much more self-assured because I have nothing to hide. I can speak out without fear of being found out for who I truly am. I have a strengthened self-esteem and sense of who I am and how I represent myself to others. I feel pride instead of shame. Many of my friends, some of whom had already guessed I was gay, remarked about what a changed person I had become. I knew this would not sit well with the Assemblies of God Church I had been attending, so I never returned. Since then I have found a new church family at All God's Children Metropolitan Community Church in Minneapolis, Minnesota. It has been a saving grace to find a spiritual home that will accept me for who I am as a whole person.

My biological brother and sister live halfway across the country, so I came out to them over the phone. They have been supportive of me, although my sister does not understand why I talk so much about gay issues. It is difficult to keep quiet when I have kept my mouth shut for 34 years! I want people to get to know the real me, to replace the facade of lies and deceit I created over the years.

My Iowa family is a different story. Prior to my coming out, it was acceptable that I was gay because "Paul's praying about it and God is going to change him." When I told them I did not believe that any more, it suddenly was not all right with them. I am still loved but I feel accepted for who I am only to a certain extent. My sexuality is, by their standards, a result of my choice to sin and be in "that" lifestyle. One of my "sisters," immediately penned a "hell and damnation" letter to me. I guess I am fortunate that they did not reject me completely, but I can not be satisfied with partial acceptance. If they can not accept me for who I am and get beyond their erroneous biblical interpretations, I wonder if we will be able to maintain any relationship when I have a significant other in my life. As it is, our relationship has become somewhat distant and, at times, strained over the last few years. This is very painful because we used to be so close. Even after I came out, I still struggled at times with understanding who I was and why. I still struggled with the whole idea of God and if God really loved me and accepted me.

I had a real turning point experience one day that settled this for me once and for all. It did not occur during one of my times of intense prayer, but out of the blue in my kitchen. I suddenly sensed God's presence and I felt God saying to me, "Paul, this struggle with your sexuality is going nowhere. All it is doing is putting a wedge further and further between us in our relationship. I want to draw closer to you, not farther apart. I love you no matter what, just for who you are." It was said so simply and I understood, not in my head knowledge for I would not have believed it, but inside, in my heart. I knew it, but I could not quantify it or place any logic to it. I finally realized that there was truly nothing I could do to be any more accepted and loved by God. My many years of trying to be a good Christian boy, to do the right thing, to pray the right way, and to think or even to feel the right thing was in vain! I had come full circle, and that is the entire message of God's love to begin with: "For God so loved the world that God gave God's only begotten Son," (John 3:16, King James Version, Inclusive). It is a free gift of love that we cannot in any way work for or earn because we are good enough or do the right things. Our life experiences teach us that we have to struggle and work hard to be acceptable, yet God does not demand that of us. I have also come to realize just how simple our relationship with God is. *We* make it complex and difficult!

I often wonder why it took half of my life to come to this place and I still deal with the anger of lost years, but I continue to believe that everything happens for a reason. I look forward to the day when the reason will be plain. I would also like to help others come to a life of acceptance and wholeness. Young gay and lesbian people would not need to go through this struggle if only they could be accepted and supported for who they are. May God use me as an instrument to truly show God's love to other gay and lesbian children!

Paul Deeming resides in Eagan, Minnesota, with his "son," Willie (a poodle) and currently attends All God's Children Metropolitan Community Church. He is a vocational rehabilitation counselor, working with both blind and deaf-blind clients, and also works as a certified sign language interpreter. In his spare time, he enjoys nature photography, scuba diving, and desk top publishing.

5

From Shame to Shalom

Jim Helmuth

I grew up in a Mennonite home near Louisville, Ohio. Ever since I was a young child, I was interested in church, God, and spirituality. For the first number of years my interest was closely related to my need for acceptance, recognition, achievement, and love. I attended church services very willingly and even asked to go. I would listen, do assignments or readings, and pray aloud in prayer groups. I had a sense of pride in being spiritual and secretly felt I was more spiritual than other people. My piety was reinforced by my mother, ministers, and church teachers.

When I was 10, there were tent revival meetings in our community. An evangelist spoke eloquently and sincerely about the wounds of Christ because of his crucifixion. He emphasized how we should not keep Christ waiting and, if we did, it might be too late and the consequence would literally be hell. I felt drawn to Christ who died for me but I also felt afraid of hell. I was very aware of the Russians and the threat of nuclear holocaust in the news back then. I went to the altar and was led in a prayer of confession and acceptance of Christ by an adult volunteer.

I felt a release of guilt deep within and felt Christ's presence. When I got home I knelt by my bed and reaffirmed my total commitment to Christ as my Lord and Savior. I went through the instruction class at church and was baptized at age 11. During the instruction class, I judged that some of the others

25

were not as sincere as I and that I was a better Christian. My ego was using my new commitment to Christ to serve my sense of personal superiority.

I was aware of being different from my older brothers at an early age. I was more interested in house work, electronics, typing, and reading than they were. More importantly, I was less interested in sports than my brothers and my male cousins. This was most uncomfortable for me at family gatherings or times when my siblings wanted me to play sports with them. I would hide so they would not pressure me to play with them.

I was fairly well coordinated and could play sports quite well but was just not interested most of the time. I felt I had to hide my interest in cooking and actually would sneak out of the house on Saturday mornings to do housework and cooking with a female cousin. Her mother paid us to clean and bake while she taught music lessons. I got $5 for five hours and that was great money back then for a young boy. I did outside farm work and construction during my adolescent years but did not like it.

I felt alienated from other boys at church who told dirty stories. I laughed at the stories but I did not really understand them for a long time and could not identify with their interest in girls. Rather than knowing my own sexual feelings, I again put myself in a superior position and felt better than those bad boys. Inwardly I felt inferior because I did not feel accepted by them.

There were many opportunities to become accepted. I led prayer meetings and became involved in the church's youth group. Most of this was very positive and I was as sincere as I could be. I memorized scripture easily for personal use and quizzing. I memorized the entire books of Philippians and 1 John and a number of Psalms. I became involved in various religious groups like Youth For Christ, Faith at Work, Navigators, Young Life, and a Coffee House Ministry. For a brief time I was involved in charismatic groups and spoke in tongues under the baptism of the Spirit. Some of these groups emphasized evangelism in a way that I felt was arrogant.

There is an underlying assumption in this form of Christianity that I could not accept then and do not accept now. It grew out of my awareness of my ego gratification in relation to being a Christian. The assumption is that having a personal faith in Christ puts the Christian in an *us* category and the rest of the world in a *them* category. We were taught we must bring these people to our way of believing. The implication was that they would be punished by God if they did not believe the same doctrine we did.

At age 18, I served on the first Mennonite Youth Fellowship Life Team sponsored by the denomination's youth office. This was a very gratifying experience in faith development. At Hesston College the next year, I talked with a psychology professor about my feelings of sexual attraction to men. It took great courage to speak about this and I was petrified. He did not know what to make of what I told him but it helped me to talk about my fears. I hoped all this would change if I were married. I certainly would not have accepted then that I was homosexual because I was a Christian and therefore, by definition, could not be homosexual.

I knew what Christ meant to me. Inborn in me, though, was the increasing awareness that to be Christian meant we were better than others who believed differently (this is inherent in the Jewish concept of election). I really respect the Quakers' quiet faith in God and their great respect for individual differences and beliefs. They affirm that there is that of God in every person and that God has not left us without any inner witness to truth. That resonated deeply with me and still does to this day. This way of believing truly respects all people as being on a journey to finding that Light and that Truth.

I went to a Quaker seminary, Earlham School of Religion. I was not interested in becoming a pastor, although I struggled with that at times. I wanted to study in an environment where there was genuine openness to God within the individual and also a commitment to intellectual honesty. I found this at Earlham. I grew spiritually as I studied the cultural, linguistic, historical, and theological roots of Christianity and other religions with a truly open mind, but not an empty mind. I also found a warmth and deep spirituality at Earlham that has been very important to me.

After studying various theologies and views of scripture, I could not accept a literal interpretation. It would have been intellectually dishonest for me to do so. Also, I could not accept the judgmental attitude that is inherent within it. I was asked to defend my view of scripture and beliefs by my mother who feared for my salvation. However, the experience of distrust from my mother only made it more clear why that view of the world and God was not acceptable to me. Manipulation with guilt violates a very fundamental value I hold in the sanctity of the person and the presence of God in all people and it is just as abusive as other boundary violations.

I left Earlham with a renewed faith in the presence of Christ within all people and within myself. I understood that Christ came to me through my parents, church leaders, teachers, and the Bible, but these only awakened what was already there, though unknown. I knew what was real for me but I no longer tried to get others to believe as I did.

In my studies of the Psychology of Religious Experience at Earlham, I learned how faith functions psychologically for different people, particularly the role of fear, guilt, shame, and personal superiority in belief.

My first two years of marriage were parallel with my studies at Earlham. My wife and I got along in most ways. However, there were sexual problems that I blamed on my wife. I could not face the truth that I did not really feel the kind of close psycho-sexual bond with her that I presumed most heterosexual couples feel. I was increasingly angry and frustrated. I was becoming more aware of my sexual interest in men and went for counseling with a respected psychologist and theology professor at Earlham. As I look back on that counseling now, I think the doctor was afraid to really tell me what he and I both sensed at a visceral level. I was either bisexual or homosexual. Again, repression won out for awhile but the psycho-sexual issue never went away.

After moving back to Ohio, I sublimated my sexual feelings into nurturing our two children, involvement in church activities at Summit Mennonite Church, and completing my Ph.D. program in counseling psychology at the University of Akron.

I attended a Masters and Johnson workshop for therapists in Chicago in 1981. It became very clear to me, both by information presented there and by personal experience, that my sexual orientation was probably homosexual or at least bisexual. Again, this was very scary to me. I was both panicked and excited at the same time. I began feeling some depression.

Soon after that seminar, a man at Summit Mennonite Church, whom my wife and I got to know in our house church group, acknowledged that he was gay when I asked him. I told him about my attraction to men. I also told my wife for a second or third time about my feelings for men but she could not really hear what I was saying. Until then, I had never met anyone who acknowledged openly they were homosexual and who felt good about themselves. Our small group studied the book, *Is the Homosexual My Neighbor? Another Christian View*, by Letha Scanzoni and Virginia Ramey Mollenkott. That helped me take a look at the issue and myself in a new way.

One afternoon, on a desolate beach on Cape Cod, away from any human ears, I screamed out to God and to myself, with an anguished voice, that I was gay. In that moment I came out to myself and my self-acceptance as a gay man was born. To my surprise, no whale swallowed me up! No bolt of lightning hit me! The hiding was over. I broke free.

The years between 1983 and 1988 were filled with struggle and intense emotional turmoil. In my detailed journal of those years I used the metaphor of being pregnant, of being in travail, and looking for a birthing room. Some awareness was growing and unfolding within me that I could not stop because stopping meant I would have aborted a part of me, divided myself, and then chose celibacy. I was suicidal at times during those years. A motorcycle accident in 1988 paralyzed my left arm and shoulder for almost a year. In 1989, I came out to my wife explicitly and revealed to her that I had involvement with men.

It was hell coming to terms with what was happening. My journal was my therapist, along with several other paid therapists who tried to understand as much as a heterosexual could. If only I could have talked to a gay therapist and had a positive role model, it could have helped tremendously.

In the fall of 1989, I met and fell in love with a man who lived in another state. He was a loving "mid-wife" and this relationship lasted nine months. He honored my pain and allowed me to release it. He and I attended a Connecting

Families weekend at Laurelville, Pennsylvania, for gays, lesbians, and their families. This experience of being affirmed as a gay man by other Christians was deeply moving and healing as I affirmed both my sexuality and my wholeness in Christ.

For the last 20 years, I have had a private practice in psychology here in the Akron, Ohio, area. I have listened to the pain and hurt of individuals struggling for integrity in their lives. I have encouraged my clients to be themselves, to accept who they are and to listen to and respect what they know to be true for them. It would have been hypocritical for me to do any less. The acceptance of being gay was my life drama and one I could not dodge.

I did give birth to this inner awareness of being gay and it was and is a beautiful loving child, playful and free, a tender, sensitive boy, wanting to be loved just as he is. I am at peace with myself now. I know God loves me and I am one of God's own. I have felt the presence of the Holy Spirit speaking to me in very clear and affirming ways at critical moments in this difficult process.

Now, I know who and what I am. I am usually no longer ashamed of that, but occasionally my guilt and anger can and does erupt and I react. I can now affirm that my sexuality is not my identity but it is a significant, core part of who I am. It cannot be ignored without dire consequences.

On April 1, 1990, I met Richard, a wonderful person who has been my best friend, lover, and companion the last eight years. He is a music professor and organist. I want to acknowledge the working of soul and spirit in the bringing of Rich and me together to share life. Our relationship has changed over the years but the love remains. He also had been married many years and has two grown children.

You may be asking, but what about your ex-wife and the children. Yes, they too have had to struggle with the consequences of divorce and seeing me in a new way. My ex-wife used this unwanted change as a wake-up call for herself. There was a huge mountain of pain and grieving for her to face. Nevertheless, she completed her Masters Degree in Counseling and has started her own counseling service called New Beginnings to help women reclaim their own lives. My children have grown in acceptance of the situation and we are still a family of four on some holidays.

I continue to provide a wide range of counseling services to people and to groups. Both my ex-wife and I counsel gay and lesbian individuals and couples. About half my clients are gay and I lead a gay men's support and therapy group.

My parents, brothers, and sisters have each had to choose how they were going to look at and relate to me with their new awareness of my being gay. The son and brother they have always known never really changed in his spirit and being. What has happened is that in my coming out to them they learned something about me that was always true, but hidden and denied before. Each has the opportunity to struggle between love and fear in their responses. Each has responded somewhat differently initially and over the years. I have felt love and understanding from them most of the time even though some of them do not agree with choices I have made.

My soul is on a continuing journey, traveling from guilt, shame, anger, and self-hatred to a place of true inner peace and deep spirituality. My path is mine and I affirm it. It would be wrong for anyone to adopt it for themselves for that would violate them. Each of us is on a somewhat different path. The challenge is to remain open and honest through it all and to grow and affirm the presence of Christ within.

This is my journey. It is where I am at this time. There will no doubt be changes and turns on the road ahead, but with God's Spirit as my guide, I can go forward with confidence.

Addendum: On June 26, 1998, I revisited Race Point Beach in Provincetown, Massachusetts, and went to that same sand ledge where I had come out to myself and God many years earlier. This time, in peace and reverence, I could say aloud, "I am gay." Spontaneously, I allowed the cold Atlantic waters to wash over my feet and then, after much hesitation, my whole body. I felt guided to write on a piece of paper, "Love is all there is, God is Love." I dug a hole in the sand and put the paper in it along with objects from my wallet and beach bag that symbolized money, sexuality, intimacy, and vocation. I prayed a prayer of thanksgiving and release and slowly walked back to my bicycle and left.

Jim Helmuth is a licensed psychologist from Akron, Ohio. He has had a counseling and consulting practice there for 20 years. Prior to his coming out, he was married for 21 years and has two grown children. He now lives with his partner, Richard. They have been together eight years.

6

Born Again — Again!

Donna Brooks

I was raised in a non-Christian, homophobic family. I became a Christian when I was nine years old. After watching a Billy Graham crusade on television one evening, I went into my bedroom and asked Jesus to come into my heart. From then on I listened to every radio and TV preacher I could find and read the Bible and Christian literature voraciously. I was always attracted to women, long before I knew there was a name for it. The message I got from my mother was, "Someone should line them (homosexuals) up against a wall and shoot them." When I discovered the name for my feelings, I knew I had to keep them a secret in order to be safe in this world.

In college, I called long distance to Jesus People USA in Chicago. I got the number from a Christian record album; it was the only place I knew to turn for help. They put me in touch with Outpost in Minnesota and thus began my five-year involvement in ex-gay ministries. During that time, I spent countless hours getting counseling by phone, mail, and in person. I read books, tracts, and newsletters, bought audio tapes, and went to conferences. Fifteen hundred dollars later, nothing had changed. My sexual desires had not diminished or been redirected to men. I began to be skeptical of the messages I was getting from the ex-gay ministries. They saw the homosexual condition as one that was the result of early emotional trauma, such as sexual abuse, growing up in a dysfunctional family, or the famous "lack of love from the same sex parent" theory.

My disillusionment with the ex-gay movement began when I realized that there are many heterosexuals who have been sexually abused. If abuse is the cause, then why were they not homosexual? If a lack of love from the same sex parent causes people to be gay, then what causes them to be straight? Does it mean they lacked the love of the opposite sex parent? Who did not grow up in a dysfunctional family? I now know gay people who have grown up in loving, stable homes, and straight people who grew up in chaos. The profiles just do not fit and there are enough exceptions to make me wonder if there is not more to sexual orientation than can be "healed" or even explained.

Following is a chronological account of the events that led to my actual healing, not from homosexuality, but from depression, fear, and self-loathing:

June 1986 — I attended a week-long Exodus International Conference. That summer marked the height of my involvement in ex-gay ministries.

August 1986 — I went to Reading, Pennsylvania, for a week-long training in the 12 Steps of Homosexuals Anonymous (HA) and was certified to start HA chapters.

October 1986 — I attended an Outpost Conference in St. Paul. Two weeks later I attended a Mobilized to Serve Christian Singles Conference. I was feeling desperately lonely, and squelching any expression of sexuality, until it began to surface in unhealthy ways. While working at a Christian TV station, I would stay after sign-off and tune the satellite dish to porn channels, waiting for scenes with women together. I felt frustrated and degraded every time I would do this.

The pornography was not satisfying and I started to realize that I really longed for companionship. I had always believed that as a Christian, sex outside of marriage was sinful, so I tried to believe I had the gift of celibacy. However, I longed to slow dance with a woman, to kiss a woman, and to do the kinds of things most Christians do with their heterosexual dating partners before they get married, without any guilt or condemnation by the church. I saw this as a double standard and rather than attribute it to society, or the church, I wrongly attributed it to God.

I began to be angry at God for my condition. God seemed cruel and sadistic. Why would God curse me with sexual desires, and give me no legitimate way to fulfill them? Why would God require a higher standard of me than of my heterosexual friends, who could date with the hope of marriage? To deal with my anger issues, I sought counseling with a male pastor. He soon manipulated me into talking about my sexual orientation and trying to change it. I responded with more repressed, seething anger. At one point, he suggested I have sex with a man, saying, "You'd love it. You'd *love* it."

January 1987 — I was at a breaking point. I had sex with the first available woman. I had warned her to stay away from me because I could not handle the temptation. She did not, and I gave in to my pent-up frustration and lust. This was the beginning of yet another five-year period. I did not want a one night stand, so I decided to try to make a commitment to this person. It was a disastrous relationship that ended when she left me for another woman. Although terribly painful, our permanent separation in May '92, was one of the best things that ever happened to me.

June 1987 — I had a nervous breakdown and spent a month in the hospital for depression. When I got out, I felt forsaken by God and was not sure what I believed anymore. I lost my job and my church, and had nowhere to live. (My partner and I had separated, even though we later got back together — an incredibly stupid mistake!) I was not out to my parents who were clueless as to what was going on. I was staying in a motel, trying to find a place to live in a new town, with a car that kept breaking down. I thought often of suicide as I had for the previous several months. Thank God I never went through with it!

While I was in the hospital, some people who did not see homosexuality as sinful and incompatible with Christian faith, visited me. This was a surprise to me, and I was skeptical for over three years. During that time I stopped praying and reading the Bible. I did not listen to Christian music or teachers, and I did not go to church.

Then one day, God broke through my defenses with a verse from Hebrews that popped into my head: "I will never, ever leave you; I will never, ever forsake you" (Hebrews 13:5, my paraphrase). My long process of healing was beginning. I realized that I had always accepted what I had been told about homosexuals. I never questioned. I never studied the passages for myself or read any different interpretations of biblical passages. I just always accepted that the Bible condemned homosexuality. I began to see that it was not the conviction of the Holy Spirit, based on my own reading of the Bible, that was forming my opinions about my sexual orientation. Instead, my own sense of low self-worth was determining how I felt about my orientation.

I distinctly remember as a child always feeling guilty that I was not a better daughter. I also remember in college feeling that God loved everyone but me — that I was too bad! It was all disparaging of self, but anything but humble. How egocentric! I needed to repent of my pride — the pride that dared to say my lousy opinion of myself overruled the opinion of the God who loved me and gave God's self for me! Years of accumulated self-hatred, guilt, and internalized homophobia were lifted from me.

I gradually began to integrate the sexual and spiritual parts of me. What I once viewed as a curse has now become a gift. I am celibate for now, but it is not a mandatory, life-long celibacy imposed on me by God or by others to prove my relationship with Jesus Christ or my love for God. It is, instead, an expectant waiting, knowing that God, who knows what I need, will bring a godly woman into my life when she and I are both ready. I know that God wants the best for me. I also want the best for me and am willing to wait for her. I now know the difference between healthy sexual desire and lust. No longer afraid of my sexuality, I accept my femininity and my body. I lost 50 pounds, let my hair grow long, and began dressing in ways that were more flattering to my figure.

I feel as if I am back from the dead! I see life in Christ as not just being born again, but being born again and again and again! I have a faith that is my own and an optimism about the future because I have seen time and again how God uses bad things to bring about our growth and ultimate good. My anger has been replaced by overwhelming gratitude! Those who know me understand that I am not looking for a license to sin — I am looking for a license to serve!

I am convinced that the Bible does not condemn homosexual identity or orientation, neither does it condemn all homosexual behavior, any more than it condemns all heterosexual behavior. I believe God has the same standards for everyone. The church, like the Pharisees, has too often been guilty of heaping burdens on others' backs while not lifting a finger themselves. Christians regularly impose standards on gays that they would never impose on heterosexuals or embrace themselves.

It is as if there are two gospels. The one for heterosexuals goes like this: "If you confess with your mouth the Lord Jesus Christ, and believe in your heart that God has raised Jesus from the dead, you shall be saved. For God so loved heterosexuals that God gave God's only begotten Son, that whosoever believes in Jesus should not perish, but should have the approval of the church and the world to marry, to be sexually active, and to tell everyone about it." The one for homosexuals goes like this: "If you confess with your mouth the Lord Jesus Christ, believe in your heart that God has raised Jesus from the dead, commit yourself to lifelong celibacy, and never allow yourself to have a same-sex romantic feeling or thought (or at least every time you do, if you feel guilty about it, and confess it as sin immediately), you shall be saved. For God so loved heterosexuals that God gave God's only begotten Son, that whosoever believes in Jesus and forsakes human companionship might become heterosexual, too!"

I also believe that sometime in the future Christians will look back and be amazed that we could ever have interpreted the Bible to prohibit all homosexual activity for all time in all contexts, just as we look back with disbelief and embarrassment today at the churches that vehemently defended slavery and later, segregation, in the name of biblical faithfulness. I hope my story helps to hasten that day!

Donna Brooks lives in Columbus, Ohio, where she is a professional art model, house and pet-sitter, tiller of the soil, and tender of all things green. She has worked on a farm and in an orchard, and now provides lawn-care and gardening services. She has a B.A. in Communications from California University of Pennsylvania, and has worked in small-town radio and television. For seven years, she was a live-in supervisor of adults with mental retardation. She is a networker, writer, and speaker concerning sexual orientation, the Bible, and the Church, with a special emphasis on scripture, peacemaking, prejudice reduction, and the ex-gay movement.

To contact her for interviews, requests to speak, other articles, or information, send e-mail to: Pansona@aol.com or write: Donna Brooks, P.O. Box 206, Alexandria, Ohio 43001, USA.

7

My Calling

Anonymous

I was born in the 50s to two good Southern Baptist parents. I was raised in fundamentalist Baptist churches and came to know the Lord early in my life — it was a natural thing to do. My life was bathed in prayer, love, and the church. We were at church twice every Sunday and every Wednesday evening for prayer services. I knew before I was a teenager that the Lord had a unique purpose for my life. I was determined to live my life for God and make a difference.

I also knew at an early age that I was not the same as everyone else. My brother and I used to spend many hours looking through the family's encyclopedia set. We would giggle nervously at the pictures of nude statues. My brother searched for Venus and Aphrodite. I looked for Apollo and Zeus. When I was five years old, my brother gave me a wallet for my birthday. It was an ever so cool wallet made of vinyl, whipstitched to look like hand-tooled leather. It had a place to hold pictures. For the next five years my wallet carried the pictures that meant the most to me — my siblings' school pictures, my best friend's picture, and an advertisement I cut out of my mother's *Better Homes and Gardens* magazine. The ad was for a weight loss program, and had the picture of a muscular man wearing only his swim trunks. I was not quite sure why, but that picture did something for me!

So, I started a life of finding men physically attractive while **not** being much attracted to women. I had the normal growing up crushes, but mine were all for men — my youth pastor, my male Sunday school teacher, and on television, Mr. Novak, Ben Casey, and that handsome man who played Adam on *Bonanza*! In high school, I had a crush on my algebra teacher and driver's education instructors, as well as certain football heroes.

I knew I was sexually turned on by attractive men and not by women, but I was convinced that if I found the right girl, I would change. I told myself that I was attracted to men because they were the image of what and who I wanted to be. I prayed that God would change me. From the time I was thirteen years old, I spent inordinate amounts of time on my knees praying that God would give me a lust for women. I bought heterosexual pornography, but the pictures did nothing for me — *nothing*. I knew I was a horrible person. My church told me I was an abomination. I stayed firmly and deeply in the closet.

I dated off and on throughout my fundamentalist college years. That was very convenient since we were not supposed to (or expected to) touch the opposite sex. It was a simple thing to retain my virginity through college. The first time I got serious with a young woman was just a few months before graduation from college. Everyone expected us to marry. I expected us to marry. But holding her in my arms felt awkward and clumsy. Kissing her actually made me queasy. I was not attracted to this woman physically. I kissed her and held her because I knew she needed that affection and it was the right thing to do. I prayed long and hard that God would give me a desire for her, but that desire never came. So, I broke off the relationship without a good explanation. I **knew** I had to break it off so she could find someone she deserved who would desire her with his heart.

I repeated this story over and over again for the next ten years. The women I got involved with just did not connect. I felt no passion for them. Each of them were attractive to me for their minds and their strengths. These were women that I wanted in my life for the rest of my life — as friends — but try as I might, and pray as I did, I could not make myself want to touch or to kiss or to desire them. To marry them would have meant to lie. So, one after the other, the relationships ended.

Finally at 33 years of age, and still a virgin, I had to admit to myself that God had not changed me. God had not given me a desire for women. I was gay! The first time I ever said those words was to another man — a man of strong faith who happened to be gay as well. It was an emotional and vulnerable evening and I left his home feeling true to myself for the first time in my life. I was not lying to myself anymore. That night, as I slept, I had a dream where Jesus came to my bedside. I was lying next to another man in my dream. I could not see the other man's face as he was sleeping face down next to me. Jesus looked at me and smiled. He held out his hands to encompass us as a couple and smiled a smile of love that let me know it was okay.

A few months later I began the further steps of coming out. For three years I had been extremely active as a leader in a new church work. I sang with the church band almost every week and helped develop and coordinate services based on multimedia and a strong sermon from the Bible. When I chose to come out to two of the other leaders of the church, I was stripped of all responsibility. "God could not use me," I was told, "because I was gay!" But, I had always been gay and God had used me plenty! I still wrestle with the pain of not being welcome at that church. It seemed wrong to me and still does, that to be used by God in that congregation, I had to lie about who I am. However, I believe God is a God of truth. I could not lie just to be acceptable to them. I knew I was acceptable to God.

After a lifetime of being used by God, four years of college with a theology degree, and two years of seminary with a Master's degree in Christian Education — I was a gay man who had been deserted by God's people. It was during this time that I read in the mainstream news media that attendance at churches was dropping. I noticed churches in my vicinity were renting their facilities for other uses just so they could keep their doors open. Also, I read in the gay press that there were a growing number of gay and lesbian believers longing to worship God, but not being allowed in the doors. The church was turning away the penitent. I was one of the many without a church home.

With the help of a local Evangelicals Concerned group, I found a handful of churches in my area that were accepting of homosexuals. So, I started visiting these churches. When I heard that the local Mennonite church was willing to let me worship with them, I was happy because I shared Anabaptist roots with the Mennonites and that heritage was terrifically important to me. On Epiphany Sunday in 1990, I climbed the stairs to enter this Mennonite Church and found my home.

I have been a member since the summer of 1990. There are other members who do not understand. There are those still opposed to my membership in the church because I am a gay man, but they are willing to put their problems aside and allow me to "work out my own salvation" along with them.

For the past three years, I have been the single foster father to four little boys with special medical needs. Two have AIDS, the other two have disabilities as a result of abuse. I could not possibly have made it in this wondrous ministry to the most needy of God's children, without the support and encouragement of my loving church. I thank my God daily for this group of caring Christians who allow me to continue my pilgrimage with them, without the need for lies and deceptions. They encourage me to follow my calling to make a difference in the lives of children.

8

Son of a Preacher Man

James Randolph Snelling VII

I was born during the great depression, the only child of a loving Church of the Brethren (COB) family in Portland, Oregon. My father was a Welsh immigrant and my mother was from many generations of Brethren. My father was in the "free" ministry of the COB and a barber by trade. I learned at an early age what prayer, faith, and trust were all about. We lived in trust and faith that our God would provide our basic needs. Any extra that we had was given to the church. Since we were to be separate from the world, my mother took me to and from school, so I would not be tainted by the world. My parents insisted that my friends had to be part of the COB, and most of the children who were my age lived miles away. My life revolved around the church. We were at church all day on Sunday, on Wednesday night for prayer meeting, on Thursday night for choir practice, and on Saturday night cleaning the church.

During the war years (my preteen years) the Portland COB increased in size. At last I had friends near me, with whom I was allowed to play. I was raised to be a pacifist (always turn the other cheek and go the extra mile), so I became a wimp, always dominated by my friends. Around the age of ten I realized that I liked boys better than girls, but socially I related to the other gender.

At 11 or 12 years I had my first sexual encounter with an older male and it happened at church camp. I was consumed with guilt, waiting for fire to rain down on me. I also was intrigued and allowed it to happen whenever I was around this young man. I found that girls were fun too.

I want to stress that I had the most wonderful, God-fearing parents that anyone could have, however, there was no way that I could approach them about my dilemma. Discussion about sex was taboo and very little information was available. I prayed and prayed that God would deliver me from my wanton desires, but, I continued to allow myself to be seduced by older teens of both sexes. It was their fault not mine, was it not? I spent more time on my knees praying and was filled with guilt and self-hatred.

My dream was to be a fashion designer. My father said that it was a worldly occupation and would not be compatible with the simple lifestyle which we espoused. So, I started to work in the neighborhood grocery store and that became my profession for 45 years.

When I was 16, a 14 year old Mennonite girl with beautiful red hair moved onto our block. We started dating and she started to come to the COB. Her parents had been recently divorced and they were not welcome in the Mennonite Church. We fell in love and I praised the Lord that my prayers had been answered. We made a vow that we would not let our sexual desires get out of control. We married soon after her 18th birthday and we had kept our vow. A year later our first son was born. My dad and grandfather were elated for we now had a James Randolph Snelling VIII to carry on the tradition. In the following ten years we had two more sons and three daughters. During that ten year period I was seduced a few times by older men. Much guilt and remorse always accompanied these dreadful interludes. I was so afraid that God would punish me in some way through my beautiful children. I thank God that never happened!

My wife was an excellent mother and we both worked hard at being good parents. Of course, I followed the same pattern as my parents had taught me: the church comes first. The sixties were upon us, attitudes were changing, a sexual revolution was at hand. My wife became a liberated woman, she wanted more than just being a mother. She started to do her own thing and I was too busy with church to see what was happening.

During the time of the Vietnam war I became a draft counselor at Portland State University. There I met a Christian bisexual man (I thought I was the only one). We became close friends, discussed our feelings, and explored our minds, but never our bodies. God had at last answered my prayers, I was beginning to understand myself. I also began to learn the great lesson to be patient and wait upon the Lord.

The gay revolution was also starting. I soon met more men and women like myself. Most of them could not understand how I could still have such a strong faith and trust in God. Most of them had been rejected by their families and the church. During a mission retreat of the COB, God revealed to me that it was time to come out. I could no longer live a lie! "But, God, how can I do this?" I asked. "What will happen to my wife and children? What will my church family think? I am a deacon, youth director, church moderator, and Sunday school teacher." Again, God spoke to me, "You can not love Me and be dishonest to yourself or to anyone else. You have trusted Me all of your life. Where is your faith?"

So, one Sunday morning in the fall of 1969 I came out to the adult Sunday school class. I had already come out to my wife after she had admitted to having an affair with a minister. Before coming out to the Sunday school class I told my parents that I was bisexual. Even though my father was in a pastorate in another part of the state, I knew it would soon hit the phone lines and I wanted them to hear it from me first. Believe it or not, my self-disclosure was a positive thing for the majority of the church family. However, as my terms of office expired, I was not nominated for anything for quite a few years. They loved me because they had witnessed my faith and trust in God, but it was hard for many to understand my bisexuality.

I have had opportunities to speak up for the rights of gays and I have also appeared on national television. Our state governor appointed me to the task force on gay youth and I was president of the largest gay organization in the northwest.

It seemed best to my wife and I to separate, the children stayed with me. Our divorce was finalized on my 40th birthday and I received custody of the children. When my ex-wife remarried several years later, we agreed that our two youngest daughters would live with her.

About three years later I fathered a son for a lesbian friend. Even though we never lived together, she, her lover, and son were a very integral part of my family. When this son was 15 years old, his mother died from a brain tumor. Not long after that the mother's partner and my son came to live in my household so we could provide the nurture he needed.

In 1977 I fell in love with another bisexual man. God blessed Victor and me with a wonderful relationship that lasted 17 years until God called him home three years ago. He died of brain cancer. God provided a way that I could stay home the last six months of his life to take care of him. During that time my mother became ill, my father had died several years earlier. I moved Mother to our home and took care of her until God took her home just a month before her 84th birthday. Victor had passed away three months earlier.

God gave me strength to get through that very trying time. I also had the support of my children and older grandchildren. God continues to bless me with a great relationship with all of my children and their spouses. I also have very good rapport with all of my 14 grandchildren. My grandchildren who are old enough know about my sexual orientation. They know too, that grandpa loves God and God comes first in my life. I tell them about my faith journey and the faith of their forefathers.

Today, I am married to a lesbian who has been my friend and confidante for nearly 20 years. We are raising her 15 year old grandnephew, so I am still a papa. We have a happy, loving, caring, and platonic life together. About eight years ago, God enabled me to make my adolescent dream a reality, when I established my own fashion design and consulting business named Iago. I am now semi-retired from the grocery company that I have worked with for 26 years. Besides my Iago business and relating to my grandchildren I spend a lot of time at the sewing machine. I do volunteer work for an AIDS charity group and have represented them in 16 major cities this past year. I am again very active at the Peace Church of the Brethren, serving on the board and as a deacon. I am involved in the Welcoming Congregations organization of Portland and had the privilege to attend three Brethren and Mennonite Council/Supporting Congregations Network conferences this year.

At 63 I am a very happy man. I know that being honest with oneself and God is the only way to live. I also know I have been one of the fortunate persons of diverse sexual orientation. I have not suffered a lot of discrimination. Many of my brothers and sisters have shared with me their painful stories in their struggle for acceptance and freedom. I empathize with my gay brothers and lesbian sisters in their on-going struggle to live their lives in open honesty. I believe that God wants each of us to be true to God and to ourselves.

I have confidence in God that what God has planned for my silver years will be best for me. Each new day is full of God's blessings if I take the time to receive them. "Now faith is the substance of things hoped for, the evidence of things not seen. . . But without faith it is impossible to please God, for [the one who comes] to God must believe that God is and that God is a rewarder of them who diligently seek God" (Hebrews 11:1 & 6, King James Version, Inclusive). Over the past weeks, as I have labored to write my faith story, an old chorus keeps singing in my mind: "Every day with Jesus is sweeter than the day before." I am thankful that Jesus is a very real presence in my life.

James R. Snelling VII, was born in 1934 in Portland, Oregon. He was raised and baptized in the Portland Church of the Brethren and has been active in the COB all of his life. He is the father of seven children and has 15 grandchildren and numerous foster children. When he was divorced, after God led him out of the closet over 25 years ago, he received custody of the majority of his children. He has a very close relationship with his entire family. Jim has been very public about who he is — a Christian and a gay/bi man. He has been happily married for two years to his best friend, who is a lesbian. Though semi-retired, he is still very active in the COB and the greater gay community.

9

A Life and Litany of Gratitude: The Faith Journey of a Gay Mennonite Sexagenarian

Dan Leatherman

If asked, even five years ago, to share my faith story, I would have eagerly emphasized in elegant chronological detail my personal pain, struggle, and bitterness. However, life is too short and space here too limited for that. Moreover, in recent years I have experienced much healing, and turning sixty the month I write this (October 1997) puts me in a retrospective, reflective mood. Looking back now, what I honestly feel most deeply is **gratitude**.

First, since I was destined to become an outsider, I am grateful to my family and community of origin for teaching me how to be one. Many gays and lesbians report feeling vaguely different from siblings and peers in childhood and youth without knowing why. Born and raised an eastern Pennsylvania Mennonite, I learned early and well that "nonconformity to the world" (as defined in the 1940s and 1950s) meant being different is okay because "peculiar people" are especially loved by God (1 Peter 2:9, *King James Version*). The *New Revised Standard Version* calls them, "God's own people."

I entered first grade in the middle of World War II, not only left-handed and a bookworm, but also as a Mennonite pacifist. Even among Mennonites, our family was partly outsiders. Poorer than many, we kept our 1933 Chevrolet until long after others had purchased postwar models. Because three of my four grandparents had been converts, we had many non-Mennonite relatives who early on gave me a wider window on the world. Ironically, I felt most like an outsider when totally with my own people in seventh and eighth grades at a Mennonite parochial school. Ever since, spending too much time in any one group — even those I objectively belong to or strongly identify with — makes me claustrophobic. I quickly become an in-house critic. This early training provided intellectual and psycho-spiritual armor that proved highly useful decades later when I deviated from accepted norms in church or society, for instance adopting interracial children, taking a draft-resister to Canada, quitting college teaching to become a letter carrier, and finally, coming out as gay.

With a strong need to belong, I usually behaved like a good boy, but my mind could not help asking my parents and Sunday school teachers unusual or embarrassing questions out of purely innocent curiosity — such as, "Why can't two men or two women marry each other?" Even when most angry at or estranged from church or society, I never rejected, or felt rejected by, God/Jesus. Somehow, I could criticize human shortcomings and hypocrisies without blaming the Divine Source. Even regarding sexuality, I never took on the heavy guilt trip we were supposed to. I joined the church at the young age of eight, not because I felt lost and feared hell, but to belong officially to God's Kingdom. After that major commitment, I refused to say the Pledge of Allegiance to the Flag at my one room school. I stood in respect but did not say the words. Ever since, I have sought that kind of middle-ground compromise whenever possible.

Three favorite Sunday school songs both symbolized and helped to create and sustain this combination of outsiderness, moderation, and closeness to God:

> Dare to be a Daniel,
> Dare to stand alone,
> Dare to have a purpose firm,
> Dare to make it known.

> Be careful little eyes, ears, hands, etc. what you do
> There's a Savior up above watching over us in love.

Earthly friends may prove untrue,
Doubts and fears assail,
Still there's One who cares for you,
And He will not fail.
Jesus never fails.
Heaven and earth may pass away,
But Jesus never fails!

Bishop John E. Lapp modeled God for me as a child — big and powerful, but with kind eyes, a gentle voice, and a warm handshake. God/Jesus watched over us not as a judge or spy but as a loving parent.

Second, I am grateful to Goshen College, a Mennonite institution in Indiana, where, first as a student, and later as political science professor, I absorbed and tried to practice the Anabaptist Vision. This was a wider view of Christian community, still different, but involved with rather than apart from the world. Too timid for a secular university, but too much a rebel for Eastern Mennonite in Virginia, which most college-bound Mennonite youth from my area then attended, I chose Goshen because it had a more liberal reputation. There I learned to know and appreciate many kinds of Mennonites plus other kinds of Christians and some people of other faiths. Without the intellectual stimulation and spiritual liberation I found there, I almost certainly would not be Mennonite today, perhaps not even Christian. Ultimately, of course, my search for wholeness found Goshen's self-absorption too narrow.

Third, I am grateful to the United States Postal Service for providing a steady, secure income, a job one can not lose simply for coming out as gay, and a chance to educate coworkers about greater acceptance of gay people. Given economic security, I could tolerate considerable harassment, and being able to leave job concerns at the time-clock, I could use off-duty energy to work in and with the local gay community. Too few of us have the talent or skills for such work combined with the freedom to be out of the closet.

After leaving teaching in 1970, I first tried to enter the gay world in 1971 in Chicago. However, losing family, church, and economic security all at once and finding only the stereotypical *Boys in the Band* gay scene (where I was still an outsider) produced a major mid-life identity crisis. When the postal job opened, I returned to family and church in Goshen as a double outsider. At the post office I was a Mennonite and an ex-professor. At College Mennonite Church, where I was formerly a professor, now I was a blue-collar worker. Ten lonely years later, including 1980 — a year of tortuous counseling and decision — I finally came out fully and proudly in January 1981 as a gay man.

Fourth, I am grateful to the Good Shepherd Parish of the Metropolitan Community Church in Chicago and the independent Open Door Chapel in Fort Wayne, Indiana (gay-orientated congregations) for providing the spiritual nurture and fellowship I so desperately needed my first few years of openly gay life. At my very first Good Shepherd service (May 1980) we sang Harry Emerson Fosdick's powerful hymn, "God of Grace and God of Glory. . . . Grant us wisdom, grant us courage for the facing of this hour . . . the living of these days." It was extra powerful for me in the middle of that wrenching year. A friend thought I would find Open Door too evangelical, but for several years I took a van load of gay people to its services every Sunday evening. I needed a church, was able to contribute, and learned to appreciate a wider range of worship styles.

Fifth, I am grateful for having been a husband and father, even though I finally had to leave my marriage after twenty years in order to live out what I felt inside. Sexually, by age nine or ten I was already aware of my attraction to males and engaged in the usual adolescent experimentation with other boys my age or a little older. In a few years they started noticing girls but I did not. I never dated in high school and only sporadically in college. However, craving intimacy of heart and mind with another person, I married two years after graduation, knowing my attraction to men, but thinking I could control any gay urges because I loved my wife. Such was then the only conceivable choice, especially given the career I was destined for — teaching at a church college. As husband and father I experienced much joy and also learned to accept and fulfill responsibilities that many singles (gay or straight) often do not. My ex-wife and I are on speaking terms and I have gradually reestablished rapport with our children. I am also grateful to two long-term gay partners (one five years, the second, six) for broadening my spiritual insights and experience in many ways.

Sixth, I am grateful to Assembly Mennonite (Goshen, Indiana, 1986-88) and to Southside Fellowship (Elkhart, Indiana, since 1992) for being congregations of refuge for me when, after years of gay activism, I had to return to my spiritual roots, like Elijah to Horeb, for refueling due to burnout. After a year of study and discussion, Southside accepted me as a full member in January 1994, even if I would reenter a committed gay relationship. Such acceptance has led to marvelous spiritual healing for me, while jeopardizing the congregation's own membership in a district conference. Another very meaningful connection, especially in the early 1980's when I had no local church home, was the Brethren/Mennonite Council for Lesbian and Gay Concerns (BMC). Now I relate more closely to its Supportive Congregations Network.

Seventh, I am grateful to Church of the Good Shepherd in Exile, the little gay congregation I helped found in 1988, that met first in Elkhart, now in South Bend. Co-pastored by an ex-Lutheran minister and a former Catholic priest, it has members from widely varied religious backgrounds and a wonderfully ecumenical worship style and fellowship. For a while, I was "bi-churchual" — Mennonite roots Sunday morning and gay Christian wings Sunday evening. But such a schedule became too heavy, I gave up the gay one and retained the Mennonite one. In my opinion "ghetto" churches of any kind should be only temporary to meet the spiritual needs of marginalized groups until mainstream churches accept us as whole persons.

Finally, I am grateful to gay and lesbian Christian authors such as John McNeil, John Boswell, and Carter Hayward, as well as Jewish, Buddhist, Wiccan, Quaker, and Unitarian writers and personal friends of both genders who have greatly enriched my spiritual life. Though he himself seems to have succumbed to cult figure status, I am especially indebted to Matthew Fox's *Creation Theology*, which calls for both "deep ecumenism" and "deep ecology." To save the planet from socio-ecological disaster, Christians must dialogue not only among themselves, but with people of other faiths, and humans once again must see ourselves with other species as part of, not outside or above, nature. The same ideological arrogance that ruling classes use to justify exploiting groups defined as marginal also considers lesser species expendable when pursuing human needs.

When I retire in 2001, I hope to build a self-sufficient, solar-powered home for sustainable, simple, senior living/ loving somewhere in the Southwest — where, quite likely, organized gays and Mennonites will not exist. However, to paraphrase Dr. Martin Luther King's Memphis speech, "It won't matter to me then, for I've been to the mountain top and seen the Promised Land." I will no longer need to define and defend these partial identities but can integrate them into a larger human vision and task that I feel God has been preparing me for all along. I once romantically hoped to find a committed partner who was Mennonite or willing to convert. Now I wonder if that is even desirable as long as the two of us are spiritually compatible.

Whatever my geo-social location, I can claim *Beth El* (God is in this place). "No storm can shake my inmost calm while to that Rock I'm clinging." So, "Lead on, O cloud of Presence . . . in wilderness and desert our tribe shall make its home." The journey, not just the destination, is important. Tradition provides structure and stability, but, like the heartwood of a tree, is essentially dead, life and growth occur only in the outer ring, and a grapevine produces fruit only on this year's new growth. While I accept and appreciate my past with all its struggles, I eagerly anticipate the future and its promise of even greater growth toward wholeness.

Dan Leatherman was born in Lansdale, Pennsylvania, in 1937. He is a graduate of Goshen College, Goshen, Indiana, and the University of Chicago. He served as a professor at Goshen College (1963-69) and at Stetson University, DeLand, Florida (1969-70). In 1971 he changed professions to become a letter carrier for the United States Postal Service with retirement scheduled for 2001. He was married for 20 years and is the father of four children, three of whom are adopted, and he has four grandchildren. Dan is a member of Southside Fellowship (Mennonite) of Elkhart, Indiana.

10

From Sadness to Joy

Anonymous

It fills my heart with sadness when I look back and realize that for most of my life I felt forced to keep the real me hidden from the rest of the world. I was born a lesbian child in a Mennonite family. As a child growing up in a rural, conservative part of the country, I did not even know what a lesbian was. I just knew that somehow I was different from everyone else in my world.

My growing up years were spent on a farm in Lancaster County, Pennsylvania. I was the only girl in a neighborhood of boys, so I spent my time doing stereotypically boyish things — building forts, playing ice hockey and baseball, and of course helping with the farm work. As I grew older, differences became apparent between the boys and me and I began to spend more and more time alone. I did not have many close friends in school, because farm chores limited after school sports and parties. Instead, I lost myself in school and learning. My closest friends were at my church — a moderately conservative Mennonite congregation. I became very active in the youth group, serving as president for several years. I also attended the local Mennonite high school, which served as an extension for the church and the teachings of the church. During the time of my growing up, I allowed the church to dictate my beliefs. I did not know that I could think through issues for myself, and draw my own conclusions.

I dated little during my teenage years. It felt too awkward. I preferred to be by myself or with a group of friends. During this stage of my life, I still gave little thought to my sexuality. Like most good Mennonite families of that era, we did not talk about sex at all — in any context. Because of my conservative upbringing in a very rural area, I was never exposed to homosexuality. I remember having crushes on girls or women in my life. Not knowing what it meant, I dismissed it as a fleeting feeling. It was not until I entered college and was exposed to the world, that it even occurred to me that I might be a lesbian. After four years of private school, I chose to enter a secular state college. I was beginning to feel that I could not let someone else tell me what to believe for the rest of my life. I even turned down a small scholarship to a private Mennonite college because I wanted to experience the rest of the world, to learn new ways of looking at things, and to reshape my beliefs.

I do not remember the exact moment that I realized I might be a lesbian. I do remember that even in my childhood I felt I was different from my family and my church friends and that they might not approve of who I thought I was. After graduating from college I moved out of my parents' house and into a new freedom. I no longer had to go to church just because I lived at home and Mom and Dad said I had to go. However, with this freedom came distance, because I was afraid that if Mom and Dad knew what changes were really happening in my life, they would disown me as their daughter. So, I stayed away, or made excuses to leave family activities early. I did not want to spend too much time with them so they would not catch on. I stopped going to church because I knew from what I had learned as a child that God and the church would disapprove of my new thoughts and feelings. However, I needed friends. Not knowing where else to look, I tried visiting the local lesbian bar. I did not like it. It was dark and depressing, and I waited a whole year before trying it again. This time I was so needy for friends that I began to fit in. There I made contact with people just like me, individuals who did not feel at home in most other social settings. They were there to forget their pain and loneliness.

It was in the bar that I became aware of a church for gays and lesbians — the Metropolitan Community Church. It took a long time for me to work up the courage to go because I still felt that God did not like who I was. When a friend asked me to go with her, I agreed. I visited sporadically for a year and finally started to feel as if I had found a place to belong. I began working through who I was and what I believed. Some of the pains of my childhood began to heal as I came to grips with family issues. Up until this time, I had not talked to my parents about my sexuality, but as I grew more healthy, it became obvious to me that I had to tell them. I was very afraid that they would turn me away because of their beliefs. It took all my courage to tell them. Their reaction was that they had thought I might be lesbian, but they were afraid to ask. My dad seemed to take it easier than my mom. He gave me a big hug and said, "You are still our daughter and we love you." Mom seemed to have a harder time with it. As we parted ways that morning, she gave me a half-hearted hug, and I remember wondering if she would ever talk to me again.

Several weeks went by until I had contact with my parents again. It was Mother's Day and I felt obligated to call my Mom. She sounded very distant, as if she did not know how to deal with the bomb I had dropped on them. It was hard at first, we did not talk about it, but I decided I was going to continue just being who I was. As time went on, it became less difficult. I started to introduce my family to my church friends and I think it was through the witness of our lives that Mom and Dad decided we were not all that bad. Maybe you actually could be gay and Christian at the same time. They started reading and learning. They joined a support group for Mennonite families of gay and lesbian children. It was hard for them to change years of old beliefs and thinking, just as it had been for me, but they were trying! Unfortunately, shortly after they began this journey my dad died and Mom has had to continue on her own. It seems as if Dad's death made her even more determined to search for the truth. She has lost some old friends, but made some new ones during the process of her journey. Now she stands up for our cause, and visits our church regularly.

Sadly, not all of my family members have followed the same journey of discovery as Mom. As I was writing this story, both my ex-sisters-in-law made it very clear that they do not approve of my life-style. One of them told me of an agreement they had made about the spiritual welfare of their children. They agreed that it was harmful for my two nephews and my niece to be in my presence. My ex-sister-in-law told me I was evil, and that there was a spiritual battle going on inside of me that I was losing. She had an answer for every comment I made, almost as if she had been coached or brainwashed. I was shocked. I had no idea that she was so caught up in the rhetoric of the religious right. Up until that moment, we had never had a conversation about my sexuality. Only a few short months before, I was giving my niece rides home. It breaks my heart to imagine the hateful things that my young niece and nephews are being taught and how their lives will be shaped by the lessons of fear and hate they are hearing.

This part of my story is complicated by my entangled family history and the fact that both of my sisters-in-law are divorced from my brothers. Both of my brothers are tolerant and accepting of who I am. They both attended my Holy Union with their new wives. However, neither of them has custody of their children, and very little say, if any, as to what happens in their lives. It is very frustrating. Sometimes I start thinking that there is nothing we can say or do to change the situation. Then I recall that I felt the same way when I first came out to my parents and I see a glimmer of hope. All I can do is to wait, pray, and continue to live my life as a witness that God created me both gay and Christian.

I want to go back a little bit to share my journey with the Metropolitan Community Church. As I already mentioned, it was when I found MCC that I found a place to belong. It was a safe place to reconcile my sexuality and my Christianity. I discovered that God does still love me, and that it is possible to be gay and Christian. For the first year or two, I just sat back and enjoyed feeling welcome in a church again, but soon I felt the need to become involved. Just as I had been an active member of the church I grew up in, so I needed to be active in MCC. I helped our congregation in our search for our own church building. We had always worshipped in someone else's space, now it was time for us to find our own. I also became involved on the Board of Directors, and within a year was appointed vice moderator of the Board. It was during this time that my church was in the process of a pastoral search and, as a member of the Board, I was very involved in this process. In a wonderful expression of the providence of God, the pastor we called, who came from 3,000 miles away, eventually became my spouse. Who says God does not have a sense of humor? Now, as the pastor's spouse, I am more involved in my church than ever, just in a different role.

It was at MCC that I also found friends. I thought that the people I had met earlier in my journey at the bar were my friends, but the only thing we had in common was loneliness. At MCC, I found true friends, people like me. They were not satisfied to sit around in a bar waiting for life to come to them and feeling sorry for themselves. These were people who were actively searching for answers. We may all be at different stages in our journey, but we all have a common goal, we want to learn about God and serve God as best we can.

Today I am proud of who I am, confident that God loves me, and an active member of my church. It has not been easy to reach this point in my life. I passed through years of loneliness and uncertainty, and sometimes I think that I wasted all of those years. However, I realize that they were just part of the journey that has brought me here. All of the lessons I learned have helped to make me who I am today, a Christian who happens to be a lesbian.

The 37 year old author lives in Pennsylvania. She has been living in a committed relationship for the past two years that has been blessed by her church in a Holy Union ceremony. She spent 16 years working in the retail and marketing business. After "burning out," she and a friend started their own remodeling and cleaning business. It has been very successful for the past five years. She is very much involved in her Metropolitan Community Church.

11

My Faith Journey

Russ Schmidt

I grew up in the small General Conference Mennonite (GC) farming community of Goessel, Kansas. God and the Mennonite church were at the center of every aspect of life. Virtually everyone in the community went to one of the three GC Mennonite churches in or near Goessel. All the surrounding towns were also largely Mennonite, although some of them included "old" Mennonite, Mennonite Brethren, and Holdeman Mennonite churches. Our life revolved around the church. This meant worship and Sunday School on Sunday mornings, Christian Endeavor or Youth Fellowship on Sunday nights, and choir rehearsals and Bible studies on Wednesday nights. The people I went to church with were also the people I went to school with, including my teachers. The school had to coordinate its activities with the churches so there would not be any conflicts. There were few social activities that were not associated with either the church or school, and even those groups involved the same people — that was simply the composition of the community.

Enjoyable memories from my childhood include studying Sunday School lessons and memorizing Bible verses on Saturday nights and going to vacation Bible school in the summer. The God I believed in was probably the type of God most of us believed in as children: all loving, all powerful, and all knowing. I, on the other hand, thought I was the worst of all possible sinners. I was a serious child who was shy and over-whelmed with insecurities and a sense of my own sinfulness. In

59

spite of having wonderful, loving parents I never learned to like myself. I did not like to play the rough and tumble games the other boys played and grew up being called a sissy and a fairy by my classmates. My biggest fear was that the other kids in school would find out I liked to play with Barbie dolls. Consequently, I was a loner, scared that the other kids would find out who I really was.

My life changed dramatically and suddenly when I went to our church's summer camp just before I started high school. During our closing morning worship service by the river, there was suddenly what I then could only understand as an outpouring of the Holy Spirit on our group. I was overwhelmed by emotions. I felt a pouring out of God's love and an inner peace that I had never known before. God suddenly was not just out there, but was deeply a part of my very soul. For the first time in my life, I truly felt that God loved *me*, and I comprehended the story of Christ dying for *my* sins. I knew that the sin and shame I felt about my life was forgiven. I was free, and I tasted the eternity of God.

Overnight my personality changed. I was no longer shy and ashamed of myself, but felt like a new creation — bold and confident in my status as a child of God. Some of the other kids who had shared the same experience by the river that morning decided to get together on a weekly basis for Bible study, singing, and prayer. I became a leader in this group. Because of the intense desire to recapture the spiritual high of summer camp, I went to many evangelical revival meetings and eventually became involved in the charismatic movement. I was also constantly reading the Bible. By the time I finished high school I had read through the entire Bible, book by book, and read through the New Testament many times.

One of the overwhelming aspects of this period in my life was believing that Jesus would return at any moment. I became an expert on rapture theology. One of my favorite books was *The Late Great Planet Earth*. Of course, it was my duty as a Christian to make sure that as many other people as possible would also be taken in the rapture. Thus I always wore buttons saying "Jesus Loves You" or "Jesus is Coming Soon." I always carried my Bible to class, filled every conversation with "Praise the Lord," and carried *The Four Spiritual Laws* in my pocket at all times. I never wanted to miss an opportunity to be a witness and to possibly be able to save someone.

My theology at that time was clear — growing up in a Mennonite family and going to all the church activities were not the same as being saved, not the same as having a personal relationship with Jesus Christ as one's savior from sin. Thus I viewed just about everyone in school who was not part of our Bible Study group, let alone the rest of the world, to be in need of salvation. Looking back on this period of my life I am somewhat embarrassed. I was very judgmental of others and had no tolerance for any beliefs that differed from my own. Yet I cannot dismiss this part of my life either, for something profound was happening in terms of spiritual formation. I experienced God in a personal, yet transcendent way, that changed my personality. I became aware, at a deep level, of my relationship to the Creator of the universe.

At the same time I was experiencing this spiritual awakening, I was also becoming more aware of my sexuality. Looking back on those years, it seems so obvious that I was gay. I participated in music and drama activities instead of sports and took Home Economics classes instead of shop. I never dated any girls but I was always fantasizing about several of the gorgeous guys on the boys' varsity basketball team. Because there were no gay mentors in my community, however, I had no idea that what I was feeling was normal — if one is a gay male. All I knew is that I was not like most people, and the only way I knew to interpret this reality was to call my desires sinful. I can now see that my fantasy of being raptured off the planet into the arms of Jesus had a certain erotic element that I was trying to suppress. I think my religious fervor at this stage in my life was in part due to the fact that Jesus was the only male who it was safe for me to openly love.

As I became more and more aware of my sexual attraction to men, my walls of denial went up just as quickly. Although I do not remember any raging homophobes in church or on television declaring how sinful gay men were, somehow I picked up the belief that homosexuals had abandoned God for their own depravity. I knew, however, that I was a good person who loved God, so that meant I could not be a homosexual. Still I had these thoughts and desires. I remember hours of prayer and days of fasting to have God change this part of my life. I went to many revival meetings and spiritual renewal retreats, always rededicating my life to Christ and begging God to transform my sexual desires. Yet my fervent prayers were never answered. I remember by the end of high school that I frequently read Jesus' words in Matthew 5:30, "if your right hand causes you to sin, cut it off and throw it away, it is better for you to lose one of your members than for your whole body to go into hell" (New Revised Standard Version). Since my prayers and fasting were not working, I began to contemplate suicide as a way to avoid going to hell.

The conflict I felt between my spirituality and my sexuality only increased when I started college. I majored in Bible and Religion at Bethel College in Newton, Kansas, and planned to go into the ministry after graduating. I was also president of the Western District Conference Young People's Union, which traveled to all the Mennonite church youth groups in Kansas and Oklahoma. I studied Greek so I could read the Bible in the original language. At Bethel, I was challenged by college friends and professors regarding faith and political justice issues in the world. At the same time, I found a corner grocery store in town that sold gay male pornography and accidentally discovered several places where gay men picked each other up for brief, anonymous sexual encounters. Thus I developed a double life. I remember sneaking off campus to have sex with strange men, and then doing incredible mental gymnastics telling myself I was not gay. I continued to believe I just had a problem — one that would go away after I became married. I kept believing I could not possibly be gay — just look at all the good Christian things I was doing.

After graduating from Bethel I went into the Mennonite Voluntary Service program in Cincinnati. Two days a week I did housing renovation work for low income families in the city's poorest section. The other three days a week I worked as the staff person for the Cincinnati Coalition for Peace Education. This was the beginning of the Reagan years and I helped develop and deliver programs on alternatives to the arms race for churches and schools. I also helped organize demonstrations and peace marches, and was active working with a wide range of political, religious, and social groups.

During my years in Cincinnati I began questioning the beliefs with which I had grown up. Increasingly Christianity did not make sense; its answers to cosmic questions just seemed too easy. During my free time I enrolled in a class at the Hebrew Union College, the seminary of Reformed Judaism in Cincinnati. I considered converting to Judaism. I also began reading a number of books on Zen Buddhism. I found that I was agreeing more with these other religions than with Christianity. Eventually I decided to stop calling myself a Christian. Ironically, I felt alive in a new and deeper way as I continued to explore spirituality through these other traditions.

Something else was happening during this time in my life. I finally came to accept that I was gay. The event that triggered my coming out was receiving a letter from a woman I had known since junior high school. I had always assumed she would eventually become my wife. In the letter she told me she was engaged to someone else. I remember holding the letter, stunned, and saying, "I am gay." I suddenly realized that I had been using the fantasy of marrying her to deny my true sexual orientation. With that fantasy suddenly shattered, the blinders fell off and I could see I was not just going through a phase.

Real acceptance, however, did not come for several months until I saw the movie *Ordinary People*. In that movie, the main character is a teenage boy who survived a boating accident in which his brother drowned. He is overwhelmed by feelings of guilt and attempts suicide. The turning point for him comes when he finally accepts that he was not responsible for his brother's death. For some reason this movie triggered the realization in me that I did not do anything to make me gay. That is how God had created me — I was not responsible. If God made me that way, then there was nothing sinful or wrong with that. I remember very clearly the next day I stood before a mirror and said to myself, "You are gay." And I saw my image smile back at me.

Slowly I started coming out to friends and only found acceptance. I finally decided to tell my family. I flew home to Kansas and told my parents I had something very important to discuss with them. I did not think they would reject me, but was sure the relationship would be severely strained. Although I had prepared a whole speech in which I wanted to convince them to accept me, I only got a few lines into it before they stopped me. They both came over to me, hugged me and kissed me and said they loved me just as they always had. They asked if I was happy, and they could see that I was, and that was enough for them.

After my two years with Mennonite Voluntary Service, I moved to Berkeley, California, to study at the Pacific School of Religion. My original intention was to study comparative religions with the hope that I could eventually travel to Tibet and become a Buddhist monk. I quickly came to the realization, however, that I could not just change worldviews and religious myths like one changes one's clothes. I realized that the symbols and rituals I had grown up with in the Mennonite Church were a deep part of me. I had to deal with them if my spirituality was to have any integrity. I also learned the meaning of metaphor in religious life and realized I could take the Christian language and symbols I was not comfortable with and give them my own meanings. So my years in seminary ended up being a time for me to reclaim my Christian faith and Mennonite roots and to integrate that with the new spiritual and sexual reality I was living.

For my Masters thesis I tried to articulate the problem I had with traditional concepts of God and build a new way of thinking about God based on my study of a wide range of theologies and my experience as a gay man. Although it has now been over ten years since I wrote that thesis, I find that my theological framework remains the same. Although it would be presumptuous to call my work a gay theology, I have found affirmation from many gay and straight friends. I share the following as a way to let others know how one gay man thinks about God.

First, to me God is what Paul Tillich calls "the Ground of Being." In other words, the God I believe in is not a Being, but *being itself.* Frequently we use the phrases that God is love, or God is life. What is usually meant is that God is a supernatural being who loves and God is a supernatural being who creates life. What I am saying is that for me God is love itself. God is life itself. In my mind, that is a big difference. Although God is experienced as personal, God is not a person.

Second, I understand God's relationship to the world through the process philosophy articulated by Alfred North Whitehead. In this worldview all reality is inter-related. Every event and every molecule ultimately affects every other event and every other molecule. Every encounter one has with another person changes both of them, which in turn affects all their future encounters. Reality, thus, is a constant state of becoming. God is included in this reality. We are shaped by God *and* at the same time we shape God. God is not a supernatural being who is ontologically separate from creation, existing immutably beyond space and time. Who God is and what God is able to do in our world is partially dependent on who we are and what we allow God to do through the world we create.

Finally, the God I believe in is best understood through the power of mutual relationship, also known as love, rather than through coercive power. The God I believe in does not have the power to prevent holocausts or bombings or tornadoes. We, as a part of creation, are not puppets on strings that can be manipulated so easily. Still, I believe God is the greatest power in the universe — but that power is manifested through the persuasive power of loving relationships. Jesus is the primary example of this power. Through the relationships he established with his disciples and through his struggle for justice for the poor and oppressed, people recognized the loving power of God and declared Jesus to be the Christ.

Because love is the strongest power in the universe, I believe God is better addressed as Lover, rather than Lord. My experience as a gay man enters my theology at this point. I think same gender relationships can be a model for understanding our relationship to God. I do not think it is a mere coincidence that our culture, which for millenniums has placed men above women, has a male deity and a female church. The image of a male God who is all powerful, who can do whatever "he" desires, and a church that is supposed to submit to the will of God and do whatever "he" says, has been instructive at a mythological level for male-female relationships.

While I certainly do not believe that heterosexual relationships are inherently hierarchical, there is something about gay relationships that I believe can be instructive for theology, which in turn can impact all human relationships. In a gay love relationship the gender of the partners is the same. Sexual roles of dominance are completely inter-changeable and must be negotiated. There is a sense of equality in this reciprocity that I believe can be a model for theology.

In such a theology, God is not the only creator, we are creators too. God not only exercises power over and through us, we also exercise power over and through God. Who God is and what God is able to do is limited by what is actually possible in the real world. Just as a person's adult reality is shaped and limited by childhood experiences (being raised in a loving home versus being sexually and physically abused, for example), in the same way who God is able to be in our world today is shaped and limited by the world we create for God. For example, God was not able to be the deliverer and savior during the holocaust during World War II because a silent world did not make that an option for God.

When God is seen as our Lover (and I mean lover, not legal spouse), rather than Lord, I believe theology changes dramatically. We no longer must submit to some eternal will, but enter into a dynamic relationship with God. We open ourselves to passion, searching, questioning, exploration, and growth. We are also able to have lovers' quarrels with God and negotiate compromises. I am who I am because God is the life inside me. Who God is, is partially because of who I am and the types of relationships I have with other people and the environment around me. Thus, God and I are lovers in a dynamic relationship within a particular segment of this time-space continuum known as my life.

I am grateful to have a church (First Mennonite Church of San Francisco) which supports both my spirituality and my sexuality. Although neither falls within the boundaries of traditional Mennonite faith and life, members of my congregation accept me. They challenge me to grow in my own direction while keeping my roots planted in the Mennonite tradition. Although there are times when I get furious at the larger church conferences and institutions (especially on the issue of homosexuality), I am firmly committed to my local congregation. They are my family. They are my community. Christian faith as I have come to understand it in the Mennonite tradition is based on this type of community. It is from this group that I am both nurtured and challenged to keep growing. My prayer is that the larger Mennonite church will come to see its gay, lesbian, bisexual, and transgendered brothers and sisters as a valued part of the church and encourage their participation and growth.

Russ Schmidt was raised on a dairy farm in a small Mennonite community in central Kansas. He earned his BA in Bible and Religion at Bethel College in North Newton, Kansas, and later his MA in Systematic Theology from Pacific School of Religion in Berkeley, California. He worked for eight years as an administrator in substance abuse programs in San Francisco, California; Reno, Nevada; and Providence, Rhode Island. He then changed careers and received his MS in Nursing from San Francisco State University. He is currently working as a registered nurse in San Francisco in both hospital and outpatient settings. Russ is active with the First Mennonite Church of San Francisco where he serves on the Voluntary Service Support Committee and as church treasurer. He enjoys photography, movies, traveling, and chocolate.

12

Queer Journey — Continuing

Gloria Kropf Nafziger

Approximately seven years ago, while in a traditional Mennonite marriage with three young daughters, I came out to myself as **lesbian**. I eventually also came out to the entire world, or so it seemed to me, as **lesbian**. Some reflections on that time, written now seven years later, as well as some of my journal writings from that time follow.

I married one of my best friends when I was 19 years old. I celebrated my good fortune in being able to fit into the community norms, and being able to be with someone who would let me be me! I believed that we would be one of those couples who celebrated our 50th, perhaps even our 60th wedding anniversary. While following the traditional norms of the time, working part-time, supporting his work, staying home with the babies, I certainly found much happiness and contentment. Mixed with this was a strong yearning for something more. This something more could hardly be expressed, much less understood. I found female friendships extremely important and supportive in my constant exploration and questioning of the world I had come to embrace as my own.

The Mennonite faith community was my world, my faith tradition. I found the community to be supportive, though irritating at times because they refused to consider my questions. This tradition was the world of safety and familiarity. I trusted them to meet my needs and hear my questions — to engage in the process of living and growing. I knew what was expected and I knew how to get approval. And I got it!

However it seemed no matter how much I got, it was still never quite enough. The nagging in my soul pushed me to question my faith, the patriarchal world in which I lived, and the very basis of my life-community sanction. I realized that I could only find peace within myself and my own personal relationship to the spirit-god world. This was in many ways what my community taught me, however, there seemed to be a contradiction.

Personal faith was important but it needed to fall within the guidelines of the larger community. I learned that my questions were accepted, but when I asked too many, I was laughed at, or told they were not legitimate questions, or *worse yet*, that I was no longer in relation to God. How, I wondered, could they question my relationship to God when they did not even know or ask to hear my story?

The day I named myself as lesbian I felt a freedom and a recognition of the greatest of divine love for me in a way that all the working in the church had never provided me. I also recognized the reality of my "otherness." I would never be able to be a part of these people whom I loved. The loss, while at the same time being full of both pain and celebration, pushed me on the continuous journey of spiritual development and awareness and is moving me from the dualistic understanding of my youth. The journey has only just begun. Through the journey I recognize a

> Bag of dreams —
>> Collapsed and Broken —
>
> Dreams
>> Illusions
>> I the token
> Learn and grow to realms beyond
>> Where oh where can peace be found?

Struggling to find peace I see dimly as . . .

> The fog blankets the earth
> I see dimly through the mist
> Unsure of truth
> I seek a way through the fog
>> to better worlds of hope
>> to lands of clarity

                    hope
                    truth
Is it a dream this voyage through the fog?
What is reality?
            Is it in the fog
        dreams and hopes and fears
the fog illuminates it —
        the dream encompasses
                the hope, the belief, the reality?
Peace, continued struggle?
    And so I travel on
            Dreaming, hoping, fearing
Attempting to find peace
    Attempting to break
            through the fog

I fear the walk, I fear the journey yet untraveled and yet I look with anticipation to a bright and hopeful dawn where peace may come. I feel used — misunderstood like I am a being who meets the needs of those around me to help unscramble felt, acknowledged, and even unacknowledged realities. I hoped for more. I wanted more. Wanted lasting truth, but know none, none can claim the truth and so I walk unsure of truth but struggling to find realities hoping in the process not to hurt those so dear and precious on the journey. I grieve for pain, both yours and mine, and I am wishing it were not so but truth says in the pain will come my growth.

Emotions are the wellspring of my being and yet — I long to deny their reality — their truth. The what of who I am, the passion of what I feel, where I belong — who I long to be —
        FREE to be all that I am meant to be
open to the growth   the opening doors   the slamming doors
        that I can't and won't be locked behind!
Truth what is it?
        a young tree growing toward maturity
        to be cut down, to be trimmed
                to be used for chairs,
    perhaps a cross to bring life

to bring hope
truth in the sacrifice

a child wanders alone, unafraid
giving, sharing — till told
don't go, watch out, don't trust
you'll be hurt
truth in the innocence

a flower blooms brings forth nectar
for honey sweet giving to bees, giving to humanity,
painlessly, painfully,
sacrificing life's essence for growth,
for wholeness

truth in the sacrifice
truth in the innocence
truth in the pain

Knowledge comes forth

. . . and so the journey continues, the ups the downs, all a part of the becoming, the growing, the learning — about who I am in relation to this world I live in. I celebrate the possibilities, the options, and the limitations (sometimes)! Today, as I prepare for a public celebration of relationship with the woman who I look forward to spending my gray years with

I wonder at the ecstasy of being
of loving of living of celebrating
I wonder at the joy the miracle
the wonder of life,
bounteous mystery
ebbing and flowing
with passion and wonder
through shallows and deep
while I mysteriously ride forward
in love
in celebration
of you, of me,
of us, family,
of community.

In Part Two, **Lora Nafziger**, Gloria's daughter, shares her experience of church and family around the time of her mother's coming out. See page 240, Chapter 45.

Gloria Kropf Nafziger enjoys the variety of roles that life offers her. She lives in Kitchener, Ontario, with her partner, Liwana, and three daughters, Lora, Lisa, and Kaitlyn. (Lora is presently serving a term in Voluntary Service in Oregon.) They participate in the life of Olive Branch Mennonite Church. Gloria has found that being the mother of teenagers is exciting, rewarding, and exhausting! Besides being involved in the lives of her family, Gloria is also involved in the local chapter of the Brethren/Mennonite Council for Lesbian and Gay Concerns (BMC-Eastern Canada). As a psychotherapist, she enjoys working with people about a variety of issues, parti- cularly those where the journey includes finding and reclaiming spirituality.

The opportunity to share her story in a variety of settings, both personal and professional, pushes her to continue her own journey with the Divine.

13

My Spiritual Journey

Dubose McLane

I am a 74 year old gay man, who was raised by Presbyterian parents in South Texas. My father was an ordained Presbyterian minister and was president for 40 years of a home mission school for Latin American students from Mexico and Texas. My twin brother is also an ordained Presbyterian minister. My older brother was a university professor before retiring.

I discovered I was gay about the age of 25. At that time I was working as production manager for the Southern Presbyterian Church at the headquarters of their Board of Christian Education in Richmond, Virginia. I was in charge of all of their printing. Being gay bothered me a great deal, knowing that all the churches of America condemned my sexuality as sinful and disgraceful. I had no one to turn to, since I was ashamed to talk to my parents or anyone else.

Due to my overwhelming feeling of guilt and unworthiness, I suffered a severe nervous breakdown. After three attempts at suicide, I spent the next two years in a mental hospital. I was subjected to electric and insulin-induced shock treatments, which caused permanent loss of memory. The doctors highly recommended that I give up working full-time for the Presbyterian denomination or I would never get well! They said the conflict was one of the reasons for my mental breakdown.

Six months later I moved to New York City and began a new career as production manager for several book publishing firms. I was not affiliated with any church, but occasionally visited Marble Collegiate Church. Their assistant pastor was in seminary with my twin brother in Texas many years earlier. He was also a therapist and counselor, and was willing to counsel with me. At the same time, I started to see a psychiatrist on a weekly basis. This lasted three years and was not at all successful.

While living in New York City, I read a short story in *The Advocate* magazine about a pastor who had started a new church in Los Angeles for gays and lesbians. His name was Troy Perry, but they did not give the address or location of the church. I was so intrigued by this idea that I wrote a letter to Troy Perry, and asked the editor of *The Advocate* to forward it to him. Over six months went by and I had no answer. I assumed that the editor did not forward my letter or Troy decided not to answer it. I felt estranged from mainline churches because of their attitude toward gays and lesbians, therefore, I quit attending them altogether. However, I wanted to know a lot more about this new Metropolitan Community Church (MCC).

Then one eventful day I received a telephone call from Rev. Howard Wells, who said he had just arrived in New York City and Troy had given him my old letter! He was the former pastor of the MCC of San Francisco and Troy had sent him to Manhattan to begin a church there. From that moment on, I became an active member of MCC of New York City and am the last remaining charter member of that congregation. I served on the first Board of Directors and subsequent boards as well. I was also the treasurer for many years. Often I had the privilege of representing our congregation as the lay delegate to the biannual General Conferences across the country because I could pay my own expenses. The church could barely afford to pay to send the pastor.

It was the message of love and acceptance by MCC that kept me from further attempts of suicide while living in New York. That church literally kept me alive and able to function on my job in a successful way. No other church ever told me that God loved me just as I was — a gay male who could rejoice in his sexuality as God's gift. This changed my life forever! I learned to know Jesus, who stressed love as a definition of God and never said one single word in condemnation of gays and lesbians. However, he said a lot about how all people should conduct themselves. For the first time in my life I felt good about myself, and worthy of God's love and blessings.

MCC in New York City celebrated their 25th anniversary in early 1997. I am so pleased that I could be a part of that group for all those years. Though I have lived in another state for several years now, I always return to MCC New York at Easter time for the services because it has become tradition for Troy to preach the Easter message.

Over 20 years ago I came out to two generations of my family. They accepted me and whenever they visited me in New York City they always attended MCC with me and enjoyed the fellowship there.

In 1990, I moved to a neighboring state and to a city where my nephew and his wife are living. My nephew and his wife attend a Mennonite Church. They suggested that I check out this church as a possible new church home in my new location. I had never been inside a Mennonite Church in my life! That was seven years ago, and I have never attended any other congregation in the area since then. I immediately felt warmth and love from everyone — pastors and members — that really surprised and uplifted me.

Six months after I began attending this church I wrote a letter to the editor of *Gospel Herald*, the official periodical of the Mennonite Church, in which I outed myself to the whole denomination, including everyone in the local church. I was very apprehensive about this, but there was no sign of stigmatism or condemnation by anyone in the congregation. Just the opposite was true. What a joy! My letter was congratulating the Mennonites for their Listening Committee to hear the concerns of gays and lesbians in their churches.

After six years of weekly attendance, and participating in various church activities, I decided to officially join the church in January 1997. Again, I expected opposition, but found none. I was overjoyed when I stood up in front of the whole congregation and officially became a Mennonite! I have never regretted it, because these fellow church members practice God's love in their relationships with other church members. Watching them carefully for six years made me want to follow in their footsteps. Their idea of service and love was something I wanted to emulate.

I am now aware of how the broader denomination can be very hurtful and legalistic in their interpretation of sexuality. The dismembership of some congregations because they have accepted same-sex couples living in committed relationships makes me extremely embarrassed and angry. What a way to treat fellow Christians! However, I am hopeful that the day will come when all gays and lesbians will be fully welcomed into any Mennonite congregation as full partners and members in good standing. God is at work, and I know God will prevail in the end. I have hope!

Three years ago I became a founding member of the local chapter of Parents, Families, and Friends of Lesbians and Gays (PFLAG). This has brought me an enormous amount of joy. It gives me an opportunity to share with interested persons what it was like to come out, not only to my family but also to my church. I enjoy offering support to parents (and their children) as they discover for the first time the sexuality of their children. I am thankful for the many opportunities I have in the city I live in to meet a wide range of people searching for help and understanding.

Dubose McLane was born in Kingsville, Texas, in 1923. After serving three years in World War II, Dubose spent his entire career in book publishing, first for the Presbyterian Board of Christian Education in Richmond, Virginia, and later for 30 years for secular book publishers in New York City. The last 20 years were with the college division of The Macmillan Company. It was in New York City that he began his association with the Metropolitan Community Church. In 1990 he moved to a retirement village in central Pennsylvania to be close to family members. He is a member of the local Mennonite Church.

14

Growing In Thanks For My Gayness

Keith G. Schrag

Rural Stouffville, Ontario, Canada, in 1938 seems very far away from Ames, Iowa, in 1998, 60 years later! Being a man who celebrates my gayness and my wonderful connections to God, faith, and hundreds of supportive people around the world is another dream come true. Knowing that I am completely loved by God, that Christ's Spirit and Presence dwells within me and leads me, is incredibly important.

Although I spent many years in search of this reality and several decades teaching and preaching it, I had to actually leave the confines of the Mennonite Church to gain the freedom to be myself. I grew up in the (Old) Mennonite Church (MC), the oldest son of a preacher, who was also the oldest son of a preacher. Being part of my extended church family, particularly of the Mennonite Church, was of tremendous importance to me. Being included was a basic yearning and focus of my energy from my earliest memories. My dad seemed to be deeply appreciated and connected. My mom seemed to work very intensely to conform and to be approved and accepted. I carried both of my parents' attitudes in the depths of my being. At my core I deeply felt the inherent contradiction.

Until I was almost eight, my parents were involved in mission work in two rural areas of Ontario. We would call this church planting today. Our friends and the support of other congregations were an integral part of daily life. Visitors were frequent. They would bring joy and provisions (food and other goodies) into the life of my family. This was our sustenance.

Going to church conferences and larger meetings nurtured my soul profoundly for most of my first 55 years.

The church, especially the wider Mennonite Church, including the General Conference Mennonite Church, is the place where I have also had some of my most painful exclusions and alienation. Naming my gayness and owning it as a basic aspect of my being, not only my sexual awareness and expression, but also at my spirit core, brought me crashing into the impermeable walls of exclusion from the life and enjoyment of my extended church family. True, our tiny congregation was still a member of the General Conference Mennonite Church (GC) which was not as ready to expel us from Central District Conference as had the Iowa-Nebraska Mennonite Conference (MC) in the late 1980's. However, the GC leadership had informed me that my continuing service in conference leadership or in the broader denomination would no longer be appreciated or welcomed. I was not being shunned because I openly admitted that I am gay, but because I had finally come to the conclusion that I could not remain a celibate gay man.

For almost 40 years I worked toward being celibate with less than satisfactory results, including lots of pain, shame, guilt, and obsessing. This included much spiritual and psychotherapeutic work. I finally asked God in profound exasperation, "Okay, God, what **is** your word to me? I have tried all these years and decades to live in the power of your Spirit above and beyond the call of the fantasies and yearnings that have been part of me since age 12. What gives?"

God's response to me was, "My dear child, don't you see that I made you in my own Divine image? I did not make you an aberration or a freak! I made you just as you are!"

I said, "Impossible, Lord! Don't tell me that. It is contrary to all I have been taught, to all I have read in Scripture since I was a toddler! What gives?"

God said, "Yes, my son, What gives? I have written my word in your heart. You are not evil at the core as you have feared. I created you good, in my Divine image. Now, love with all your heart, soul, mind, and body."

I said, through my gushing tears, "My Lord, do you mean that all this time I have tried to live a life that you never really called me to? I thought my life was right because of my own training, my reading of Scripture, and my listening to many of my friends and mentors? I heard other people, including Christian leaders, say that 'gay is also part of God's plan,' but, I could not find it possible to believe them. All along, was it really *you* talking to me?"

The Lord said, "Yes, is that too hard to believe?"

I replied, "I certainly hope *not*! It is so wonderful!"

The Lord answered, "Yes, exactly! Now, go and sin no more." And, finally I knew that God meant, "Go, and do not try to remake what I have already given you as an incredible gift. To do so is to live in sin." Then I felt a wonderful peace, such as I had never felt before. It flooded over me in such great waves that I cried and sang some of the most wonderful Gospel songs that I had sung as a child, but now they had wonderful heart energy — "Wonderful Grace of Jesus!"

I do not see celibacy as a fate worse than death. It is just not the gift the Spirit gave me. My "fate worse than death" was trying to get that gift when the Spirit gave me another. My goal has always been, and remains, to serve God and neighbor. Just because I do so in a way that some consider sin is by no means any indication that they understand my goal in life — or me! Perhaps they are merely confused as to what the Bible really does say and are reacting from their distress. I believe I am a wonderful person, created in God's glorious image, and given the mandate to serve God and others. That is really a pleasure — God gives so many pleasures.

My testimony of "gracedness" in my decision to live openly and clearly, with inner integrity, was accepted and appreciated by some people. The joy was obvious, even inviting, to some of my friends in the leadership group who announced the decision of the church to me. Some of them have continued to appreciate me and my journey and to support me since that time ten years ago. Yet, in their leadership role in the church they have had to dissociate themselves from me.

Divorcing my wife of 25 years was very painful for me. Although my local pastor was quite attentive and supportive, many other church leaders were not nurturing of that pain. Needing to leave decades of involvement at numerous levels of district conference, regional, and church-wide service was also painful. These structures and persons were not there to minister to my grief. I needed to find these aspects of healing ministry from many other sources, both inside and outside my family of faith. While both Mennonite Church and General Conference Mennonite Church bodies continued to debate the status of members and congregations who "openly and publicly affirm the gay lifestyle," my soul was being nurtured elsewhere. My profound pains and sadness were appreciated and salved by some within the church and its structures, but the same structures kept deepening that pain and sadness as well.

I found solace in my own tiny congregation, Ames (Iowa) Mennonite, which had been there through many years of this struggle with me. I found wonderful support and affirmation in the Brethren/Mennonite Council for Lesbian and Gay Concerns (BMC) from its earliest days in 1977. I found life-giving support from my wife and some very close personal friends during those decades of terrifying and lonely struggle for air to breathe and for direction as a human being and as a Christian man. Many of my friends are no longer in the organizational church. Many are from spiritualities far removed from my first 50 years of spiritual awareness, sometimes referred to as pagan or godless.

As I have followed my inner light, where the love of God resides, I have been drawn to groups of friends who would be considered to be without God and untrustworthy by the church of my childhood. Integrating spirituality and sexuality has been a struggle for me. I was appointed to serve on committees of the Mennonite Church for a time. But there the subject of sexuality in general and of homosexuality in particular was "too controversial" to treat openly and honestly. There was no room for questions and dialogue there. The Mennonite Board of Missions harshly canceled a project in process in 1981, one that its Student and Young Adult Services Committee had set into motion. We were forbidden to retain any materials we had written or received! That was a very painful blow.

Among friends in the American Friends Service Committee, Spiritual Frontiers Fellowship International, National Organization for Men Against Sexism and Racism, and Midwest Men's Festival, I was to find more kindred souls. My growing understanding of unknown realms was fostered, cheered, and cherished by these groups. I found I could trust them with some of my deepest longings and fears. I was beginning to change my tribal loyalty. At the same time, I was not being pushed to desert the core Christian faith that still nurtured and blessed me. All during this time, however, I experienced incredible support and love from my family of origin: siblings, parents, and children. For that I am eternally grateful!

It was also deeply supportive to be active in the Brethren/ Mennonite Council for Lesbian and Gay Concerns (BMC) and to have a period of six or seven years on its Board. This was a group where both my roots and my current pilgrimage could be shared and celebrated. As we traveled around the continent and the constituency I often felt an "at homeness" that I did not experience in the same way anywhere else. There we could talk the language of church and faith, while at the same time experiencing the special language of gay culture with its campiness and pizzazz. We could sing familiar hymns and share communion in profoundly spiritual ways. We could integrate spirituality and sexuality.

It was during this time that the Mennonite Church, later joined by the General Conference Mennonite Church, appointed a Listening Committee on Homosexuality Concerns. This group of courageous persons listened intently to the journey, the joys, and pains of many of us in the church, including our families. They showed personal respect that many others in our denominations chose not to share. They became the bridge for us to other church leaders and the larger constituency. However, they too, were finally ignored and experienced a measure of the marginalization and distrust that we have long felt.

My current profession as a Marriage and Family Therapist has given me many opportunities to heal further. As I have held leadership positions in state and profession-wide organizational roles I have had opportunity to educate and advocate for the inclusion of orientation issues in our training and practice as educators and therapists. Both in the American Association for Marriage and Family Therapy and the National Council on Family Relations I was to find open readiness for this perspective. Although certain of the membership in both organizations were not ready to hear or receive my points of view, I was not to find the constant double-talk and disenfranchisement that I often experienced from my own faith family in Mennonite and General Conference Mennonite Church settings. While I thank God for the avenues open to me, I grieve the response from the majority of my faith family and its leaders, a pain that is all the more severe because we make such high priority on community and family.

Unfortunately, the church is slow to change. Although I find the gospel incredibly clear on Jesus' identification with the disenfranchised of society, and Scripture unequivocal on the ethic of love for all believers, a large segment of the church continues to hide behind certain proscriptions and laws that I believe Jesus would not own if he were here in person. It dims the church's message of clarity and consistency when this exclusionary path is followed. The spiritual loss to the world as well as the church is huge.

Yet, many refuse any longer to even discuss these issues. In 1986 and 1987 when the two denominations developed their historic statements on Human Sexuality, which were highly debated at the time, there was much open talking about our need to be clear as a church that homosexual behavior was sin, but that we also needed to continue in dialogue and to confess our judgmental attitudes. Although those assembly meetings were at times painful, they also were times of great movement, of finally being able to discuss these explosive and controversial items publicly. Yet, in the ten years following, the church made clear that confessing judgmental attitudes was to be very short-lived and the dialogue was to be quite brief and shallow, for the most part. The behavior of the church recently indicates that the church does not trust the Spirit to lead in our dialogue. We only trust traditional understandings and practices. What a heavy indictment!

A major concern of mine at present is that Mennonitism is trading in its historical focus on love and justice for a quick-fix on controversy and a hiding behind the assumed security of a "firm position," a polity statement. This is a move that has much broader implications than merely our denominational stance on homosexual activity. It points to a central flaw, a readiness to respond in fear and to erect boundaries at times of insecurity rather than deepening spiritual roots and trusting the Holy Spirit to guide us in love and hope.

I pray that our denomination, as well as the many other denominations that are making similar moves, will yet find the courage to risk failure in insight rather than failure in love and be ready to cast a wide net to include at the table people who have variant viewpoints, and who are centered on Christ and the power of love to heal and guide.

This is the legacy I want to leave my children and grandchildren. This is the Good News that brings hope and salvation to all youth and all others who seek wholeness.

Keith Schrag lives in Ames, Iowa, where he is in private practice as a Licensed Marital & Family Therapist and a consultant and spiritual/healer/educator. He enjoys supervising new therapists and mentoring spiritual healers. He was born near Toronto, Ontario, grew up in Lowville, New York, and graduated from Goshen (Indiana) College and Goshen Biblical Seminary. Keith pastored for 20 years in Texas, Kansas, and Iowa. He has three adult children and three grandchildren. For hobbies he enjoys traveling, music, and nature.

15

This is Who I Am

Lloyd Bowman

Author's Note: This essay was originally written at the request of the editor of Shalom!*, a small, quarterly Brethren in Christ publication focusing on topical issues of peace and justice. The issue the article was going to be included in dealt with the topic of homosexuality. The editor asked me to write "my story" to provide balance to the issue. I was pleased with the opportunity to tell my story and to lend my voice in a publication dealing with homosexuality. After receiving the article the editor said she could not include it because it was written by a self-affirming homosexual. Publishing it, she felt, would endanger the existence of her publication. The issue was printed but included no articles by gay or lesbian people, though it did include the story of an ex-gay person.*

To me this demonstrated an ongoing, glaring, and tragic irony: the church only deals with the subject of homosexuality by completely excluding the stories of gay and lesbian people.

Being part of the church and being Christian have always been part of my life. Before I was born my father was a minister in the Evangelical United Brethren Church (EUB). That denomination merged with the Methodists to form the largest Protestant denomination at that time, the United Methodist Church. My parents were never comfortable in that denomination so they moved to the Church of the Brethren (COB) when I was 13 years old. While I was a student at

Messiah College I made the choice to join the Grantham Brethren in Christ Church.

I accepted Christ as my personal savior at a young age and developed a deep spiritual life. Weekly church and Sunday school, with other activities throughout the week, were a vital part of my life. I was also a youth group leader.

When I reached my teens, my sexuality began to blossom. Rather than finding myself attracted to people of the opposite gender as I expected I would, I was attracted to people who happened to be of the same sex. This scared me very much. Not only was I aware of my parents' beliefs about homosexuality, I held those beliefs too.

I believed that homosexuals were sick people who needed professional psychiatric help. Homosexuality was one of the examples of sin in a fallen world. It was my firm belief that this position was supported by the Bible. The Bible said homosexuality was sin, so it was sin. Since my sexuality was sinful, I hated my sexuality.

I tried very hard to be good, endeavoring to be the heterosexual that every one believed I was supposed to be. I believed it also. I dated persons of the opposite sex through high school and college, hoping that by trying to do the right thing, my sexuality would change. In spite of these relationships, years of lonely prayer, and attempts at healing, my sexuality never did change. In fact, trying to be something I was not felt terribly wrong. I felt deceitful and dishonest masquerading in relationships as someone I was not.

As I neared the end of college, I began to understand I could no more deny my sexuality than my spirituality. I could no sooner cut off my sexuality than I could remove my heart. I could no more deny my sexuality than my need for oxygen.

Deep within me, I knew what sin and evil felt like. I realized that damning my sexuality, trying to shut it off, punish it, and disrespect it was hurtful, harmful, destructive, and sinful. I came to appreciate my sexuality as an essential, integral part of me, part of my spirit and soul. In fact, they felt interrelated. Both felt like an important part of me as a whole, genuine, real person.

I understood that my sexuality was a treasure and gift that God had fashioned within me as part of God's design for my life. To disrespect it was to disrespect myself and my Creator. Once I came in touch with this, I no longer hated being gay. There was no reason to. I understood my sexuality as part of my identity. From this point on, I have sought a challenging journey that honors the relationship between my spirituality and sexuality.

Along with many other gay people, I have been dismissed by the church. Most of the institutional church has decided what the position of the church should be toward homosexual people without seriously engaging the gay and lesbian people within it. While the church claims to love us, it refuses to seriously consider our point of view on scripture or our spiritual experience unless we already agree with the majority viewpoint.

In addition, the church works politically to deny lesbians and gay men the same rights to housing, jobs, and family that other people have. Gay people are fired and evicted without any other reason than another person's hatred.

A friend has compared the love of the church to that of a boss who tells his secretary that he loves her and proceeds to make unwelcome, hurtful sexual advances toward her. The problem with this sort of love is that it is unequal and exploitive. Only one side of the relationship gets to define it.

Only one side of the relationship gets to decide how gay and lesbian people should be loved by the church. As a gay man, I am left harmed by this so-called love, but when I cry out, I am told that I have no say in the matter.

I am fortunate that I live in a church and civic community that isolates me from most of that kind of harm. I attend church where my partner and I worship and work freely and enthusiastically. I hold a job with an organization that has policies forbidding discrimination against lesbians and gays. I live in a city where I cannot be denied housing because of my sexual orientation. I have spousal benefits through my partner's job, I have a wide circle of friends whose sexuality is irrelevant to the friendship. In short, I live in a community where gay and lesbian people are as much a part of the social landscape as Sunday school and prayer meetings. I wish more lesbians and gay men could share this experience. Unfortunately, I have achieved this life in spite of the church, not because of it.

In my congregation our trustees, committee members, lay leaders, Sunday school teachers, child care workers, and those entrusted with the vision of our church include both gay and straight individuals. Of course, they include women and men, young and old, Jew and Gentile, married, divorced, and single. We understand that each is a child of God, learning to know and walk with God. I am accepted neither in spite of my being gay or because I am gay. I am accepted for who I am — all of me.

Lloyd Bowman is a computer systems analyst at the University of Pennsylvania. He has a Master of Science degree in information systems from Drexel University. He and his lifelong partner, Douglas Brunk, reside with their Norwegian Elkhound, Peder, in the Germantown section of Philadelphia, Pennsylvania. Lloyd and Doug attend Germantown Mennonite Church.

16

Still Standing

Terri M.

But we have this treasure in earthen vessels that the surpassing greatness of the power may be of God and not from ourselves, we are afflicted in every way, but not crushed; perplexed but not despairing; persecuted but not forsaken; struck down but not destroyed.

2 Corinthians 4:7-9,
New American Standard Bible

A couple of years ago, I was speaking to a young people's support group. Most of the youth identified as gay, lesbian, or bisexual. Two of them were struggling with gender issues, so I was asked to share my experience with transsexualism. As I shared, I mentioned my church frequently. My Christianity is such an integral part of my life that it comes naturally to speak of it.

When I opened the floor for questions, one of the young men in the group asked me, "You speak about your religion. During all the things you went through in your life, did you ever lose your faith?" It was one of those moments that occur infrequently in one's life where some factor in your life becomes crystal clear. James Joyce calls these moments epiphanies. John Bradshaw calls them *kairos* moments. Whatever you want to call them, they help define your life.

Without pausing I answered, "Never. How could I? When I was 15 years old and lay in bed with a knife poised over my throat, ready to plunge it in, only the hand of God stayed my hand. When I was surrounded by six thugs in high school and the leader of the gang hit me across the jaw with a steel bar, it was only God's hand that kept me from harm and allowed me to walk away without injury. When I was pushed headfirst down a flight of stairs, it was a miracle of God that righted my body and allowed me to land on my feet. Through all the abuse, confusion, and pain of my life, when everyone else had deserted me, when I felt all alone in the world, I always knew I could go to the throne of grace to receive comfort. How could I turn my back on that? It would be like a person seriously ill running from the one doctor who could save their life. No, when faced with a trial, I could never run from my faith. Rather I can only run toward it." About 15 minutes later I finished. (I come from a long line of Pentecostal preachers.)

There have been two constants in my life, my experience with God through Jesus Christ and my transsexualism. I was born on a Sunday and the next Sunday I was in church. I have missed few Sundays since then. When I was four years old, I knelt at an old-fashioned altar with my mother on one side of me and a child evangelist on the other side and prayed the sinners prayer. I asked God to forgive me of my sins and for Jesus to come into my heart. It was a simple prayer, because God did all the hard work on Calvary.

When I was seven years old, I received the baptism in the Holy Spirit, an experience difficult to explain without having a common base of experience. Basically, it is letting the Holy Spirit enter into your life in power and giving yourself over to that power. The initial evidence of this experience is speaking in an unknown tongue (Acts 2:4, New American Standard Bible), and I was given that gift.

From my earliest memories, I have been in church. And, from my earliest memories I have had a female gender identity. I felt there was some great mistake. I felt that I should have been born a girl. I felt like a girl inside. I wanted to be a girl, but everyone kept treating me like a boy. So, I played the boy game. I did not play the game very well and by the time I was in high school, I was labeled a "fag." I was also labeled a nerd and a holy roller. Any one of these was enough to get you beaten up in my school and I had all three. I faced every level of abuse from verbal abuse, to beatings, to terrorizing, to rape. Some people have flashbacks of Vietnam. I have flashbacks of high school.

By the time I was out of high school I was socially isolated except academically and in terms of ministry in the church. My brain in both places became my social currency. I became useful. I was involved in numerous ministries. I do not regret any of the time I spent in them. There are people in the Kingdom today as a direct result of what we did.

However, I always felt like an outside consultant. Looking back, this was largely due to my own fears and not because people did not reach out to me. Meanwhile, I was learning more about transsexualism and trying to tell myself it would just go away. I dated sporadically, with six dates in ten years. I never even held hands with my dates. It is hard to be a really good date when you are more interested in where the woman got her dress than what is under it.

After the last of these disasters, I came home and realized the futility of my desire for it all to just go away. I cried for about half an hour. Then I said to myself, "Well, if this is what I am, how am I going to handle it?"

It took another ten years before I could seriously address that issue. I had moved to Fresno and finally had a good job teaching at Kings River Community College in Reedley. However, I still felt I had to test things out — take things slowly. I do not handle risk well. So, my idea was to come home from school and one day live my life as a man and the next as a woman, alternating through the week. I even attended two churches one as a man and one as a woman. Well, after about a month of this, I came home from school one day, took off my suit, and could not for the life of me remember what day it was. So, there I stood stark naked staring at my closet at a loss for what to wear.

In desperation, I looked up and said, "God, I give up. I give up! I can not keep up this testing. And I can not hang onto some hope that someday this will disappear of its own account. So, I am not going to deal with it any more. It is in your hands now. If you want me to be a man, you put those feelings in me. If you want me to be a woman, you put those in me. But I am not going to try either way anymore. I am going with the assurance that you alone can give."

Then, in my heart, the Lord said, "Well, finally! Do you know how long I have waited to hear that?" There was no doubt in my mind from that point on. There was no need to test any longer. I reached for a dress and never turned back. Within a week I discovered Genderline on Compuserve and met other transsexuals for the first time. Within a month, I had made an appointment with Luanna Rodgers, a gender therapist in San Francisco. I began full-time cross-living in about fourteen months and had surgery about two years later.

Miracle after miracle has followed my transition, in fact it became somewhat legendary in certain corners of the gender world. God has been good to me. My current church is an Assemblies of God Church in Fresno, California. I write for the church news letter, manage the church's web page, write the Bible study materials for our home Bible study program, and teach a Sunday school class.

Talk about miracles! And no, it was not easy for any of us! But, we worked it out together, learning from each other, and loving each other. It has been an interesting life. And if 2 Corinthians 4:7-9 is my scriptural theme, my theme song is "Standing," written by Debbie Branson, which goes:

> Like Shadrach, Meshach and Abednego
> Through the fire I have been;
> Like Daniel and the Lions
> I've been thrown into a den.
> And, I've faced my share of Giants;
> Like Job, I've had my share of pain;
> But Jesus delivered yesterday
> And, today he's still the same.
>
> And, I'm standing, I'm still standing;
> Standing with my hands
> Lifted high to the Lord.
> And, I'm standing, I'm still standing;
> Standing unashamed
> of the Gospel or His name.
> Every day he's still the same,
> And, I'm still standing!

God is Faithful!

17

Born Blessed

Anonymous

I was born blessed. God blessed me with two parents who love me and love each other, a luxury that is all too rare in today's world. I owe much of my faith and perseverance to them.

I was born blessed. God blessed me with God's Son, who suffered and died so that all of my past, present, and future sins could be forgiven. I owe all of my happiness to God.

Due to the unfailing love of my savior and my parents, I have come to a point in my life where I can finally be open, truthful, and at peace.

My dad and I spent a great deal of time together working on the small farm that he ran in addition to working at his office job. As a little boy, I was Dad's assistant. I ran for tools, cleaned tractor parts, opened farm gates, and joined him at our town's coffee shop where he would swap stories with the other local farmers. He referred to me as his "portable tow motor," and I loved spending time with him.

My mom did all those wonderful things for which mothers never get credit. She stayed up late nights with a heating pad when I had ear aches. She made me chocolate milk shakes when I had a sore throat. She forced me to clean my room, even when I complained. Through dentist appointments, swimming lessons, band concerts, driver's education classes, and trumpet lessons, Mom was always there.

Far too few children have the luxury of experiencing a childhood like mine. My parents built a home together that was free of anger, abuse, violence, drugs, alcohol, and hatred. I grew up in an environment of pure love. I have known my whole life that my parents are as close to perfect as they come.

Because my mom and dad raised me correctly, I turned out right. In my 22 years I have never gotten into any kind of serious trouble. I did well all through school and will soon graduate from college with honors. I will be receiving a degree in music education and hope to secure a job as a high school or junior high band director. In the summers I work in a group home with severely mentally disabled children. I am a devoted Christian and was recently baptized into the Church of the Brethren. I consider myself to be an honest, decent, loving, moral, young man. I am also gay.

I want to make it very clear that there was no choice involved in my sexuality. There is absolutely no doubt in my mind that my sexual identity was determined long before I had the cognitive ability to understand it. If I had been granted a choice, I would have chosen to be straight.

I can not pinpoint the exact moment when I realized the truth. I had known since first grade that I was somehow different from the other boys in school. I had no idea what it was about me that made me feel different, but at the age of six, I already felt that difference.

Looking back, it was all too obvious. I was labeled a sensitive child. I was that kid in elementary school who cried when someone else got yelled at. While my peers asked Santa for He-man figures, I had my eye on my sister's tea set and an Easy-Bake Oven. Yet I quickly conformed, as many in small, conservative towns do, to the expectations of the society around me. By the age of eight or nine I was consciously behaving in ways that would ensure I would be seen by those around me as a normal boy. I was passing for straight, and I did not even know I was gay.

Realizing the truth about my sexuality was a gradual process for me. Through junior high and most of high school, I considered myself to be bisexual, which allowed me to deal with things fairly easily. I would be married, have a family, and live happily ever after. My secret would go with me to the grave.

My orientation did, however, seem to be in direct opposition to my religious upbringing. My adherence to Christianity had come about by a sort of cultural osmosis. My home town, with its large Amish and Mennonite population, raises its children to be Christians by surrounding them with an ultra-conservative environment. My parents taught me to serve God by being honest, godly people and by providing a home full of genuine Christian love. I have been a true believer for as long as I can remember.

As a result of the conservative environment in which I was raised, I considered homosexual acts to be morally wrong. Because I knew that my orientation was not chosen and I planned to never pursue a gay relationship, it did not really create much of a religious conflict for me. Only on occasions when I felt that my gay side was winning the tug-of-war over my sexuality did I become concerned. I would then pray to God to be healed and would try my best to steer my thoughts toward girls. As the years progressed, I realized that I was losing the battle.

The turning point finally came during my sophomore year of college. I became friends with a fellow student who lived in my building. As the months progressed, we became closer and closer. We talked for hours on end, and he quickly became the closest friend I have ever had.

By February 1996 I had told him everything about myself, except my sexuality. I realized that I finally had found the person in whom I could confide. I was frightened by the prospect that our relationship could become uncomfortable after he knew I was not straight. However, I was also desperately looking forward to having someone with whom I could finally be completely honest.

As it turned out, I worried needlessly. To my complete surprise, I found out that my friend was gay also. Once the truth was out, we both soon realized for the first time that ours had been more than a friendship for quite a while. I had fallen in love for the first time. I had fallen in love with the mind and soul of another person, and that person happened to be a man.

The months that followed were the most wonderful, yet confusing, I have ever experienced. On the one hand, I was in love. When I spent time with this young man everything seemed right. I was amazed by how *normal* our relationship was. I was able to experience with him the wonderful relief that comes with acting naturally.

All the negative stereotypes about gay people that I had simply accepted as facts were proven to be completely false. Gay relationships *were not* all about sex. Gay people *do* have committed partnerships. Gay people *can* love, yes *truly love* each other on a level that extends far beyond the physical. These revelations helped me to see myself differently. The issue of who I was physically attracted to became unimportant when I realized that I was meant to bond emotionally with men and only men. I had to stop clinging to the hope that I could live a heterosexual life. The time had come for me to accept the truth. The time had come for me to embrace what I had denied for my whole life. I could no longer force myself to believe my own lies, and I could not continue lying to those I love. I decided that it was time to tell my parents.

On December 26, 1996, I was home from college on Christmas break and knew that I could not continue lying to my mom and dad. I sat in our living room watching television with my parents, trying over and over again to gather the courage to start the dreaded conversation. Time after time I inhaled and opened my mouth, fully planning to speak, but I just could not. With each failed attempt, the dread and frustration grew until finally I found myself lying on the couch crying silently while my parents sat a few feet away, oblivious to my suffering. It went on for hours.

"Mom, Dad," I finally said with a quivering voice. "I need to talk to you." Turning, they both recognized that I was upset and came over immediately. Mom sat at the end of the couch by my feet and Dad sat on the floor by my head, with a hand on my shoulder. "What is wrong, son?"

Trying to hold back tears, I began, "I want you both to know that you did not do anything wrong, that you are wonderful parents and that I could not have been raised better."

"You think you might be gay," Mom interrupted.

It was over just that quick. Mom had ended all the years of hiding the truth and all the months of dreading to tell them with that one sentence. I guess that in that moment I should have felt relief, like a great weight had been lifted from my shoulders. I should have felt happy that I could finally begin to be honest with the people whom I love more than anyone in the world. However, I had looked at her face as she said it, and in the time it took her to speak those six words I saw her whole world fall apart. I saw the pain in her eyes and was ashamed to know that I was the cause of that pain. It was the most horrible moment of my life.

I was then, as I am today, truly sorry for the pain that my parents suffered in learning that their son is gay. It is not fair that loving parents have to realize that the child for whom they have cared for 21 years cannot fulfill many of the expectations that they had naturally, lovingly set for him.

Mom had suspected for several months that I might be gay and had prayed and hoped that she was wrong. Her adjustment in the months that followed was a slow and painful one, but like all good mothers, she stood by her son. I never doubted that she would.

Dad was shocked by the news, but accepted it and accepted me with a speed that still amazes me. He immediately made it clear that he would *always* support me, no matter what.

The support of loving family and friends and the continued, unfailing grace of my Lord and Savior have brought me to the present. I am 22 years old, I am gay, and for the first time in my life I am beginning to feel true peace within myself.

I know that my struggle is far from over, however. While I am completely out and accepted at college, things at home have had to move more slowly. I have come out to many of my closest friends from high school. Nevertheless, I hesitate to go public in my conservative hometown in order to protect my parents who do not deserve to be dragged through the mud. It is for them that I write my story anonymously.

Wherever I find a job and make my home after college, I will live openly and honestly. My life will not always be easy because I will never be comfortable hiding in the closet again while decent, honest people like myself are subjected to continuing discrimination. I will not, through silence, contribute to the suicides of gay and lesbian teenagers who are left with no allies and no one to look up to when gay and lesbian adults are unwilling to stand up for what is right.

Most importantly, I refuse to let the word of God be twisted into hatred. God's word is today being mistranslated and misinterpreted to condemn homosexuals, just as it was mistranslated and misinterpreted by Christians of the past to support slavery and the oppression of women. *God is love*, and twisting God's word to support hatred is just as wrong today as it has always been. The subject may be different, but the results are just as ugly. I believe that any interpretation of God's word that breeds hatred, murder, suicide, and inequality among God's children is a false interpretation.

My future will not be all about struggling, however. I have many wonderful things to which I look forward. In ten years I can see myself in a committed, permanent, loving relationship. I see myself as a father of happy, well-adjusted, Christian children. I see myself worshipping with my family in a church congregation that glorifies Christ and accepts me for who I am. These are my hopes and prayers for myself and the thousands like me.

I was born *gay*, and God still provided me with two parents who love me and love each other.

I was born *gay*, and God still saved me by the grace of Jesus Christ, in whom I have found true peace.

I was born *gay*, and I was still born *blessed*.

The author graduated in May, 1998, with a degree in instrumental music education. He will be looking for a job as a junior high or high school band director during the summer of 1998 and hopes to soon be starting his career as a teacher. During his internship semester a student came out to him about his struggles with his own sexuality. The author feels that he was able to be the mentor to this student that he would have liked to have had when he was at that age. His relationship with God and with his parents continues to be wonderful.

18

An Undaunted Hope

John Linscheid

The young, according to the prophet Joel, will see visions and elders will dream (Joel 2:28b). But I am a middle-aged gay man, too old to see visions and too young to dream.

In my youth, I lived by visions. I envisioned the church as flawed but essentially good at heart. I pictured the body of Christ as bound by love despite disagreements over nonessentials and willing to let the grace of God make up for the differences.

I also had more mystical visions. Once, when I was studying for pastoral ministry, Christ enveloped me as I walked across the seminary lawn. I practiced prayer and meditation and the Holy Spirit visited me with seeming regularity. In a vision of the night, Christ appeared to me as Lady Wisdom, in a long flowing dress. I remember this vividly because I found myself strongly attracted to this strange woman. I found it odd because, as a gay man, I had never been attracted to women. But when I approached her she whispered to me, "I am Jesus." Then I understood. (Several scholars, I later discovered, believe that the early church understood Jesus as the embodiment of Sophia — the person of Holy Wisdom in the Hebrew scriptures.)[1]

My struggles with my sexuality seem ancient history now. During college, I had a nervous breakdown due to my despair at God's failure to answer my prayers to become straight. I saw

[1] *Wisdom's Feast, Sophia in Study and Celebration.* Susan Cole, Marian Ronan, Hal Taussig. Kansas City, MO: Sheed & Ward, 1997.

God as a sadistic torturer who would not rescue me from the very urges for which God would condemn me. But early in my seminary years I came to experience the grace of God's unconditional acceptance. I surrendered myself to the arms of God and stopped worrying about my sexual orientation. Although I was still convinced that I would need to remain single and abstinent to pursue pastoral ministry, I no longer felt condemned. I was gay, and that was okay with God and okay with me, even though it would not be okay with the church or society.

As my communion with God deepened, so did my acceptance of my sexuality. As I accepted and embraced my sexuality, I found myself more able to accept the love and grace of God.

Then the battles over homosexuality intensified in the Mennonite Church in the early 1980s. I had become a pastor, but I had remained closeted except to close friends and family. The debates put me in a bind. Church people sought my views on the sexual debates. Yet whenever I expressed them I felt disingenuous because I was not revealing the personal impact the issue had on my life. So I decided to come out publicly.

I was, to my knowledge, the first gay Mennonite pastor to come out of the closet and seek to remain a pastor. The congregation engaged the issue nobly. But before the congregation could decide how to faithfully respond, the denomination intervened and revoked my pastoral credentials. I met my lover, Ken, in the midst of this coming out process.

The cost of discipleship has been high for all involved. The congregant who led the opposition to my continuing as pastor had been a favorite student of my father. My father died before that relationship could be fully healed. For Ken, whose own ministry had been torpedoed by the United Methodist Church years before, these events opened old wounds. My mother's relationship with her brother was strained when I was the only cousin not invited to her nephew's wedding. My twin brother, who works for denominational offices, has to bear the constant strain of being in the middle, between a church that rejects gay and lesbian people and a family that embraces me.

Ken and I moved to Philadelphia in 1985, and the costs mounted. I became a member of the oldest Mennonite congregation in North America, Germantown Mennonite Church. But the membership of gay and lesbian people in that congregation occasioned a prolonged dialogue process with the regional Franconia Mennonite Conference. The conference's leadership at first quietly tolerated and later publicly attacked the congregation for accepting us. Members of the congregation watched as family, relatives, and spiritual brothers and sisters from churches they had grown up in rejected their congregation and eventually excommunicated them from the Mennonite Church. My lesbian sisters and gay brothers for the most part have moved away from the church as they sought spiritual paths and communities more likely to nurture lesbian and gay souls. The pastors who served and stood by our congregation now face the revocation of their own credentials.

On the institutional level, I saw formerly progressive leaders, including some women, who pioneered in entering the pastoral ministry, forget the controversial nature of their own journeys and preside at the expulsion of congregations friendly to gay and lesbian people. Church leaders I had once counted as professional colleagues, now wield the knives that cut the body of Christ to pieces over issues of sexuality. The few quietly supportive officers of denominational institutions mostly fall silent.

In these years of struggle, I took the role of a "Christian soldier marching as to war" in the fight for justice and for the vision of an inclusive church. I battled for understanding and unity in diversity. But now I look over the field and mostly see the casualties. I look around at those who lived by these visions and we seem to be the shell-shocked survivors of a spiritual genocide. The right-wing victories mount in the campaign to rid the church of gay, lesbian, and supportive believers. And we are left disillusioned and confused about how to proceed.

The visions I lived by, of a flawed but basically good church and of a united though diverse body of Christ, have faded. My conviction that integrity in one's journey of discipleship will triumph seems disproved.

I still love Christ. But I cling to faith only by the slender thread of God's grace.

For now, I await the advanced age that will produce the dreams that Joel promises. And while I wait, I live by the hope (too weak to call a conviction) that Job expressed in his despair: "My redeemer lives," and whether I stand or fall, that redeemer — for me the Christ, the lover of my soul — will stand at the last.

John Linscheid had his pastoral credentials revoked in 1984, seven months after he publicly revealed he was gay. He was the first North American Mennonite pastor to come out and seek to retain his pastorate. Since then, he has published articles and presented talks which interpret biblical passages from a gay perspective. He and his lover, Ken White, lead occasional retreats on gay-male spirituality. He currently earns his living as an administrative assistant at the University of Pennsylvania Department of Chemical Engineering where he helps undergraduates negotiate the university bureaucracy. He received his B.A. in Bible and Religion from Bethel College (North Newton, Kansas) and his M.Div. from Mennonite Biblical Seminary (Elkhart, Indiana).

19

Faith Journey: A Son's Perspective

John Flickinger

When I came out to my parents fourteen years ago, we were sitting together on the lawn at Fresno Pacific College, taking a break from the activities of the Mennonite Central Committee relief sale. They had driven from Phoenix and I came from San Francisco, where I had just begun a term of voluntary service with the Mennonite Board of Missions (MBM). I had been tense for days, planning the conversation and worrying about it. As it turned out, few words were necessary. We spoke what was in our hearts. From me, an emotional and incoherent outpouring from a well of frustration and insecurity, from my parents, a few simple questions that were expressions of their love and care for me. Yet it was a baptism and rebirth far more powerful than the one I experienced at the age of 14, standing dutifully with my catechism classmates in front of First Mennonite Church of Phoenix. In one moment, I washed away years of deception and self-doubt, and invited my parents to know me as I had come to know myself. Fortunately, they accepted that invitation.

Since that time, I have told many others that I am gay, although I do not share this with everyone. Some have made themselves at home with the information, while others pretend it was never given. I do not want to make things uncomfortable for others or myself so I do not push it. Well, maybe I do push more and more as I settle into my identity. I have a strong sense of justice. I know these things take time and that change happens slowly, but time is precious. We only have this life and these relationships in which to work it all out. Before we know it, the time has slipped away.

Family

It was not long after my coming out in Fresno that my brother, Dan, and my sister, Su, also came out to the family. I had mixed feelings. I love them and was grateful for their honesty, but why should our family have three gay children? It was uncomfortable enough for me to accept my own sexuality and its consequences for my family. Their coming out only increased my discomfort, and it took some time before I finally let go and accepted it. Finally the game, that fearful hide-in-the-closet game, was over for us. Since integrity is one of the values we were taught to hold dear, it was a relief to be able to reclaim our integrity. It was the beginning of a long journey of reorientation and education for the entire family. We worked to educate each other and ourselves. We exchanged books and articles. We wrote letters. We asked questions. We argued. We cried. We went to meetings. We participated in studies at the National Institutes of Health (NIH) and we made new friends, even as we lost old ones.

There has indeed been loss on this journey. We lost a dream — that dream about what life should be like for our family. We lost a community — few in the Mennonite Church community in Phoenix, that had been our home for so many years, were supportive. We lost a sense of security and the ability to relate quite so comfortably and casually with our extended family and society. We experienced anxiety and fear and we worried about discrimination, alienation, and possible violence. However, for me, the losses I have experienced have been balanced by immeasurable gain. A much larger view of the world has opened up to me — a world that is shared with people as they are, not just as I would like them to be.

Heroes

For years after I realized I was gay, I resisted calling myself a gay man. I told myself that labels were for people who were insecure and wanted the world arranged in neat little boxes. I was bigger than that. However, there came a point when I had to acknowledge that my resistance was not because I disliked labels, I was resisting because I was afraid of my own identity. I was afraid of claiming that part of me that was attracted to other men. I was afraid of admitting that my attraction was not merely admiration or wanting to be like them, but because I wanted to love them, and I wanted them to love me. Part of what helped me acknowledge this were gay men and lesbians who had already figured this out for themselves.

Since homosexuality has been hidden in our society, finding positive role models is a huge hurdle for gay people who are coming out. Even though the media has increased its coverage, it still does not talk about mainstream gay men and lesbians. They are the ones teaching our kids, delivering our mail, playing basketball in the gym, having a picnic in the park, or sitting in our church pews. I desperately needed someone when I was younger to communicate to me that they understood what I was feeling. I did not feel it was safe to ask, and apparently no one felt it was safe to tell.

Heroes fill us with courage and vision. They emerge from life on the edge, where the risk is great, but conviction overcomes fear. I have been privileged to know men and women who have been on the edge of what was safe and acceptable, and they have chosen the more difficult path. They have acted with conviction that is grounded in both self-respect and love for others. They have shown me a way to be in this world that respects everyone, including myself.

Partner

My partner, Doug, was one of my early gay heroes. We first became acquainted when I interviewed for a voluntary service assignment. Doug was the West Coast director of Voluntary Service (VS) for the Mennonite Board of Missions (MBM) at the time. We had several phone calls while I was deciding where to go, and finally met in person after I moved to San Francisco. A few weeks after I settled into the VS house and my new assignment, we set a time to meet together at Café Flore, a popular Market Street coffee bar. After chatting a bit, he told me that he was gay and was being forced to resign from his position with MBM because it had become public knowledge. MBM was being pressured to get rid of him. I told him that I, too, was gay, and that was the start of a relationship that has lasted to the present. It was also the beginning of the end of my VS career, since MBM did not look kindly on intimate relationships, and especially gay ones. The process of dealing with church agencies and church leaders during that time was painful, but neither Doug nor I had much to lose at that point, since there was no longer a future there. That is not to gloss it over, it was a very real loss, and we still grieve it occasionally.

Doug and I still live in San Francisco, in a Victorian row house in what has become a trendy neighborhood. Our neighbors are of a variety of ethnic and economic backgrounds. The Catholic Church down the block houses a novitiate for Mother Teresa's Missionaries of Charity. It was also the setting for Whoopie Goldberg's movie *Sister Act*. The primary school across the street is being sold and will be turned into housing. A neighborhood grocery has a huge rainbow flag painted on the side of the building. Our neighbors work for Silicon Valley computer firms, for non-profit organizations, for legislators, and as doctors, lawyers, homemakers, and parents. They are plumbers, construction workers, and shopkeepers. One of them owns a tattoo parlor and raises pit bulls. One of them has a boat docked in Half Moon Bay and occasionally brings us a salmon he has caught. A few of them are gay, most are straight. Some have lived here for generations, others have just moved in. We have good friends here. We are members of the San Francisco Mennonite Church, we attend church conferences, and we take trips to visit friends and see new places. We are surrounded by a community of straight and gay people that care about us and whom we love.

Sex

Sexuality impacts how we relate to each other. As society has come to accept different sexual orientations as a biological fact, the inclusion/exclusion criteria for gay and lesbian people is often based on whether or not they have sex. In the Mennonite Church, some people are allowed to be sexual and some are not. If you are straight and married — no problem. However, if you are single and do not want to or are not allowed to marry, then there is a problem. Sure, some choose to be celibate. But for many, the choice is between sex and the spiritual community. Why should it have to be a choice? What has the Mennonite church gained from members who are frustrated and unhappy with themselves and their relationships? What does the church have to lose by encouraging loving, healthy relationships?

Not only am I gay, but I am sexually active. Sex is a beautiful and precious thing, but it is hard to understand how a simple biological event can have so much power. Perhaps it is precisely because society mystifies and sensationalizes sex that people are sometimes irresponsible and irrational about it. In spite of that, most people I know deal with sex in very responsible ways, probably because of the education they have received about sexually transmitted diseases, unwanted pregnancies, and respecting other people and themselves. I firmly believe that our education about sex is ongoing, it did not stop when the Bible was written, or some persuasive speaker pounded the pulpit. We have so much to learn.

The Values Game

I am often amazed how people can believe that someone saying, "I am gay," is an attack on the traditional values of the church and society. There is a game that begins with a phrase like, "We all know the truth about homosexuality, the Bible is very clear." It is an appeal to a common set of values. We all play a similar game with one subject or another. Chaos is lurking just around the corner, and we need to be able to trust each other. We need to believe that our community will keep the world together around us, even if it is falling apart somewhere else. The problem is that the basis of this values game is fear, rather than love, control, rather than caring. Consequently, if someone challenges a prevailing assumption, we do not stop to ask why we are being challenged. We throw it back in their faces and label them sinful, or disrespectful, or harmful, or whatever it takes to shame them into toeing the line and helping us feel safe again. Coming out as a gay man has been a process of facing the fear of something unknown and learning to love that part of myself. Then it is taking that love, putting it together with my values, and seeing where that takes me. My search for truth is essentially a matter of faith, and I am still on that journey. I will try not to be guided by fear.

It is not easy to be finished playing the game before everyone else. You look around and see what an ugly game it can be. Some players feel they are dealt a bad hand, and twisted with anger and pain, they will lie and cheat in order to hurt other players. Some live in denial that they are even playing a game, yet they sit there with a full hand, playing their cards in turn. Some only want to win, and they play their hand of Bible verses or statistics ruthlessly until the other players fold. Some see the game for what it is, but are afraid to stop playing before everyone else. It is a frightening thing to realize that the majority is wrong and to align oneself with a minority. Suddenly, you are vulnerable. Then you look around, find others who share your values, and build a new community. As Mennonites, that is what my family has done for generations, and that is what we are still doing today.

In Part Two, **Sid Flickinger**, John's mother, shares her story about her gay and lesbian children. See page 212, Chapter 39.

John Flickinger graduated from Bethel College in North Newton, Kansas, in 1981. He worked as a graphic artist for several years before moving to San Francisco, where he served as a volunteer under the Mennonite Board of Missions. Following that assignment, he began working with an AIDS education program and is currently the administrator of an AIDS research facility at the University of California, San Francisco. He and his partner, Doug Basinger, are members of First Mennonite Church of San Francisco.

20

Spirituality Versus Religion

Jacqueline Marish

My religious life began in childhood and ended in early adolescence. This was because my mother was shamed by the Eastern Orthodox Church priest for our small weekly contributions. The church service was in the Russian language, which we did not understand. The church was going to add the word Catholic to the church name. My first assertive action was to question the priest about this and state my unacceptance of such a move. My mother was shocked by my arrogance. I never again affiliated with a church that held dogma based on fear, limitations, and "isms."

My spiritual life began after I left the church. I had a mystical experience at age 12 that I shared with no one until age 25. The mystical experience revealed the truth about death, the truth about homosexuals (a term I had never heard before), and revealed my life to age 40.

I make a clear distinction between religion and spirituality. I am spiritual, not religious. I have a well delineated philosophy based on what makes spiritual sense to me. I believe in divine energy that is alive and without gender. When necessary to give it gender, I always use the female gender, for I believe in balance, not in hierarchy. I believe that inanimate forms possess living energy. I celebrate nature as sacred and the earth as a living entity that sometimes cries in pain.

I know my life has sacred meaning and a sacred purpose. I know that I am a truth sayer and a change agent. I know that I am a role model. I know that the second half of my life is when my sacred purpose will manifest itself in the larger public domain. I have the great blessing of knowing that if I died today I would leave feeling I have given a lot to the world.

A second mystical experience occurred at a professional conference when the keynote speaker took us through two guided visualizations. My spirituality blossomed. This occurred about 14 years ago when I was about 38.

I have a strong faith, a fearless faith. I am not perfect in my faith and I realize that no one can be. However, I can trust my faith. I have witnessed and experienced many, many miracles. I know that I am a spiritual being in human form not a human being with a spiritual core.

In the professional work I do as a counseling psychotherapist and hypnotherapist I honor each person's religious or spiritual philosophy. I find that many people do not have a philosophy by which they live and thus they have no anchor to hold onto while going through life's struggles. My role is not to proselytize, but rather to help people find the truth that they can honor. Self-esteem is soul-esteem, an honoring of the Creator.

I was never in conflict with my sexual orientation. My heterosexuality was as natural to me as my lesbianism now is. I am certain that being lesbian is my orientation until death. I have never had to undergo the emotional torture that so many lesbians, gays, and bisexuals experience. The mystical experience blessed me with absolute clarity and forever resolved any possible conflict.

I believe religion lost its way because it became political. To become political meant it had to be hierarchical and fear-based in order to control and dominate. Religion is based on closed and controlled thinking.

I believe spirituality is based on universal truths of nature and observable processes. I believe spirituality is life-affirming not death and war oriented. I believe spirituality is open-thinking and always celebrating and encouraging awe, wonder, and joy of sacredness. And everything is sacred — you, me, the earth, plants, animals, everything.

Jacqueline Marish is a 53 year old woman who lives and works in Bethlehem, Pennsylvania. She holds a Master's degree in Counseling Psychology and maintains a private practice in Bethlehem where she, her partner, and their feline live their spirituality with grace, dignity, and compassion.

21

The Call Remains

David M. Glasgow

The LORD gave me a message. [God] said, "I knew you before I formed you in your mother's womb. Before you were born I set you apart and appointed you as my spokesman to the world."

"O Sovereign LORD," I said, "I can't speak for you! I'm too young!"

"Don't say that," the LORD replied, "for you must go wherever I send you and say whatever I tell you. And don't be afraid of the people, for I will be with you and take care of you."

Jeremiah 1:4-8, New Living Translation

It sometimes strikes me as ironic that the moment when I first came to know God — when I first looked with belief to the Being whose existence defines undefinable holiness, righteousness, and perfection — that at that moment I, with the blind egotism of a 13 year old, felt as though the whole of creation had been working toward *this* moment in *my* life; as though *I* were the only concerto in the Master's repertory, the only tapestry on God's glorious loom! How could it be, I wonder now, that after seeing the face of the Most Holy Judge, I could dare to feel important, special, *loved*?

It happened in Garden City, a small town on the beach in North Carolina whose streets flooded after only an inch or two of rain. The sidewalks there always had a gritty, sandy crunch to them, and the breezes that chased styrofoam cups among the stilts of the summer homes always smelled slightly of bilge. Not the stuff romance novels and tourist brochures are made of, but then, God was not out to win awards — just my heart. So, on that night, as I stepped out onto the porch with a heart full of questions, I looked out over the ocean and saw a single, bright star, like a peephole from heaven. Through the peephole I saw hope. I saw caring and compassion. I saw God. Suddenly, life made sense.

*   *   *

Julie[1] was there too, that night. We had been going out for a few months then, so when the youth fellowship had announced the week-long retreat, I had seen it as a perfect opportunity to spend some good quality time with Julie. Well, with Julie and Stan. Stan was a year older than Julie and me — already in high school — and I idolized him mercilessly. I called him my best friend. I think Julie knew, even then, that it was more than that, although her kindness prevented her from calling it a crush — at least, out loud. Julie has always been a model to me of a true friend, always able to listen (and hear), ready to set aside her own priorities for another person's needs, willing to offer her beliefs and opinions only on request or necessity. In another ironic twist, it was Julie who, after we had been dating for several years, first suggested to me that I might actually be gay, and that it might actually be okay with God.

High school was, I suppose, as high school is for all of us: a time of fervent fun, band trips, and snow days peppered liberally with growing pains, calculus exams, and ends of the world, in various forms. I tried drama, and liked it; I tried college-level English, and did not; I looked forward to Mexican pizza in the cafeteria and dreaded prom night. Julie was there through it all, even joining the color guard just (in my mind, anyway) so she could be with me at marching band competitions and away games. We shared popcorn at the movies, passed notes during the sermons in church, and laughed together at the peanut butter topping I spilled in my lap at Friendly's. Julie and I grew closer and closer, and yet I still could not bring myself to kiss her.

---

[1] This and some other names have been changed.

"That's okay," she would say, "I don't want to push you into something you're not comfortable doing."

*   *   *

By the time we started college (Julie in Maryland and I in Pennsylvania), I was so good at pretending we were an item that it came as a genuine shock when, over Christmas break, Julie told me she had started seeing someone. Not just "someone *else*." "*Someone!*" She did not sound flippant, by any means, and was obviously concerned about my reaction, but the matter-of-factness of it struck me hard nonetheless. We had never really been in love, had we? Suddenly, my cover was blown. With Julie at my side, I had not had to work hard to make excuses for my glances at other men, my bent for theatrics and the arts — but now? How would I keep my secret safe? I suddenly felt very vulnerable, very conspicuous. And very alone. What Julie had been to me, I needed now more than ever. I needed a friend.

In the world of refrigerator magnets and tasseled bookmarks it is often said that "When God closes one door, God opens another." In retrospect, it is not surprising at all that when Julie ended our relationship and set us both free from an untruth we had been clinging to for far too long, I practically tripped over someone God had set right in my path. His name was Jim and he hung out with a couple of the girls who lived downstairs.

Jim had once wanted to be a Catholic priest, but was not sure he was cut out for it and had opted for premed in college. He loved languages and music and the poetry of life. I liked him. I liked the person I became when I was with him. I liked Jim's ability to find humor and joy in everyday struggles. I liked his focus — the way he worked without thoughts of play and played without thoughts of work. Most of all, I liked the way he made me feel comfortable sharing my life with him. I could cry, laugh, shout, whisper, sigh, or scream at Jim and he took it all in stride. Something about him reminded me of that star I had seen over the beach that night. But I still could not tell him my deepest secret.

One night Jim rented a movie, so he and I and a bunch of our friends all piled onto someone's bed in the dorm to watch *Maurice* (a film version of the E. M. Forster novel). I did not like the movie all that much. When it became clear that the hero of the film was a gay man, I felt a sudden need to avoid all movement. It seemed as though any revealed emotion might bring me to the center of attention and my secret would be out in the open. I sat breathless until the tape ended and Jim and I could return to his room for our usual late-night talk.

"Do you know why I wanted you to see that movie?" Jim asked me during a break in the conversation.

I hoped I did.

"Well," he started, and for a few seconds I was afraid he would change his mind. Then he sighed, and with both resignation and relief he said, "It's kinda my life's story."

"Really?" I almost gasped. "Mine too."

*   *   *

When our sophomore year began, our different majors made it difficult for us to spend much time together. Jim was running off to biology labs first thing in the morning and I was spending late nights in the music building practice rooms. The romance whose bud had broken through the snow that night after the movie soon withered for lack of attention. I found the old unwelcome loneliness of my life before Jim returning more desperately than ever.

I began to wonder if maybe I had been "blinded by sin" (a phrase I had never used before, but which sounded appropriately damning now) when I had thought Jim was sent to me by God. Now I wondered if I had been fooling myself into following a path to hell, when I thought I was being led closer to God's plan for me. The questions finally grew so loud that they kept me from sleeping. One Sunday morning, feeling angry, confused, and frustrated, I went to church early and asked to speak with the young associate pastor. Ironically, only my cynical enjoyment of self-loathing was keeping me from suicide.

Pastor Chris welcomed me into his office and closed the door. He asked what he could do for me and that opened the floodgates. I do not remember exactly what I told him, but somehow I told him that I thought I might be gay and I did not know what God thought about that or what God wanted me to do.

I must have taken Chris by surprise because he sat there in silence for the briefest of moments. Then, rather than trying to analyze or comment or criticize or even answer, he spoke out of pure Christian caring.

"You look like you need a hug," he said.

Then he stepped out from behind his desk and hugged me. The pure, non-sexual, non-judgmental love of it made me finally, gratefully, weep.

* * *

Chris was the one who hired me, soon after, to direct the youth choir. I used to marvel that my call to serve came from the man — I sometimes see him as an angel — who knew all of my weaknesses. As I have grown, I have come to realize what Chris saw in my anxious face that morning. He understood that what I needed was to feel loved by God — and that the best way for me to feel God's love would be, like Jeremiah, to acknowledge God's plan for my life.

Chris was transferred to another church a few years later, the destiny of all Methodist pastors, but I never forgot his lesson. Shortly after he left, I felt called to write a musical for the immensely talented group of kids in the youth choir. I saw in them a perfect avenue to share the message that I had come to believe is the heart of the Gospel: God made us flawed. God loves us anyway. Our only responsibility is to love one another as God does. I called the show *Love in Christ*.

Love in Christ dealt with several touchy issues — premarital sex, parent-child relationships, loving strangers and sinners — illustrating all with examples from Scripture of how Jesus responded to similar situations. Halfway through the show, one of the characters reveals that he is gay and another character affirms that God still loves him. I guess I still needed to hear it myself too.

If I had any idea how controversial that show would be, I would not have sent the press release to the city papers or allowed them to give us front page coverage. I received angry phone calls condemning me as a child molester and notes of concern that I might be spreading AIDS to the young people with whom I worked. Anonymous letters demanded that I resign from my positions as Youth and Children's Choir director. One caller told me I should be ashamed of myself for trying to seduce the young men in the choir. A letter-writer told me she would pray for my deliverance, just as though I were trapped in a burning building. In another display of God's delicious irony, though, the same musical that ignited the storm of controversy across the city and brought phone calls, letters, insults, and accusations brought a new friendly voice into my life.

I answered the phone tentatively (I had come to fear its ring since the hate calls had begun) but this new voice sounded as nervous as I was hesitant. "My name is Mark," he said. "I liked your show and I was wondering if maybe we could meet somewhere to talk over dinner."

* * *

I look around myself sometimes and wince at how blessed I am. Mark and I celebrated our third anniversary — and our fourth mortgage payment — in March 1998. I am still directing choirs at the church and, for a year now, have been the worship leader of a weekly contemporary worship service. There are still those who would rather I not serve the church, saying that Mark and I are living in sin and that I am not capable of spreading the Gospel. I ignore them most of the time, but when I find it hard to ignore the voices of hatred, I pull out a Bible and flip to Romans 8:18-25:

> I consider that our present sufferings are not worth comparing with the glory that will be revealed in us. The creation waits in eager expectation for the children of God to be revealed. For the creation was subjected to frustration, not by its own choice, but by the will of the one who subjected it, in hope that the creation itself will be liberated from its bondage to decay and brought into the glorious freedom of the children of God.

> We know that the whole creation has been groaning as in the pains of childbirth right up to the present time. Not only so, but we ourselves, who have the first fruits of the Spirit, groan inwardly as we wait eagerly for our adoption as sons and daughters, the redemption of our bodies. For in this hope we were saved. But hope that is

seen is no hope at all. Who hopes for what one already has? But if we hope for what we do not yet have, we wait for it patiently.

New International Version, Inclusive

That is the passage one of the cast members quoted in a letter she wrote to me after the musical. She also offered me some personal encouragement:

Since the first day I met you, I have been constantly amazed and inspired. No pastor or preacher could have ever brought me closer to Jesus. And now, nobody could ever make me believe that the musical and its message and its author are anything but miraculous.

So thank you. *Love in Christ* has been a milestone in my journey toward Christ and no matter what happens I'll never forget it or stop thanking God that I was a part of it.

Reading those words for the first time was like looking through a distant star into the face of God — seeing love.

In Part Two, **Patricia and Michael Glasgow,** David's parents, share their story about David's coming out. See page 203, Chapter 37.

David M. Glasgow is not nearly as melancholy as he would like you to believe. He received a B.A. in Music Theory and Composition from Dickinson College in 1993. He serves as Director of Contemporary Music Ministries at a United Methodist Church. He and his companion, Mark Boggs, have purchased a home in Carlisle, Pennsylvania.

22

In God's Presence

Stephanie Sue Davis

How blessed is the person whose strength is in You, Lord;
In whose heart are the highways to Zion!
Passing through the valley of Bacca [weeping],
They make it a spring, the early rain also covers it with
blessings.
They go from strength to strength. Every one of them
appears before God in Zion.

Psalm 84:5-7
New American Standard Version, Inclusive

"Oh God," I pleaded with tears, "please take this away. I can't be gay. I just can't!" My own words fell upon me as a haunting echo, a nettle in my side that I tried to ignore. It was utter taboo to even say the word, let alone admit to its struggle. *Homosexuality:* the subject that made everyone in church cringe and quietly shift in their cold, wooden pews.

I was a closet Christian silently being eaten away by my attractions to women. It was not a subject about which many in the church cared to talk. It was sin to them and that was all there was to the issue. Out of desperation, I went to Christian counselors, even counselors who were ex-lesbian. I prayed. I confessed. I wept. I begged God with tears of repentance. I raked over my childhood to no avail. I had believers lay hands on my body to pray over me. But even after all these things,

God was still silent in my pain. There were no answers to be found.

How could this be happening to me? I had loving Christian parents and a loving family. I had experienced a "Saul of Tarsus" conversion at age 19 that would forever imprint on my heart the desire to serve Jesus. I was a well-respected young Christian woman and college church leader at what some called the "Bible Mecca," Grace Community Church in Sun Valley, California. I had even served God overseas as a missionary in Ecuador. I loved the Lord. Now, years after being saved, I found myself once again facing desires of which I thought God had rid me. How could this happen to me? Why was I struggling?

I had long forgotten the battle in my earlier years, growing up as a tomboy. When I was little, most girls, although attracted to my enthusiasm, did not play with me. In part this was because I was playing with the boys. I identified more readily with the boys — climbing trees, playing sports, rescuing girls in distress on the playground, and fishing for crawdads in the nearby water canal.

I did not care for playing dolls and house with other girls my age. Or, should I say, most girls did not prefer to play dolls with me? I was not a delicate flower of a girl. I hardly could stand the all too domestic, tame, boring scenarios that girls would come up with for playing house. I was the rough and tumble type. When I attempted playing with dolls, I found myself playing Ken to another girl's Barbie. My Ken doll could never just sit and have a cup of tea. He had to be jumping off of roof tops, chasing after imaginary spies, and sweeping other Barbies off their feet in romance! Needless to say, my creativity often frightened the other girls away.

My emotional, and even physical attraction to the same sex was very intense and very apparent even at a young age. I was constantly in search of a kindred spirit and a fair maiden to rescue. This caused me to pursue friendships with other girls in elementary school. Once I found someone to be a "bosom friend," as Anne of Green Gables put it, I would give my utmost loyalty. I would follow her around the playground, sit next to her in class and at lunch, beat up boys who teased her, and spend all of my after school time pursuing a closer friendship with her.

Like every other girl, I dated boys in junior high and high school. However, deep inside, I never felt complete. Something was missing. During my sophomore year in high school I began to realize why I lost several girl friends. I was too intense. I wanted to go out on dates, buying them gifts, courting them as a boy would court a girl at that age. I never understood that my behavior was abnormal to them. I thought everyone felt the way I did about girls.

It was not until I had a crush on my best friend during my junior year, though, that I began to realize my attraction to girls *was not* like everyone else. Frightened of the overwhelming rush of adrenaline and butterflies, I confided in my boyfriend at the time. He dismissed it as not being a big deal. I sighed with relief and tried to forget about the crush. I did not want to be different. Deep inside my soul, though, I had begun to awaken to the reality that I *was* different.

As a young adult, having obtained my bachelor's degree in Southern California, I moved to San Francisco to begin my graduate work. I had left behind my close network of Christian friends, my ministry, and an outward holiness that I had hid behind for so many years. It was here that God began to bring the issue to the surface once again.

I became increasingly depressed, confused, and isolated. Soon I stopped attending church under the burden of my silent pain. I continued to pray that God would take it all away. But it never went away. The more I kept silent, the more agonizing the struggle grew. Finally, out of desperation for an explanation and resolution to this gay problem, I turned to people I knew who would not judge me, to others already in the gay community.

I will never forget the day that I stood outside the door of the Lesbian, Gay, and Bisexual Alliance on San Francisco State University's campus. For weeks I walked by the room, but never went in. I was still longing to be cured, but the church had no answers for me. God had given me no cure. Finally one afternoon I could not stand the pain of my struggle any more. It was a cold September day in 1995. With much fear, I grabbed the doorknob and turned it. As I opened the door, I walked into a new identity while walking out on what had been familiar to me all my life. It was not too long after that day on campus that I began living a double life — part time Christian, part time lesbian. The deeper I became involved in the gay and lesbian community and relationships, the more I had to lie to cover up this new identity that I was now secretly wearing. One of my closest friends had already threatened that I would be excommunicated from the church. I felt hopeless and alone. Other brothers and sisters in Christ would condemn me for living as a gay woman. I was told, "Live as a gay woman and you will be walking out on God, you will demonstrate that you are not truly a believer."

I was terrified of the threat that God would forsake me. I knew I could not live without God. However, I also knew that this deep seated sense of who I was would not go away. I continued to be tormented by what the Church presented to me as the only choice — deny a part of who you are or deny your God. There is no greater pain for a child of God than to believe you turned your back on God.

After almost two years of this double life, God began to gently draw me back. After my lover left me for another woman I was devastated. This, however, was just what God needed to get me in the place where God's healing grace could begin to be shed on me. I began to face the truth that God needed to be in control of my whole life, including my sexuality.

The loss of my lover caused me to run from being gay. I sold my belongings and moved to Oregon, went to seminary, entered a ten month intensive ex-gay program, and continued to receive counseling. Despair and tears consumed me. For months, I wept daily. I confessed. I prayed. I was required to cut off all contact with my community of gay friends. I surrounded myself with the familiar Christian community and its lifestyle of outward holiness. This was supposed to free me from my gay tendencies, but no amount of behavior modification or aversion therapy could take away my pain or my attraction to women. Night after night I writhed in pain. I would go alone to the chapel to beg God to touch me, speak to me, heal me . . . anything. I was dying inside.

Just when I thought I could bear it no more, God broke the painful silence, "Come to my Presence and drink." In a vision that repeatedly came to me, God invited me to drink from the River of Life. There at this river, Jesus himself cupped the water of God's presence in his hand and put it to my parched lips. For the first time in years I felt hope in my heart. God had not forsaken me and had not condemned me for my struggle. God simply wanted to make me whole again and wholly God's. Fear and condemnation left, and in its place came a renewed joy and thirst for God. As I began studying God's word on homosexuality, praying for God's guidance, I found my story within the pages of the Word. There was a place of God's acceptance and celebration of me — not condemnation as I had been taught for so many years.

Shortly after coming to a place of acceptance of my own God-given identity, I left seminary and the ex-gay program. I began attending a nearby Metropolitan Community Church. I have met a godly Christian woman, something I never dreamt possible. We even have plans to have a holy union. My partner and I serve on the worship team on Sunday mornings and yearn to grow in our service to God. I still have a hunger to serve God by reaching out to the disabled, afflicted, and oppressed people — both heterosexual and gay. One day God will open a door for me to minister God's love to such people with my partner.

The Christian writer, Neil T. Anderson, once wrote, "Satan knows that if he can keep you from understanding who you are in Christ, he can keep you from experiencing the maturity and freedom which is your inheritance as a child of God."[1] It has been a painful process of healing, as the Lord has begun to show me who I am in Christ. As I have drawn deeper into the presence of God, I have found a new identity, a true identity in Christ. I found that I am valued and chosen. I am loved by Christ and am secure in that infinite love towards me. As God daily breathes healing into my life, I can say with confidence and an unswerving hope that God has created me as a gay woman. It is not a disease or a handicap. It is not a sin or a hindrance to my spirituality. It is not a shame or a burden. It is not the whole of me; I am more than just a lesbian. My existence

---

[1] *Victory Over the Darkness: Realizing the Power of Your Identity in Christ.* Neil T. Anderson. Ventura, CA: Regal Books, 1990. Page 10.

and value goes beyond my sexuality. I am a child of God whose inheritance is freedom and strength and joy in Christ.

The battle of who is right and who is wrong wages on. Friends still send books and tapes on Sodom and Gomorrah. Family members still struggle with the end of their dreams for a son-in-law. I continue to be at the center of debate, scorn, and at times, even pity. However, after the Bible passages have been exhausted, after the friends have left, after family members have turned their backs, and after all the loud storms have passed over, then the still, small voice of my God spoke reassuring words. God will make springs from my weeping. I will go from strength to strength. I will be God's witness to this world where love has grown cold. Then when my life here is ended, I will appear before God in Zion as I was created — a gay woman whose purpose in life has always been to love God and all humanity.

There is a seed of faith in all of us who are gay, lesbian, bisexual, or transgendered people. It is a faith almost strangled, but still alive. Will the Church nourish such faith? Or will it allow our faith to be snuffed out by making Christ inaccessible to us? My prayer is that God will put away our petty doctrines and divisive theologies so that we may truly see that the love of Christ is for *all* people.

Stephanie Sue Davis holds a master's degree in Early Childhood Special Education and currently works in the educational field. She keeps busy by volunteering for a gay and lesbian youth mentor program, providing care to people living with HIV/AIDS, and staying active with Portland Metropolitan Community Church ministries. Currently, she is planning with her partner for their upcoming holy union ceremony and writing a devotional for gay and lesbian couples. In her quiet moments, she loves studying the Bible, playing the guitar, and taking long walks with her partner.

23

The Process of Coming Out

Rabbi Rebecca Alpert

The process of coming out begins with the enigmatic phrase *hatznea lechet im eloheha* from the biblical book of Micah (Micah 6:8). Traditionally, this has been translated "walk humbly with your God," but more recent translations have suggested it to mean to walk modestly or with decency. I interpret this statement to be about the way an individual understands her own place in the world. I assume that the way in which a person approaches her own life will determine her ability to behave ethically towards others. A central Jewish precept demands that we love our neighbors as ourselves. Commentators have understood this to mean that we can only learn to love our neighbors if we learn to love ourselves.

Walking with God is a metaphor for the way each person approaches her own life. It is a way to conceptualize one's innermost feelings and thoughts. It is not necessary to hold a traditional concept of God, or to imagine God in human form, to appreciate this metaphor. To see oneself walking with God requires a vision of God as the most important value in life, that which is with the individual always and everywhere. God may be in the image of a human being, but God could also be a power, force, feeling, idea, or anything that helps one perceive holiness in the world.

As Jewish lesbians, we begin with the assumption that we can only walk with God if we know and accept ourselves for who we are. Walking with God begins with self-acceptance, and requires that we tell ourselves the truth about ourselves. This stance describes coming out, declaring oneself to be lesbian, as a necessary prerequisite to walking with God. Walking with God requires self-knowledge. Those who walk with God know their way and consciously claim a path in the world. They are guided by the understanding that all human beings are holy, having been created in God's image. They respect the mysterious process, whether it derives from nature or society, that makes them women who are erotically attracted to other women and who prefer to build their lives with them. This is not an easy task to accomplish. I share my own coming out story as an example:

There was no one else about when Joseph made himself known to his brothers. His sobs were so loud that the Egyptians could hear (Genesis 45:1-2). As a child reading the Bible, I was always deeply touched by the story of Joseph and his brothers. I was moved to tears when Joseph, forced to hide his true identity, was finally able to tell his brothers who he really was, and to be reconciled with them after years of estrangement.

It was not until I was much older that I identified Joseph's story as similar to my own. Like Joseph, I hid part of my identity for many years. And also like Joseph, the experience of revealing that hidden dimension of myself made me feel whole. Joseph hid his identity as a Hebrew. I hid my identity as a lesbian.

I grew up knowing that I was strongly attracted to members of my own sex. But everything I saw in society — movies, popular songs, my parents' relationship, Bible stories — pointed to heterosexuality as the norm. I often had crushes on girls and women teachers, and had sexual relationships with girlfriends in high school. Yet as an adolescent I would never have called myself a lesbian, I assumed I was going through a stage. When I was growing up, lesbians were found in bars, underground magazines, and pulp novels. They were assumed to be poorly adjusted women who wanted to be men, not courageous women who dared to be different. I did not want to be one of them.

My experience in Hebrew school reinforced my own discomfort with my sexual feelings and fostered the development of my heterosexual identity. Lessons about the importance of marrying a Jewish man and raising Jewish children were well taught, and I wanted desperately to belong. There was nothing in Judaism as I was growing up that would indicate any possible acceptance of lesbians.

For me, focusing on my Jewish identity provided a perfect alternative to exploring my sexual identity. I married, became a rabbi, and had two children. Despite my wishes to the contrary, the strong erotic attraction I felt towards women never left me. After a while I began to think of myself as bisexual. But at some point it became clear to me that I needed to make a choice. It was then that I left my marriage and developed a primary relationship with a woman.

Coming out to myself, calling myself a lesbian, was not an easy thing to do. I had achieved status and visibility in the Jewish world as a rabbi, and I was afraid that if I came out I would be forced to give that up. I was concerned that people I had worked with would be uncomfortable around me, or that they would no longer respect my ideas and judgments.

But at a certain point I developed a strong conviction that it would be better if people knew, and that I could not worry if they did or not, at least most of the time. I came out because I got tired of hiding and lying, it had a corrosive effect on my soul. In coming out I experienced a sense of pride in being a lesbian. I gained peace of mind and a sense of freedom unattainable in the closet. That year, Pesah (Passover) took on new meaning, for I had truly experienced the journey through the narrow straits of *mitzrayim* (Egypt) to freedom. And I finally knew what Joseph felt like when he revealed his identity to his brothers.

Excerpted from Rebecca Alpert's book *Like Bread on the Seder Plate: Jewish Lesbians and the Transformation of Tradition* (New York: Columbia University Press, 1997) Chapter 4, pp. 54-57. Reprinted here with the permission of the publisher.

Rebecca T. Alpert is the Co-Director of the Women's Studies Program and Assistant Professor of Religion and Women's Studies at Temple University. She is a rabbi and the former dean of students at the Reconstructionist Rabbinical College. She has taught and published extensively in the areas of women in religion, medical ethics, contemporary Judaism, and gay and lesbian studies. She is the co-author of *Exploring Judaism: A Reconstructionist Approach* (1986) and author of *Like Bread on the Seder Plate: Jewish Lesbians and the Transformation of Tradition*, published by Columbia University Press in 1997.

24

A Letter to the Church

Greg Lichti

The following letter to the Committee on Ministerial Leadership (CML) of the Conference of Mennonites in Canada (CMC) tells a significant part of my story as a gay man in the Mennonite church. I wrote this letter in November 1992 while I was a Master of Divinity student at the Toronto School of Theology and a member of the pastoral team at Warden Woods Mennonite Church in Toronto, Ontario. I had applied for CML bursary funds to attend seminary, but my application was set aside because the committee staff person had heard that I was gay. Although I was not invited to give input, I sent the following letter to the committee so that my voice would be part of the conversation.

Greetings. I am writing in response to B____'s September 10, 1992 letter. He indicated that my application for a bursary from the CML Study Reserve Fund has been set aside for special consideration because of my sexual orientation. I wanted to communicate directly with you regarding this matter. It seems to me that discussions regarding homosexuality often take place divorced from the people directly involved. Thus, I want to share some of my story with you, including the process that led me to pursue theological training. I hope that some of this background is helpful to you as you make a decision. I was quite involved in the church during my high school and university years. Listowel (Ontario) Mennonite Church provided numerous opportunities for me and other young people to test out our gifts and to grow in the Christian faith. Opportunities to provide leadership in the youth group and in Listowel Church in general, as well as church-wide conferences and events allowed me to test out those gifts further and develop an understanding of the church's broader mission. My involvement at Conrad Grebel College further clarified and expanded my interest in the church. During the time I worked for the Mennonite Church General Board, I again expanded my experience and my gifts were strongly affirmed by others. I assumed that I would spend at least part of my vocational life doing church work and many people were encouraging me to move in that direction.

It was also during my time at the General Board that the church was dealing with the issue of homosexuality and I was beginning to acknowledge the fact that I am gay. The next two years were probably the most difficult period of my life. Everything in my life seemed to be going so well. I had a very supportive, nurturing, cutting-edge faith community at Grebel, a supportive family, a good academic record, and a sense of where I wanted to go vocationally. My perception at that time was that my being gay was going to destroy it all. The possibility that a vocation in the church was going to be cut off for me was especially difficult to deal with. I cried a lot of tears and experienced a lot of anguish about that. It seemed that the vocational path I felt called to follow had suddenly been swept out from under me. Concurrent with this vocational crisis was a personal crisis of faith and self understanding. What did it mean for my own personal faith, self esteem, and relations with family and community to acknowledge that I was gay? For a time, I was very angry at God for allowing me to be in this situation. This was a very confusing time because one receives so many different messages from church and society on homosexuality, many of them condemning. I unsuccessfully explored change in my orientation. Over the course of time, however, and especially during my MVS (Mennonite Voluntary

Service) terms in Winnipeg and St. Paul, Minnesota, I began to affirm myself as a gay Christian and understand that my homosexuality was a part of the way that God had made me. After I came to that self affirmation, I came to see church and societal condemnation of gay and lesbian people as a justice issue, and have increasingly become an advocate of gay and lesbian concerns, including involvement in the Brethren/Mennonite Council for Lesbian and Gay Concerns (BMC).

How does this relate to my decision to attend seminary? For a time I had given up on the idea of working in the church after a very painful period of letting go of that dream. However, as I have increasingly come to affirm the harmony of my faith and sexuality and dialogued with other Christians who see a significant role for lesbian and gay people in the church, I have reconsidered this decision. This has also been a difficult process. Even if I feel a call to pursue work in the church and that call is affirmed by others in the church, that does not mean that the church as a whole is ready to affirm that call and will be open to my ministry after I have prepared for it. On the other hand, maybe over the next few years there will be places in the Mennonite church or particular areas of ministry where the church would be open to an openly gay man. Perhaps not. Who knows?

Determining one's sense of call to ministry in this kind of situation is difficult. My understanding of call is that one should experience not only a personal sense of call from God to a particular vocation, but also a corporate call from the faith community. Let me say a bit about my own personal sense of call and the gifts that I feel that I bring to ministry. As I mentioned earlier, I have had a long-standing interest in the church and have always been involved in its work in significant ways. It is somewhat of a passion with me and it seems that whatever issue I am working on, I am drawn to some kind of involvement with the church. My relationship with God and my faith in general is very important to me. I hope that my faith is always evolving and growing as I feel God's call and that of the faith community. An important part of Christianity for me is working to create shalom in society — a situation in which the spiritual, emotional, relational, and material needs of all are met and where all live in right relationship with each other and with God. I want to be a partner in creating this kind of shalom. My work in the church, as an advocate with low income persons, as a community organizer, and as a human rights advocate has given me some experience in this area and a sense of my path as a Christian working toward shalom. I feel that I have strong skills to bring in the areas of administration, organizing, planning and leading worship, speaking, and dealing with people. I have experience in urban ministry and relating to minority communities. I have good knowledge of the church and the issues with which it is dealing. I think that I also bring a special concern for people who are on the outside in church and society, partly because of my own feeling of being on the outside. I am at the point now where I am determining what vocation I want to pursue over the next few years and during that time, I want to have skills in the area of spirituality and personal development. My hope is that seminary studies will enhance my own personal development and ministering skills and allow me to minister to people in holistic ways in whatever vocational context I find myself.

The call of the broader faith community is also important to me, but this is a more difficult call to discern. On the one hand, I have experienced much affirmation of my gifts during my high school and university years, my time at the General Board, and since then. I feel that I need to test out my call more, especially in the context of ministry internships. At the same time, the church overall is giving a strong message that gay and lesbian people who choose to be in committed same-sex relationships are ineligible for leadership positions, despite the gifts that they bring. Some people have counseled me not to pursue church ministry because of this view. In the face of such advice, I have sometimes doubted my own personal sense of call and whether my gifts are worthy of consideration. Others in the church have encouraged me to pursue church work despite the church's attitudes toward gay and lesbian persons, with the hope that attitudes will change as the church encounters gifted gay and lesbian persons.

Amidst these differing messages, I have decided to pursue this call to ministry. I am in my second year of M.Div. studies at Emmanuel College of the Toronto School of Theology. I have found my studies to be very stimulating and faith enhancing. I have taken PLTB's (Pastoral Leadership Training Board) Church and Ministry course . . . and am seriously considering doing an Interterm and the spring term at Associated Mennonite Biblical Seminaries (AMBS) in January 1994. In addition, I am doing my field placement at Warden Woods Mennonite Church in Toronto where I have also been hired as a part-time pastoral assistant. As pastoral assistant, my duties include worship leading, preaching, pastoral care, worship preparation, and work with young adults. I am very grateful for the opportunity to test out my gifts with the Warden congregation and to work along with the other members of the pastoral team. . . .

I want to share with you some of my perspectives on my bursary application for your consideration. It is clear that there is a diversity of opinion regarding the role of lesbian and gay people within the church — this makes your decision a difficult one. At the same time, I am aware of an increasing number of Mennonite churches who are embracing the gifts of their lesbian and gay members as elders, church council members, Sunday school teachers, preachers, members of pastoral teams. These congregations include some in the Mennonite Conference of Eastern Canada who are members or associate members of CMC, including Warden Woods. Also, there are an increasing number of lesbian and gay Mennonites who are in ministries of various kinds: e.g., pastoral ministry or chaplaincy, or have been forced to leave the formal ministry, but still feel God's call, or who are preparing for ministry. Over 20 of us gathered for a day of reflection as part of the October 1992 convention of the Brethren/Mennonite Council for Lesbian and Gay Concerns in Denver, and those of us there were aware of many others who could have joined us there that day. This group includes persons who are members of CMC congregations.

I am aware that there are Mennonite congregations who are recognizing that lesbian and gay people are part of the reconciling body of Christ and that their gifts are needed for the building up of that body. These congregations, while perhaps still living with a diversity of opinion, have chosen to journey with the gay and lesbian people in their midst. They recognize the gifts that God has given them and the fact that gay and lesbian Christians can live lives of integrity and wholeness. I know that the majority of CMC congregations are not at that place. But just as some congregations are ready to hire women and some not and as congregations seek out leaders with a variety of theological orientations, I believe there will be diversity in CMC ministry settings regarding the hiring of qualified lesbian and gay candidates. Within our unity as members of God's family, we have much diversity in our faith expressions, calling for dialogue and mutual respect.

In the spirit of this dialogue and respect, I urge you to provide support to gay and lesbian applicants for CML funds. This would honor the journeys of CMC congregations who are or may be open to gifts of those persons in the future. At the same time, you would not be saying that such ministerial candidates would be appropriate for all CMC ministry settings, which is also the case with any other applicant. A decision to support the education of lesbian and gay persons would honor the gifts that we are already sharing with the church. It would also recognize that God has given spiritual gifts to all members of the body of Christ, and that those gifts need to be developed and enhanced.

This letter has become a long one. Thank you for your patience. I hope that my sharing of my journey and my thoughts is helpful to you as you make your decision. I am quite open to continued dialogue with you on these issues, either as a committee or as individuals. Please feel free to contact me at any time if you would like to pursue that.

Concluding Notes: The Committee on Ministerial Leadership chose to deny me funding for my seminary studies. This decision, combined with many other messages and actions of exclusion by the church directed at me and other lesbian and gay people, led to my decision to leave church ministry in 1994. These actions included the fact that Associated Mennonite Biblical Seminaries chose to deny a gay student admission into their Master of Divinity program. The church's hurtful attitudes and actions combined with uncertainty over my future made my life in the broader church extremely stressful. I began to see the church's actions toward gay and lesbian people as abusive, and felt a need to distance myself from that abuse. The good news that the church is supposed to embody became increasingly unbelievable. The gospel of love and reconciliation no longer had credibility for me. Given all these factors, my decision to leave pastoral ministry in 1994 felt like a wonderful liberation.

Greg Lichti lives with his partner, Garth Norbraten, in Toronto, Canada. He enjoys a rich community of friends, including many wonderful people from BMC, and is part of the Warden Woods Mennonite Church where he feels the support of his church community. He works as a fund-raiser for the AIDS Committee of Toronto.

25

Between Two Worlds

Anonymous

Before I tell you my story, I want to ask you to allow yourself to believe that the sister who is writing to you considers you her family — her valuable family. I believe you are my sisters and brothers with all your struggles, heartaches, anger, failures, and secrets, with all your joys, humor, loves, delights, and successes. Just as within our nuclear family, we all get on each other's nerves at times, so this larger family, the Church, can have feelings of impatience, anger, or regret toward one another. It is my opinion that the Church is experiencing some very difficult growing pains in relation to sexual orientation. I am writing to you because I hope I can help in some small way. It might be good for you to keep in mind that, from my perspective, I am taking a risk.

I grew up in a loving, normal home, the daughter of heterosexual parents who loved their five children and each other. Fourth in line, I have a sister and three brothers. My family took me to our Mennonite congregation just about every time the doors were open, from the time I was just a baby. Even as a child I loved the experience of church. I found the sense of family in our congregation very encouraging. I respected and loved my parents who taught me that church, and more importantly, a personal relationship with Christ, belonged at the center of one's life.

I was a good kid. I liked pleasing people, especially adults. My agreeable nature defined where I fit in my family unit. I was artistic and put a good deal of effort into developing that skill.

135

As much as I enjoyed my art, when college plans started to take shape, somehow I knew it was not my major. I focused on child psychology and finally ended up getting my teaching certificate. I have a fulfilling job in a public school.

At the age of seven, I prayed with both my parents and asked Jesus into my heart. I did not fully understand the commitment I was trying to make. I think my parents were a little concerned about that, but I know that at whatever level, God heard a little girl say, "I want to be yours." And I know I meant that. Of course, as I grew older, I was able to stretch and grow in that initial step of faith. During my early teen years I was fervent about sharing my faith, especially with those who were in difficult situations. During high school, I worked hard to understand grace better — to not put myself down so much. In college, it seemed I might have lost my faith, but now I see that was not the case. Jesus remained my best friend. It was simply a time for me to face the limits of human belief. I found that *God* was and is greater than all *my doubts.*

The aspect of myself that is most difficult to describe specifically is the fact that I always *felt different* — sometimes special, sometimes strange — but different, even as a very young child. I always attributed it to being an artist-type, but when I became an adolescent, it was not so simple to explain. I had a group of girlfriends who talked on the phone a lot, had overnight parties — all the normal girl stuff. I felt sexually aroused when I was with them, but I avoided thinking about that. I honestly believed that such thinking was impure, and "whatsoever things are lovely . . ." (Philippians 4:8). I am sure you know that verse. Somehow, I was successful at repressing my thoughts so firmly that I developed an interest in boys my age. I even went a little overboard, not morally — I was just one of those girls who was often in love. Still, I remember a day, at the age of thirteen, when a girl walked down my row at school. I must have been watching her pretty intently, she stopped at my desk and smiled. I reached out and put my hands on her waist and let them glide over her hips. She gave me a look of terror, but she had no idea how horrified *I* was! Believe me, from then on I kept my focus on boys, art, church, and school. I prayed more than ever.

By high school, I was becoming convinced that I had a great deal of self control. I got good grades, taught Sunday school at church, read my Bible, prayed, and was liked by my age group and by adults. I was a leader. Yet somehow, this boy-crazy girl found herself in the arms of another young Christian girl one evening. I hope you will believe me when I say that I had already been tempted with boys, and although it was honestly difficult, I resisted because I believed it was wrong. Well, God knows I thought *this* sexual encounter with a girl was wrong! And this might be harder to believe: I forgot the experience as it actually happened! All I remembered was a flirt, a pass, and me cutting it off. In reality, while it had its limits, I did not cut it off and it involved more than a pass. I tell you this to illustrate the morbid fear I had of the issue of homosexuality, due to my upbringing. Thankfully, I came to uncover the memory later in my life, once I saw God as magnificently merciful, once I was ready.

I deliberately give you only scanty information about my life at present, because I am trying to protect my family. I do not think I have the right to put my husband and children through the difficulties my coming out would involve for them. My husband and I have been married for over twenty years and we have a wonderful life together. Fully aware of my orientation, he has been perfectly supportive of my efforts to face it and deal with it in a wholesome way. I am learning to accept myself and he has been very helpful throughout the process. We have a healthy, whole, strong relationship — we are in love. Our children seem to be well-adjusted, happy, and successful. All of us are active in our churches and growing spiritually.

So, what is the problem, you ask? The problem is that, even though homosexuality is better tolerated than it used to be, people still fear it and feel free to joke about it as though it is the plague. They do not consider that someone could be sitting in the room who is hiding his or her sexuality. As the world begins to accept homosexuality, the Church, who could embrace hurting people better than any other group, becomes a scarier and scarier place. It hurts to watch congregations be expelled because they accept gay and lesbian persons as members. It hurts to hear people tease each other about being gay as though it were a disease. You are my church family. You should know

— the hurt goes deep! It scares me for the adolescents among us. I will always carry with me two chilling memories from my youth: the times I seriously considered killing myself.

I ask you to look carefully at what I and others like myself are hearing from the Church. I hear many of you say that you would accept a person like me. As I understand you, I am not living in sin. The only sexual encounters I have had since our marriage have been with my wonderful husband. But I am in hiding, am I not? And you know why, do you not? I hide this because the Church, which would be the best place to process my sexuality, is not a safe place to do so — not for me, not for my family. That is all I would call you to, not to agreement on doctrine, but to be a unified body of believers (with many *different* beliefs) who know they are not perfect in understanding or practice. In thankfulness for God's grace toward them, they provide a safe place for all persons. Brothers and sisters, we have the love of Jesus at our disposal! We are wasting our time! God will take care of hearts if we just open our doors and provide a place of healing instead of harm, hope instead of judgment. I assure you: God can cleanse *all* our hearts!

I continue to have strong feelings toward persons of my own gender. Often I have asked God to remove them; more often I have asked God, "how can a person be bisexual?" Someone like myself who believes in the sanctity of the marital covenant, different or same sex, can become confused and want to ask God "why?" in relation to his or her own bisexuality. At times in my life, it has felt like a joke God played on me. Fortunately, I am more sure of God's loving nature now. I know God does not joke in such a fashion.

It is not about nature or nurture. It does not matter at all whether we are born this way or not. Even the most conservative psychologist, I believe, will tell you that sexual orientation is established at a very early age. This is far younger than any of us would expect such sophisticated choices to rest upon a child's shoulders. That is where the Church has left me in the cold. I have this orientation, that is a fact. Before I had any choice, I suffered from simply being me. I could not understand why I did not have the normal feelings of those around me, the normal relationships with my parents that my siblings had. It was not my family or me that was causing the problem. It was my orientation — or rather, me trying to make sense of it within a society and a Church that offered me little help or hope. However, now I am coming to terms with my duality and finding peace. I know this is partially due to my unusual situation. Marriages of different sexual orientations do not usually fare as well as ours has. I will be frank with you: my husband and I believe that God regards fantasy differently for each individual circumstance. Therefore, he has encouraged me not to feel needless guilt for my thoughts, feelings, and fantasies about women.

So, to you who are struggling in a mixed sexual orientation marriage, who are confused about your sexuality and how it fits with your relationship with God, I just want to say: *do not give up!* God is big! I know it is hard to find a safe friend, it is an enormous risk. However, it is easier than it used to be to find love in the body of Christ. Do *not* look at the condemnation. Look for the love that Christ would like to extend to you through some members of the Church. There are many who will put their arms compassionately and wholesomely around you. There is *no* condemnation for those who are in Christ Jesus (Romans 8:1).

To you who are afraid that I and my kind are bound and determined to undermine the family, to pervert the Church, or at best, to cloud the boundary lines, I just want to say: *do not give up!* God is big! I know it seems clear to you that the Church is becoming compromised, it is a big risk to reconsider your beliefs, your standards. However it is easier than it used to be to find love in the diverse body of Christ. I and my homosexual, bisexual, and transsexual sisters and brothers will *not* make you give up what you stand for! We want to wholesomely and compassionately embrace you. We do *not* condemn you.

26

Coloring Outside the Lines

JW

...Jesus said to his disciples, "If anyone would come after me, you must deny yourself and take up your cross and follow me. For whoever wants to save one's life will lose it, but whoever loses one's life for me will find it. What good will it be for you if you gain the whole world, yet forfeit your soul?"

Matthew 16:24-26,
New International Version, Inclusive

Who decides what another person's cross is? Who decides what it means to lose your soul? Society has its definitions, but only you yourself can know what it means to live your life authentically. I could have lost my soul to other people's ideas of what my life should be. I have lost friends and I have battled through many people's lack of understanding of my life, but I feel confident that I am finding my way.

I was born into a very loving Christian family in December 1961. As I was growing up I felt happy, safe, and wanted. My father worked for a Nazarene college. I enjoyed the community of which I was a part. My mother and father were talented musicians. We often spent our weekends traveling and singing. My favorite early memories involve singing around the piano and "singspirations." All of these things drew me to a spiritual path at an early age, and as soon as I could read I became a daily Bible reader. While in high school, I had a boyfriend who was a good friend to me. He and I dated for two years, but we were not headed toward a long term relationship.

At seventeen, in 1979, I went to a Nazarene college where I majored in Christian Education and minored in music. I felt called to work with young people. I thoroughly enjoyed my study of theology. I met some people from a campus ministry group, that I would later join. In college I dated several young men, feeling awkward and self-conscious, but I wanted to be with someone. There never seemed to be any spark, even though I tried to be attractive and funny. It always felt like I was playing a game. At one point during college I was engaged, but broke it off.

When I was nineteen, in 1981, I met a woman, Ann,[1] who would have a profound influence on me. We first met at church, after I sang a song I had written. She said it touched her deeply. She had graduated from the same school I was attending, a few years before. We became friends not long after, and began sharing from the heart. I felt drawn to Ann in a way I had never known before. We would get together, eat dinner, talk for hours, and study the Bible together. We had both lost our fathers, to whom we were very close, so we talked a lot about that. We started speaking of our friendship as a triangle: God, Ann, and me.

That next summer I went on a youth mission. When I returned for my senior year at the college, Ann had decided to go on a mission that would take her away to Washington D.C. She would be working in a church that would be providing emergency services to the poor. I was devastated. It never struck me as odd at the time that I felt so badly that she was gone. Of course up until now, I had never questioned my sexuality.

While finishing up my senior year, I decided to join a campus ministry group and prepared to minister on college campuses. Ann and I remained in close contact, writing and calling, both excited about the new things happening in our lives and solving new problems together. At the end of the summer of 1983, I was off on my assignment, which was the opposite direction from D.C. in Minnesota. I was twenty-one years old. I had to raise a lot of money and I was going to a very cold and lonely place. Through all of these years I had probed

---

[1] Ann's name has been changed.

my inner self and walked an inward journey. I was unprepared for the outward journey I was to face in the years to come.

I found myself in strange churches, giving talks, and doing fund raising week after week. When I did finally make it to campus, I found that my training partner did not believe women should be in ministry. He had taught many of his students these beliefs also. Everything I had prepared for up to now had come to this, test after test. I found after two years of this, that I was spiritually and emotionally broken. It was time to go to D.C. and see Ann. She had also been through a crisis, finding out she was a diabetic. We decided that we deserved a week at the beach. After having known each other nearly four years, and being spiritually and emotionally intimate, we found ourselves exploring a physical relationship on our vacation. I remember telling her at one point that I did not know what to do with the energy in my body when I hugged her. It was so powerful and yet foreign to me.

After we became lovers, I knew my world view would need to shift and did not know if it could. Within six months I had found a new job, moved twice, and broken up with Ann. The next few years were the most confusing time of my life. I wanted to please God and my family, but suddenly I was aware of a part of myself that did not fit everything I had known and been taught. For the first time in my life I began to ask myself what was going to make me truly happy. I did not know the answers, but I just did not want to get to the end of my life and realize I had lived it for everyone else but me.

I spent the next several years trying to date others, mostly men. All this time I was comparing everyone to Ann. She had loved me unconditionally and that was a tough act to follow. I tried to expand my ways of relating to God. I still attended church, but felt the Nazarene church was now too narrowly focused, regardless of how my sexuality ended up. I went back to school to get my education degree, and made my living with a small business I created. However, I was still missing out in the relationship department. I just never seemed to connect with the people I dated.

In the summer of 1990 I called Ann. By this time she had moved to Oregon. I said that leaving her had been a big mistake and we began talking on the phone and writing all over again. I asked to come for a visit in December and we spent an amazing two weeks reconnecting. It was rather tenuous and yet that soul mate connection could not be denied. Despite all the things I had put her through, and the time that was past, we still loved each other deeply.

I had finished my degree and I told her I thought I would move to her town in June of 1991. Then maybe we could try again. The first year was tough as we rebuilt trust, but little by little we made a strong partnership. It is now January 1998 and we are in the second home we have purchased together. It is such a gift to get to be with your best friend and soul mate. We can sing and harmonize to the old hymns whenever we like. Our shared heritage and history are a real blessing. It has taken her family some time to come around, but now her mother visits for a week at a time and includes me as a dear family member. I see some progress with my family and hope that as we continue to be true to our love for them and each other, they will become more and more comfortable with our relationship.

I still hold many of the values that I was taught as a child: commitment, honesty, integrity, love, discipline, responsibility. These principles are the basis of my life. I found a job as a high school teacher, and work every day to bring hope into the lives of young people. The spiritual path that I am on continues to challenge me, as I seek every day to bring love into the lives of others. In a way, being a lesbian frees me from a lot of conventional thinking that is a trap to the spirit. Although not everyone understands coloring outside the lines, I am creating my own unique painting. I know God thinks it is beautiful, and I have a wonderful woman to walk beside me on my journey, God's amazing gift.

The author and her partner have known each other for 17 years. They have enjoyed a home together for the last seven years. They delight in the spiritual company of non-programmed Friends (Quakers). The author and her partner feel strongly that they are here to find their true meaning and purpose through their inner work, along with their work for healing in the world.

27

The Light Is Persistent

R. Robin Austin

The Light is persistent, but the Light is resistible. I heard these words nearly ten years ago at a retreat for men and women new to the Religious Society of Friends (Quakers). For Friends, the Light is God and every aspect of God. Friends believe that God created us as inherently good, not evil. While perhaps commonly held today, the belief that "a measure of God's Light dwells within each one of us" was considered blasphemous during the 17th and 18th centuries. Many Quakers were persecuted — jailed and even executed for espousing this belief. For Friends, our primary faith concern has not been salvation, but rather discerning, both individually and corporately, the continuing revelation of God's Light in and among us.

Friends have been described as practical mystics. My experiences in the Religious Society of Friends have tempered and grounded me. In my own joyful and arduous journey towards self-discovery and the often elusive, but sometimes attainable feeling of self-acceptance, I first found among Friends a place where I was totally accepted. My difference was valued and my courage in revealing myself as a gay man in a straight world was respected and supported. It was transforming! My experiences as a Quaker initiated a healing process in me that has been beyond anything I could have hoped for or imagined.

For many years, I minimized the impact being gay had on my life. I could not acknowledge my shame. I did not have the capacity to see the good that God placed inside me. I resisted

God, convinced I did not have a place in God's kingdom. For many years, I believed that homosexuality was evil and a sin.

Several years ago, I had the marvelous opportunity to read one of my short stories at a winter gathering of the Friends for Lesbian and Gay Concerns. This is a loving, supportive community of gay, bisexual, and straight Friends who come together annually for a weekend of prayer, healing, and fellowship. This community of gentle souls has been very influential in my life. While I do not see most of these Friends more than once or twice a year, I carry them about in my heart, as they do me.

I am uplifted and supported by their courage and by the shared experience of our disappointments and triumphs in loving ourselves and allowing ourselves to experience God's unconditional love for us.

Here is an excerpt from my short story, "Uncle Jimmy," that drew laughs and smiles:

> Okay, it's true! I was actually in love at age eight. Impossible, you say, but there is no other way to explain it. I was in love — real love! Well, perhaps it was "puppy love," the "I want to be near you and sit on your lap and have your strong arms around me" variety, but still I think it was love. However, there was one problem.
>
> I was in love with my Uncle Jimmy.

Uncle Jimmy was the first man I loved. Actually he was not really my uncle. Well, at least, I do not think he was. He was my mother's brother's wife's brother. I do not think that counts as a real uncle. What I mean to say is that he was not related by blood. Even at eight, I knew it was dangerous enough to love a man, but worse to want to marry an uncle. At school, I did a book report on the Russian royal family. You know, Czar Nicholas and Princess Anastasia. Mrs. Kring said it was a good report. It scared the hell out of me. By marrying a relative you could bleed to death inside. Hemophilia. H-E-M-O-P-H-I-L-I-A! I practiced that word a million times for the fourth-grade spelling bee. Of course, most stories are in some way autobiographical and, yes, I actually did win the spelling bee that year. Unfortunately, 1964 was not just the beginning of academic success, but also the inaugural battle of the war that would wage in my heart and spirit for the next three decades.

When I was just eight years old, I knew there was something terribly wrong with me. I knew that I could not share my feelings with those around me. Consequently, I began to believe that I could not trust myself because of my wickedness, a new concept I had gleaned from the fundamentalist Sunday school where my parents sent my sister and me. Ironically, my parents were themselves not at all religious. I suppose they felt it right to expose us to church. Unfortunately, the well-meaning, but overly-zealous adults who taught our Sunday school instilled in me a fear of God as judgmental and intolerant. As an adult, I now wonder if the image of God they taught us was not an extension of their own psychology. Were their fathers as unforgiving and intolerant as was my own?

Along with adolescence came the increasing realization of my sexuality accompanied by the discovery of masturbation. I was convinced that God was a little old man sitting on a cloud looking down at my genitals. I could not please God as I could not please my father. It was the beginning of years of numbness and disassociation from my feelings in an attempt to manage my own discomfort and pain. I was a sinner through and through and to feel perpetually horrible seemed God's punishment for this most reprehensible of crimes.

Sickly, and hospitalized for asthma throughout my childhood, I became increasingly aware of the fact that I could not be the son my earthly father wanted me to be. I could not play sports or rough-neck with other kids without becoming seriously ill. I saw the sadness and resentment in his eyes. Ashamed and confused, I retreated just next door to the safety of my grandparents' home, their embrace and nurture.

About 25 years before my birth, my grandmother, Mathilda Weirich, had turned down a scholarship to study voice at the Curtis Institute in Philadelphia. She chose instead to marry my grandfather. I have the most marvelous, vivid memories of them — my grandfather, a superb violist, and my grandmother's beautiful voice — making music for hours on end. On reflection, I am now certain that my love for Jesus began in her kitchen amidst the smells of freshly baked bread and pies and her gentle singing of "The Old Rugged Cross," "How Great Thou Art," and "Amazing Grace," among many others. Those were sweet forgiving sounds although, admittedly, I now find the lyrics a little old-fashioned and limited, not exactly expressing my experience of the Divine. However, it was not the words, but the Light in my grandmother's voice, the good I found there that inspired me. It was she who first awoke in me the certainty of my faith. She was real — vulnerable, loving, and difficult — but above all she always surrendered to someone greater than herself.

My parents always seemed to be preoccupied with themselves or each other. They were and are good and loving people and I have seen in them, as I have seen in myself, beautiful growth and movement toward wholeness. They, as I, are no longer as afraid of life, of loving, or of taking chances. They provided for me, nurtured and sustained me, and because of all my experiences — difficult and marvelous — I am the person I now am.

The Apostle Paul teaches us to give thanks in all things. He does not say just the good things or the things that make us happy or comfortable. He simply says *all things*. I believe that I have seen a glimmer of this kind of acceptance in the quiet resignation I observe in the elders of the Quaker faith. I understand it as their ability to embrace all of life — its joys, its sorrows — to simply allow oneself to *feel*. I also saw this in my grandmother. She was the one person in my life, and we all only need one such person, who embodies "the peace that passeth all understanding." Paradoxically, it is a kind of surrender, but not without action or movement. It is not complacent. My grandmother accepted herself, her life, and she accepted and loved those around her. However, my grandmother's life was not without turmoil and upset. She was not a saint, she could be impatient and demanding and yet, the Light radiated from within her.

In many ways, my grandmother has been so influential in my life because of this Light. I am now able to recognize the many ways in which we shared other similarities. She, as I, struggled with emotional stability. She, as I, suffered from emotional collapse because of our shared inability to express feelings, especially anger. She, as I, found God's joy in music.

Earlier this year, I took up serious study of the piano after a hiatus of 16 years. I am now conscious of the ways in which I had used music to suppress my feelings, to hide from myself and others. I realized that the reason for my early pilgrimages to my grandparents' home was to avoid interaction with my parents. For me, music is playing with the hands what is in the heart. Until recently, it was extraordinarily difficult to play because there was so much fear, resentment, and anger in my heart.

I have learned that homophobia and discrimination — in my family, my faith communities, and in myself — made it dangerous for me to acknowledge my attraction to men. I also learned that when I become involved with another man, our culture's conditioning of men has not prepared me very well for the exchange of feelings that should form the basis for emotional intimacy. I am often afraid or feel ill-prepared to reveal my fears, my self-perceived weaknesses. I firmly believe that intimacy is simply having the courage to acknowledge and confront conflicts in our relationships, our communities, and in ourselves. For me, courage is the willingness to name the conflict. The condemning teaching of the church on homosexuality as wrong and sinful creates such a conflict, which to me, seems in direct opposition to the teachings of Christ. It is absolutely unbelievable to me that this conflict persists among people of faith. I find it unconscionable that the Bible is selectively used to condemn gay men and women.

My first step towards resolving this conflict in myself was to come out to Jesus Christ. Feeling supported and loved by the Quaker community, I quickly had the capacity to develop an intimacy with Christ. I was no longer ashamed to claim him as my teacher and friend. I felt worthy and loved and boldly asked for his intervention. In 1991, I surrendered my life to Christ. It was the beginning of what has become an incredibly satisfying and sustaining relationship. This began a series of prayers about my gayness, asking for Christ's guidance. From several years of prayer and reflection, the following has been revealed to me:

◆　I know that I am created in God's image and I know to the depth of my soul that my sexuality (as one small, yet marvelous, integral part of me) is a gift from God. It is essential to who I am. As radical as it may sound to others, God made me gay.

◆　God loves me as a gay person, God accepts me as a gay person. The challenge for me, as it is for all of God's children, is to express my sexuality through loving and committed, intimate relationships where Christ is at the center. In prayer or at other times when I am privileged to experience the Living Christ dwelling in my heart or the heart of another, I never feel any measure of condemnation, criticism, or judgment. I find only the loving, encouraging embrace of a redeeming Savior who smiles approvingly at me as I journey through life.

◆　Christ continues to teach me. To embrace and celebrate my life and my sexuality is to embrace and celebrate God and creation as evidenced in what God created in me.

◆　Lastly, Christ has enabled me to see that if others are judging me harshly on the basis of my sexuality, no doubt, they are afraid. If someone in Christ's name is so compelled to judge me, to want to change me, or deny my experiences as a gay man, I need to pray that their hearts will be softened. For surely, they are afraid and have projected this fear and the resulting anger onto me.

Silent corporate worship is the central feature of the traditional Quaker service. Friends gather in silent prayer and meditation to wait on the Light. If so led, individuals will stand and share ministry, speaking spontaneously from their hearts. The silence can be both comforting and confrontational. When we slow down and let go of the busy-ness that characterizes modern life, we have the opportunity to experience the essential. Slowing down enables us to experience the Light dwelling in ourselves and our neighbors.

Five years ago, while worshiping, I remembered an event that I had purposefully chosen to forget. In 1973, in the midst of a turbulent adolescence and the beginning stages of my parents' eventual divorce, I ran away to Los Angeles, California. I had come out to my parents a few months earlier, and in their own fear, they elected to ground me indefinitely. I was allowed no contact with friends and had to come straight home from school each day (no pun intended). Unable to express myself, my frustration, and my anger, I ran away. I ran away from my family, myself, and my feelings.

In my misdirection to find love and acceptance, I unwisely chose friends in Los Angeles. I was 17 years old, scared, and eventually ended up practically living on the streets. I slowly watched my life deteriorate. I slowly watched myself make increasingly self-destructive decisions. I tried to ease my own pain through sex and drugs. I felt very far from God and myself.

What I remembered that cold January afternoon during the silence of Meeting for Worship was that I had betrayed my own feelings 23 years before. Wanting more than anything to be accepted by *someone*, I got into a car with a man I hardly knew under the pretense that he was taking me to see a friend. Viscerally, I knew he was lying, but I went. He took me to an old house where two other men beat and raped me repeatedly. They kept me against my will for three days, gagged and handcuffed. At one point, I was certain they were going to murder me. In terror, I cried out to Christ, asking for his protection. Light enveloped and protected me. Through a series of events, that in hindsight could only be Divine intervention, I am alive. I felt the presence of God that day, that certainty of faith. I knew that I was not alone, that somehow I would survive. God was that glimmer of hope inside me, the Light that relentlessly held onto me with the promise of something better.

That promise has revealed itself beautifully and steadily in my life in its own way and time. Today, I am nurtured and sustained by my friends and family, and above all by Christ. I feel reconciled and healed in so many ways I never imagined possible. I look forward to this next phase of my life: the possibility of finding pleasure and love in companionship, in loving and allowing myself to be loved by another man. I have that certainty of faith because I have that certainty of God. This enables me to have certainty in myself and the discernment to find this certainty in others.

I had not realized then what I know now. I was a prisoner of my own internalized judgments about the pleasures of loving another man. Love is not painful. Being raped is painful, but that is not love. I no longer, nor have I for many years, felt guilty or shameful about the goodness of myself as a gay man. As God's children, we have an extraordinary capacity, a deep and gentle goodness encoded deep within us. Walt Whitman wrote, "I did not know I held so much goodness."[1] Neither did I until a few years ago.

Religion is tyrannical when exclusivity is practiced in the name of the most sacred. My experience of Jesus is that he is inclusive. His message is as radical today as it was nearly 2,000 years ago. He gathered the disenfranchised, the marginal, and the unlovable around him. When I hear of faith communities passing declarations to exclude and condemn gay people, I ask myself where would we find Christ ministering today? Is it bold of me to suggest that we might find him among gay men and lesbians to help them see that they have a place in the Creator's Realm?

I know that we are intrinsically good. God created us this way. I sometimes wonder if we preoccupy ourselves with the external aspects of religious life. Do we build shrines and cathedrals, orchestrate services, and acquire regalia because of the fear of our own unworthiness, our reluctance to experience the beauty that God placed inside us? I have kept a journal sporadically for more than twenty years now. I found a recent entry that I believe best characterizes where I now find myself.

> Wow, I am alive! I am aware of my feelings. I had the best Christmas this year because I was really aware of my feelings and who I am. I feel connected to myself. Perhaps this was God's Christmas present to me this year, helping me become aware of who God created me to be, enabling me to experience God's forgiving, unyielding presence in my life. I can ask no more than this and I want no longer to resist God's unyielding love for me. Onward to my next joyful step.

I highly recommend *What the Bible Really Says About Homosexuality* by Daniel A. Helminiak, Ph.D., (Alamo Square

---

[1] "Book Seven: Song of the Open Road" from *Leaves of Grass*, by Walt Whitman. New York, NY: Random House.

Press, 1994). Summarizing extensive new scholarship and insights, the book challenges the traditional biblical interpretations used to persecute gay people. Just 120 pages, this book is a *must read* for all persons of faith.

R. Robin Austin grew up in Lenni, Pennsylvania, a tiny hamlet 30 miles southwest of Philadelphia. Raised in a family of crafts people and musicians, he gained an early appreciation for the importance of creativity. For many years he struggled with seemingly dissimilar leadings for the arts and social service. Eventually he chose the field of professional fund raising and today works full-time in hospital development and part-time as a performing musician. He is the proud uncle of three beautiful nieces and a handsome new nephew.

Robin lives in Philadelphia, Pennsylvania. He first became affiliated with Quakers in 1990. While he remains committed to the principles and practices of Quaker faith, Robin has been exploring other forms of religious expression and considers himself a member of Christ's Church that knows no boundaries.

28

Being Gay in a Homophobic Society

A true story as told to Earl Loganbill,
December 12, 1990.
The man whose story this is
wishes to remain anonymous.

I was born and reared in a west Texas town. I am a playwright and a composer of music. I contract for cabaret performances. I am a gay man. During my early childhood I usually played with girls. I was never one of the tough guys. I must have been recognized as being different. Yet, none of this seemed weird to me. On a home movie someone recorded a play scene with me dressed up as a bride; my sister played the part of the groom.

When I was in first grade I had a crush on a boy who just hated me. The imagery I was experiencing in my brain was not properly fitting into the heterosexual worldview. I really did not know what being gay was until I read an article in *Life* magazine that told about how life was changing in America. It dealt with the subject of gay liberation. I realized then that I was a gay person. There was now a name for me and I became aware that there were other men who had erotic predilections for men. There were other men like me who were struggling with their identity. I began to recognize that there were other people also who were concerned about the acceptance of gays in society.

The acceptance of myself was generally not a big problem. However, it seemed everything I liked doing was different from the norm. For instance, I *liked* to play the piano and when boys would throw rocks, I would draw pictures on rock slabs with mud. From a very early age I was a subject of ridicule. I was not accepted in many ways and was called dehumanizing names. I did not think anything was wrong with me. I figured other people did not know how much fun I was having.

I suffered great pain when people would drop me as a friend. In school I had just a few close friends. I was never popular or well accepted. In junior high I started getting beaten up. I was humiliated in physical education because I could not throw the softball very far. It was driven into me that I was different even if I did not know how to define that difference. I learned that all the traits that set me apart had something to do with being gay when I read the article in *Life* magazine.

In order to cope with humiliation I tried to excel in art and music, which I did well. My teachers in these subjects were very supportive. However, I was not supported in physical education! My self image suffered. I reacted by becoming haughty in some situations. I just decided I was better than all the others. I protected myself by deciding I was the champ and they were the losers.

At home my sister and my mother were good friends to me, but it became evident that I was not to become the ball player my father expected me to be. He shied away from me as I grew older. Our estrangement escalated until we had no relationship at all. We could not even make eye contact. It was absolutely evident that he was ashamed of me. He took a job coaching a baseball team that I was on to be sure I would learn to play ball. I remember how I would humiliate him when I failed to meet his expectations. I could tell it hurt him. We grew further and further apart. I was failing to meet his aspirations for me. I did not know how to turn that around. I could only do what I could do. Finally, it began to dawn on my father that I was not a man for all seasons.

During adolescence I knew I was gay and that, as a result, I had something to fear. I became aware of being identified by the nomenclature of a sexual taboo. Full fledged realization hit me. "I am homosexual." I fully understood that this was something that had to be hidden even though I was perceived as a sissy to anyone who wanted to beat me up. I was a gay man who could not possibly pass for straight. I was not willing to *say* I was homosexual because I thought that might cost me my life or a lot of painful encounters every day.

I went to a tough junior high school located on the wrong side of the tracks. I became haughty about many things. Being haughty in junior high did not work because others could see right through me and they were anxious to tell me every day that I was gay. I became fearful of being embarrassed or humiliated. I was so humiliated in physical education that I dropped out of school when I was in ninth grade. I was tortured by both the teacher and the students. The pain was devastating. I would rather give up high school than put up with that. The fear became a daily plague that caused a breakdown. I felt very much alone.

I changed schools to enter tenth grade. That was a fairly good move. I started recognizing traits I thought were gay traits in other men but they would not identify themselves as being gay. As far as I could tell I was the only gay person in this school of 2,000 students. I was certain that there were other gay students in the closet. I was alone, but I was marked. Consequently, if anyone else was gay they would not have anything to do with me because that association would implicate them.

The years from 15 to 20 were absolute hell on every front, even in art class, though I was at the top of the class. When I would go to the kiln room to fire clay, guys would be waiting for the chance to push me around and pick on me. I could not go to the rest room for fear of being pushed around, beaten up, and detained from class. I wish tradition and religion would teach people not to hate. I did not do anything to hurt my classmates, but they wanted to push me around to see if they could make me cry. I have been punched in the face and received black eyes. One reason I failed Algebra was because a number of young men in the class were hostile to me. I could not do a problem on the board without them making fun of me. I was aware of other people being roughed up also. I never knew when someone might attack me. It seemed that every time I stepped out I might be risking my life.

During that period I was in a roadside restaurant where gays often congregated. We heard pounding at the door.

Someone was nailing the door shut! People actually set the building on fire, intending to burn us all alive. The place was destroyed, but no one was killed. I remembered standing out in the street with tears streaming down my face, asking, "Why, why, why?" I was horrified that someone would hate us so much they would want to trap us and burn us alive! Gay people are sometimes killed for no other reason than that they are gay. A good friend of mine was beaten, stabbed 18 times, and strangled with his own belt.

You ask, "Does it hurt to talk about it now?" It does not hurt to talk about it to a caring person like you, but I feel a sense of sadness for the people who are on that hard road. At times I feel some anger too. Young gay and lesbian kids at school are hurting! Young gay people go through hell because they do not have a choice about their sexuality. Some people tell us it is our own fault. Some say it is a case of devilish deviation. I was told, "You are just trying to strike back against mean parents or something." But I know that is just not the way it is! Every obviously gay person goes through experiences like these. How is one to face one's peers? How do you communicate with parents who scorn gays? Every gay person's story is similar, but uniquely different.

Coming out to my parents presented big problems. I decided to come out about the time I started to read up on the subject. I was determined not to live a lie. My coming out was a nightmare! I went to a New Year's party where a friend of my father's was also present. I was 15 years old. This friend called my father and told him I was gay. I remember returning home the next morning at about 10 a.m. When I came in the door, my father said, "I want to talk to you! Are you a homosexual?" I said, "Yes, now can I go to bed?"

We stayed in that room, with my mother crying and my father lambasting me all day, until 10 that night. I remember the Winter Olympics were on the television, which stayed on the whole time. Intermittently my father would think of something nasty to say, berating me again and again, but he would not allow me to leave the room. I remember that was the day he said he would rather I were dead than gay. I was honest with him and told him I was sorry he would rather I were dead, but I could not alter the facts. We debated a long time about that. It was very painful! I realized for the first time that I was alienating my father simply by being who I am. I was either to live a lie or tell the truth and risk losing my father. From that time on my father and I had a strained relationship until perhaps the last two or three years. It is still not a normal loving relationship. He is a man with a lot of hurt and I am sure my being gay has contributed to his personal burden and sense of failure. I am sure expectations were that I carry on a great family tradition, but the chances are I will not have any children.

I lost a job because I am gay. When I was 17, I started to work in a design studio. I worked hard and my fellow workers were my friends. They thought I was an exciting young guy who could get the job done. Then I went out to lunch with a gay friend who was more overtly gay than I was. While in the restaurant, I looked up and there was my boss giving me a hate-filled stare. I knew when I got back to the studio that she was going to find a reason to let me go. I was arbitrarily ousted even though I had more talent than anyone in the studio. No gay persons allowed! No room for me there!

Where does the church come into this discussion on the taboo of gay orientation? I felt close to God in the church in which I grew up. I found my salvation at an early age. As I was nurtured in the church I was taught that God's grace was limitless. When I grew older I found there were conditions. One of them was that you could not be a homosexual and experience this grace. However, I had always been a homosexual even before I knew how society deals with my orientation and before I had experienced God's grace! My church, the Baptist church, always preached a personal relationship with God. Now that is what I have, I do not have a church anymore, but I do have a personal relationship with God. I treasure the Bible verse, "Judge not, that you be not judged," (Matthew 7:1, Revised Standard Version).

I look at my life as a cup. It is given to you full of things to use. The only way to get more is to empty the cup to make room. I think some of the issues that have been taken out of my cup served to leave room to hold something greater. The suffering I have experienced has enabled me to understand other people better. It has been hard and I have not enjoyed the suffering, but it has given me a great overview of humanity. I am much richer because of it. Those who want to deny me salvation are only stealing from themselves by denying me their love. They will never know me or experience the gifts I could share with them. I am willing to offer friendship, but it is often spurned. I have been able to survive a lot of the suffering by knowing it cost my oppressor so much more than it cost me. It is not I who am the criminal, the twisted knife belongs to someone else.

I believe God has been very good to me. The gifts that God has given me are God's way of saying, "See, I did not take anything from you that was really important." Being homosexual is rated near zero in importance, other life issues are much more important.

We talk about love and people's need to express love. At times we negate love if we think it comes from the wrong field. A man might reject expressions of love because of homophobia. If someone thinks I am going to hell, they might reject me because they are afraid they might go to hell if they *do not* reject me. These people are denying a certain category of love that could enrich them. Everyone needs love. The fear of retribution from God seems to inhibit love. Some people seemingly can not love, or they do not choose to love. They choose to remain safe. I think this is sad.

Earl Loganbill tells his own story on page 218, Chapter 40.

Earl Loganbill is a seventy-six year old retired community newspaper publisher. He is the straight father of a gay son and a lesbian daughter. A member of Faith Mennonite Church in Newton, Kansas, Earl's interests include theology, human sexuality, conflict resolution, political issues, international relations, ecology, social justice, and peacemaking.

29

From Confusion to Grace

Susan Kenagy

(Excerpt from a letter to relatives and friends in 1993.)

For many years — from my teens into my late twenties — I struggled deeply with my sexual orientation. Throughout those years, I felt persistent strong attractions to women, yet I assumed that I would marry a man. I had good relationships with both men and women, but I always lost interest in potentially intimate relationships with men long before they developed very far. I knew what the church taught about homosexuality, and I thought I knew what the Bible said about the subject. What I clearly wanted most in my life was to do the will of God. I thought that meant to be straight and get married, but that understanding kept clashing with the increasing awareness of how strongly I was drawn to women. How could this be, that I, who was created in the image of God, and who felt called to live in covenant relationship with another human being, could be made so differently (with same-sex attractions) than what I believed was right in the sight of God.

For years I struggled with these questions. I studied and prayed, I pondered and agonized, I tried to change and believed that I had changed . . . and was distraught when I realized that I had not changed. I studied and prayed, and continued to search my soul.

After much prayerful study, I began to realize that the biblical passages that I thought condemned homosexuality were probably written to address other things, such as to condemn rape or cultic prostitution (see Letha Scanzoni and Virginia Mollenkott's *Is the Homosexual My Neighbor?*). Eventually, I began to realize that the Good Creator loved all of me, even the part of me that loved women. Still, I went back and forth. Finally, thank God, I was struck by the light on the Damascus Road.

One prayerful, tearful afternoon, in the company of an elder sister in Christ, all of a sudden I believed. I suddenly knew in the depths of my heart and soul that God created me lesbian and that I was part of God's good creation. I knew too, that God was calling me to be in relationship with another woman, and that God would uphold me through whatever difficulties I would face as I carved out a life in the context of a church and society which condemned being gay. I will never forget the presence of God that was with me that afternoon. Nor will I ever forget the presence of God and the joy and fullness of life that have been with me in the years since.

Thank God.

* * * * *

Author's Note: Biene and I joined a local Congregational Church. We had a covenant celebration in November 1991 in which we, in the presence of God, our church, family, and friends, made essentially a marriage covenant together. Since then Biene and I have continued to grow in love for God and each other.

Susan Kenagy grew up in Albany and Corvallis, Oregon. Today she is a part-time mechanical engineer for a small manufacturing company in New York and a part-time stay-at-home mom. She lives on Long Island with her partner and their children. She and her family are active members of the Sayville Congregational United Church of Christ.

30

A Side Trip to the Wilderness

Rev. Peter A. Helt

I can pinpoint when I went to the wilderness fairly accurately. It was fun in the wilderness at times. It was lonely and desolate at times. My wilderness began when I turned away from God. I was attending Sunday worship, as I had done my whole life. The pastor got up for his sermon and preached fire and brimstone against the local Conference of the United Methodist Church because they were considering ordaining openly gay or lesbian people as clergy. "How could any good Christian allow that to happen?" They had a petition in the back for everyone to sign. Sadly, I left the church, knowing what they did not know — I was gay. I had even contemplated going into the ministry and following my father's footsteps (yes, I am a PK — preacher's kid). I was struggling with these two seemingly opposite feelings tugging within myself. Though I never remember my dad speaking about homosexuality or ever hearing it mentioned in church, I somehow knew deep within my heart that what I was feeling was wrong. After being bombarded by heterosexual images my whole life, I had no real concept what it meant to be gay, just that God did not like it.

I was in college when I began to realize I was gay. This was a difficult realization since most of the images I had of gay people were very negative. I was not even like the couple of openly gay people on my small campus. They swished and swayed, acting very "nelly." Even though I did some theater, I also wrestled and generally passed for straight. Since I did not have any positive exposure to gays and lesbians, I could only go by what I heard, which was not flattering in the least. I could not be like that, I kept telling myself, but those feelings kept coming. These feelings caused me to take the first tentative steps into the wilderness by putting my call as clergy in the closet as I learned to place my sexuality and feelings in the closet.

For many years I had felt a calling to the clergy and many people confirmed that this was a good place for me to be and that God wanted me to be a pastor. Throughout the years I had sung in choirs, taught in Sunday school, led Youth Fellowships, basically did all the things that potential clergy should do. When my father died during my high school years, it felt as if more pressure was being applied to follow in his footsteps. However, as I began finally dealing with my sexuality, it seemed to become more and more an impossible barrier to answering that call. In my confusion, I still pursued going through the process of becoming a pastor. I applied to a seminary and was accepted. However, in the end, I went into graduate school for nuclear engineering. I figured that was as far away as I could possibly get from seminary and from God's ridiculous call. I went further into the wilderness.

During the two years of graduate school, many things were put on hold. Dealing with my sexuality and my spirituality were placed far back in my mind, or so I thought. Quite often they would just seem to lurk there in the background like a ghost and haunt me. Since I was attending a very conservative southern school, I kept these personal ghosts under wraps. I was fairly lonely, but at least no one found out about me and therefore I did not have to really deal with them.

After graduate school I moved to Connecticut and started attending the church described at the beginning of my story. It seemed just like the churches I remembered and I liked it. Slowly I began to become involved in the life of that church. The pastor was friendly and knew my father had been a pastor. The church seemed welcoming and warm. I even began to think that I could just possibly pursue my calling to the clergy — until that fateful day.

I left the church that day and went deeper into the wilderness. I put God, who I knew could not love me and possibly hated me, behind me. I left the church that had been an intimate part of my life behind me. The only way I felt I could deal with my sexuality was to place God and my spirituality in a closet, and start to explore what it meant to be a gay man. The problem was I had no idea where to begin. This was still before the time that there were television programs and large sections in bookstores on gays and lesbians. Where does one find gay people? I finally noticed in the newspaper that there was an adult movie theater that showed gay films late on Saturday evening. It was really the first time I saw the word *gay* in print and finally worked up enough courage to go. The theater was dingy and not overly clean, and there were not very many people there, but I began to realize that I was not the only one. There were other gay people.

I changed companies and moved to the Washington, D.C., area. While I knew there were definitely more possibilities, I was still naive to this gay thing and had no real idea how to proceed. I slowly met a few people and began to discover the physical side of being gay. It still seemed furtive and secretive, but it also seemed comfortable and right in some strange way. After only a few months, my company was opening a field office of my particular section in California and was looking for people to move and support the office. I was a low person in seniority, but everyone else had homes and families and was very reluctant to move. I had few ties so, when it came to me, I said, "yes." California seemed quite exotic and I was young enough and adventurous enough to pick up stakes and leave. So here I was, moving to the Bay Area of California, one of the meccas of gays and lesbians worldwide, with not an idea in the world of what I would find.

What I found was a gay culture. There was much more than just furtive sex in dark places, although there was definitely a lot of that, but there were also bars, restaurants, theatre, and more. Here I came out with a vengeance. Except for my work life, I submerged myself into the gay world. I discovered many things during my short time there, both positive and negative. I attended my first Gay Pride parade down Market Street in San Francisco. Hundreds of thousands of people were there to show their solidarity with the gay movement. I listened to gay music and read gay books. I found a whole world out there. For a naive boy from Pennsylvania, it was like being a kid in a chocolate store. However, I also discovered the gay world of drugs and anonymous sex. While my religious upbringing kept picking at the back of my brain, I lived a life that was probably not dissimilar from the prodigal son of Jesus' parable. I was 26 years old and determined to make up for what I perceived as lost time. (This was before the advent of HIV and AIDS and every potential hazard seemed to be able to be taken care of with a pill.)

During this time I made one attempt to go to church. Church had been such an integral part of my life that when I heard about a church in San Jose that welcomed gay people, called Metropolitan Community Church, I decided to try it one Sunday evening. I had read the few books available on homosexuality and even fewer on homosexuality and the Bible. I still felt that tugging that I know now was from God. Much as I tried to suppress it in my mind, it still was a part of me. There were a handful of people meeting in this large church, and they were scattered throughout the sanctuary. No one talked to me or ever contacted me, even though I had filled out a visitor's card. The service was dry and fairly boring. While there seemed to be an attempt to say that God loved me, it did not get through to me. I decided that if this was the only possible church for me, I would rather spend my time in riotous living in San Francisco.

While living in San Francisco I also started to come out to my family. Our family had always been close and I wanted to share this new experience of my life with them. Slowly, one by one, I told my sisters and brother. While the reactions varied, I received no adverse reaction. The one thing they all agreed on was that I should not tell our mother. So I did not, much to my future regret. Basically it became a non-subject within the family since I was a continent away and only saw the family on major holidays.

My company again approached me to move. While in my heart I did not want to go, they said it was move or find another job. So, sadly, I continued my journey in the wilderness. I was beginning to feel like the Israelites. I became proficient in packing. I could store things away quickly, including my feelings. My time in the Bay area had been a watershed time for discovering my sexuality. As the song says, I would always leave "my heart in San Francisco." I did not look forward to this move with much relish since it was back to the south, Dallas, Texas.

While in Dallas, I began my first relationship. It was not a good one. My lover was physically abusive. To say I should have just left is to put it mildly, but this was my first attempt at a relationship and I was determined to make it work. After all, I had been raised that you put up with a lot of things to make a relationship work. "What God has joined together let no one put asunder." While this was not a marriage in the legal sense, in my mind it was. Finally, it became too much, and after counseling I gained the courage to move out.

I was no longer being physically abused, but I felt lonely. I did not really know anyone in Dallas. In the midst of this loneliness, I felt what I can only describe now as the presence of God. It was comforting, but still, in my mind, I could not let it happen. How could God love me? I had done too many things that my religious upbringing told me was going to put me in *hell*. But the nagging became stronger and stronger. Finally, I saw an ad in the local gay paper about the Metropolitan Community Church of Dallas. An evangelist was scheduled to preach. That was enough to peak my interest, being a good old evangelical boy myself. So after checking the place out by driving around it the Sunday before, but not going in, I came to hear the Rev. Jeri Ann Harvey.

When I walked into the church, I could not believe the number of people there. It was packed with about four hundred people. I took my seat and waited for the service to start. I nervously looked at the ceiling to see if it was ready to cave in on me or so that I could be ready to move quickly if the lightning struck. The organ started playing and they started the processional. Everyone was in robes or cassocks and it looked very Catholic to this Protestant boy, but I was stuck in the middle of the pew and could not get out gracefully. Finally, it came time for the sermon and this large woman got up. She lifted her Bible and boomed out the message. It sounded like fire and brimstone, but the message was totally different. It was about God's love. How could she be preaching so emphatically about God's love to these homosexuals, including myself? I knew that it was impossible. However, I continued to listen. (Remember I was stuck there. I think that shows God's sense of humor!) It impressed me enough that I came back that evening to hear her again. The evening service was more evangelical than the liturgical service in the morning, but her preaching was just as powerful and just as emphatic about God's love for me. She gave an altar call and I went forward. Someone laid hands on me (sadly, I do not remember who) and started praying. It felt so wonderful. A void that had existed in my life was being filled again. The closet door came flying open and my spirituality and sexuality came together once again. It felt like a weight had been lifted from my shoulders. I realized that in all those years that I thought God hated me, God was leading me back home again from the wilderness.

My faith journey began anew. I involved myself in the life of the Dallas church, becoming leader of a family group and organizing the children's Sunday school. While things were going better, I definitely had a long way to go. God was not finished with me. I went into another relationship that ended not much better than my first one, but life seemed to be going better. Then my company told me they had to move me to Minneapolis, the company headquarters. I could feel the ice deep in my bones. However, again, I had little choice and moved. The Metropolitan Community Church that I found there was small and dysfunctional. While working through the politics of "churchdom," I became a member of the Board of Directors and started coordinating the Christian Education program. After a pastoral change, the church began to grow and there was an excitement in the air.

During this time I ended my second relationship. It was messy and involved the church taking sides. I had the guilty impression that this was God's punishment and that gay people could never really have positive relationships. Nevertheless, through God's nurturing and the example of friends, I learned that we, as gay people, have the same possibilities and challenges with relationships as straight people do. Through this process I began to feel God nudging me with the call to clergy again. It had been a few years and I had thought that it was a dead issue. As with much in life, I have learned that God deals with things in God's own time.

I knew again in my heart where God wanted me to be. I had learned that God loved me. It was time to learn that when God calls you, *God calls you.* I looked at the Bible with new understanding. I saw God often calling the least likely people to do the work of God's grace. I decided if God could do it with them, there was a possibility that God could call me also. I had come full circle back to where God wanted me to be.

I am convinced now that while I had turned away from God during my wilderness experience, God was gently, and sometimes not so gently, leading me back. When I look back on the wilderness times, I realize how much that time contributed to who I am and what I am. Like the prodigal son, it was a joyous homecoming. The struggles of that time have given me a strong appreciation of the grace and love that God offers me. I have experienced the empowering love of God despite the things I have done. I can stand up in my church on a Sunday evening and share the Good News of Jesus Christ because I have experienced it in the depths of my soul. When I thought I was lost for ever, God found me.

Today I am the pastor of the Metropolitan Community Church of the Lehigh Valley, Pennsylvania, and know, without a shadow of doubt, that God has called me. I am still gay. I still do not have all the answers, but I try to share my faith as best I can. I finally told my mother and she has been supportive and loving. I helped marry her and her new husband, a retired clergy. I am still single, but always open to the possibility of a committed relationship. I foster parent teenage boys as an openly gay single parent, which is another story in itself. Life is not a bed of roses. There are still times when it seems that the aridness of the wilderness is taking over. The difference now, compared to my previous time in the wilderness, is that I know that I have a companion on this journey. God is my companion and "there is nothing that can separate me from the love of God in Christ Jesus" (Romans 8:38 and 39). This is the assurance that helps me help others to come in from their own wilderness journeys. I know — I have been there!

Peter A. Helt is the pastor of the Metropolitan Community Church of the Lehigh Valley, Pennsylvania. This community of faith meets for worship at 6 p.m. Sundays in the building of the Unitarian/Universalist Church, 424 Center Street, Bethlehem, PA.

31

Moving On

Douglas K. Alderfer

(This story is adapted from a message given to the Germantown Mennonite Church, Philadelphia, Pennsylvania, on March 22, 1998.)

When I was a kid, I used to sit in a corner of the living room and play with my family's big old box record player. We had a collection of thick, brightly colored vinyl records of religious and secular songs that we played on it. One of them was "Jesus wants me for a sunbeam." Actually, it was the turntable itself that most intrigued me. It had a grooved rubber surface and a large speed control knob for three different settings extending out from its base.

On the hub of the turntable I would carefully place some blocks, sometimes a tiny car or other more readily stackable toys to create a little pile of objects in the center that would spin around. As I increased the speed of the revolutions, the objects would gradually dissolve into bands of color that would hold my attention for brief moments. When one or more of the objects in the stack eventually lost their balance because of the way I arranged them or because I set the speed too fast, they would tumble and bounce off the edge. Sometimes the pieces at the top would hit the rubber at an angle to be flung in a broad arc about one foot away before coming to a stop. Thinking about my relationship to Christianity and more pointedly to Plains Mennonite Church and the Franconia Conference recently reminded me of that childhood activity.

While growing up, as I looked about and took in what was around me in the Mennonite Community, I saw much that was strong, pleasant, measured, and solidly stacked. All seemed to revolve around the Jesus center pretty uneventfully as long as you kept your carefully set position. Organized and run mostly by men, most of whom dressed rather conservatively, the Church offered near seamless uniformity. Both men and women were exceedingly polite and generally friendly. Subtle color in dress and of personality seemed to be reserved for a small minority.

As I got older I saw how this quiet, efficient, pleasant environment could dribble you off the edge or fling you against the wall if you dared move too much. There seemed to be little latitude for losing and regaining your balance. Some in my extended family had the experience of moving and falling away. A few relatives on my father's side chose to leave the traditional Mennonite Church because they liked to sing and carry on — in a God-fearing way. I can still see my Aunt Carolyn, with her autoharp, and my Grammy Alderfer in her cape-dress rolling her stool to the pump organ where they would wail away in powerful, nasal rejoicing. My siblings and I watched and participated in this with a mixture of amusement and awe. Outside of the family they were embarrassingly wacky. However, they were anything but reserved.

My Poppop Henning was pressed to give up his church membership a couple of times because he, too, liked to carry on — he liked to carry on business transactions. Apparently he was a little too willing to sell televisions in the 50s before most Mennonites had them in their homes. I am grateful for those relatives and the examples they set which opened other paths to me. In their excesses I saw freedom. I often wondered why my parents stayed in the church.

When I was old enough to make a choice I, too, left. My questions and conflicts with the church began in earnest at about age 12 or 13. I had a keen sense that I could never be at home or find my place there. I joined my friend Jon, with his own host of emotional injuries, in defiance. I also had a crush on him. There was a powerful place unequivocally reserved for my sexuality. Together, Jon and I resisted the pressure to become members of the church, but there were large obstacles, the most daunting being several, solemn in-home visits with the bishop. Some of my peers were joining the church at 13 and 14 years of age. I eventually joined, but held out until I was old enough to drive to my membership classes. Church membership very quickly felt like a sham. I had already learned the crippling skill of resenting and burying my feelings in an effort to conform. I needed to move away, naively hopeful of a new start.

Tyler School of Art provided my first real leave from Protestant Christianity. I met and was drawn to Jews, who seemed to run across a wider patch of emotions. Pleasure and pain were indulged and expressed. The culture had more recent experience with being derided, outcast, and exterminated. For the first time I felt I did not have to explain and justify a place for myself. My best new friend, my college roommate, some professors, my first lover David, as well as all three employers since college are Jewish. I avoided overtly Christian influences for more than ten years.

One of David's favorite lines was, "If you live long enough, it all happens to you." He meant it reassuringly because I often wanted to move things along in an effort to catch up with him and bridge a fifteen-year age gap. His mother's famous refrain, often cynically said, was, "You don't die so quick!" She meant that pain is part of life but also that we have great reserves of strength and "what doesn't kill you makes you stronger." Death would come to my family later on — in waves.

When David and I separated, after living together for five years, I experienced the first noticeable quake in my life. Buried hurts surfaced. As much as I was hurting, I could hurt others in return. We are sometimes hell *to each other*. It was a bleak and lonely time. In the aftermath I made it a priority to find other gay Mennonites. Through my brother Rick, I learned of the Brethren/Mennonite Council for Lesbian and Gay Concerns (BMC). I dropped by a board meeting at the old Meetinghouse in 1985, longing for people who might share some of my experiences. I was not seeking any religious connection because Christianity still felt like an odd jumble of the oppressive and the palliative. It was not a place for me to heal. In my conversations with the pastor and a few members at Plains

Mennonite Church about being gay, I felt like a specimen to be scrutinized, poked at, frozen, and set aside. When you have not had a voice for so long, the first attempts to use it are often loud and inconsistent. Talking openly felt like gnawing at already frayed religious ties. I hoped for dialogue and specifically invited an exchange of sexual experiences and evolving understandings, but some people think listening is a two-way conversation. I chewed through the remaining ties and had not even gotten to the good stuff. During this process I was referred to Germantown Mennonite Church. I terminated my nominal membership with Plains and gradually started attending Germantown. I am better at moving than being still. I can pack my goods — my emotional necessities — very tightly and am ready to go, one foot is ready to step away from where I am if I sense danger. It is harder to hurt if you keep moving. I have been driven — running ahead of a fireball of hurt, frustration, and anger. Along the way, I have run some caring people out of my life.

What is finally slowing me down is a spiritual weariness and death hitting home. Two years ago a friend sent me a poem by Rebecca Kiser-Lawrence about grief,

"Grief is an earthquake. All the boiling, liquid passion pushes up through any available crack or question and spews inner turmoil over the landscape of my carefully constructed life. It makes great cracks in the weak places of the outer crust and thrusts old history up into plain sight."

The period before and after Easter, with the coming of spring, is bittersweet to me. Three years ago, my sister-in-law, Cheryl, died of breast cancer the day after Easter, following a long illness. About nine months later my sister, Faye, already weakened, underwent delicate surgery at New York University's Tisch Hospital to remove a spinal growth. She never regained feeling below the middle of her chest. She never came back to her family and her home. In the trips to and from New York, between February and May, we saw spring make its way into the grimness, yet Faye got weaker. Nature's magic did not come to her body; she died in May. Faye and Cheryl, both in their mid 30s, both of them mothers, wives, sisters, friends, daughters, and teachers, finally had to let go. They did not *stop* caring, they did not *stop* loving, they did not *stop* trying, but they did give themselves over, and in that I can see possibility. Short of a bodily death, I have many options. It shows me that my anger must have some bounds and some direction, that the fireball cannot sweep at everything inside me if I am to allow some places for love and grace to move around in my life. I need to express it and let others feel uncomfortable at times. However, I also have to make a place for pain and powerlessness so I can go about my business. Like Faye and Cheryl, I serve in many roles to many people. My nieces and nephews, parents, family, friends, and I need each other's honest and full involvement to support each other's inner strivings and to help make sense out of chaotic and frightening times. I cannot do that if silence and stuffed resentments bloat me and sap my energy.

Talking helps. Laughing helps. *You all*, this community, helps — especially through singing. And time helps. But we are never the same after great loss. There are no words that even come close to exaggerating how different life is in the aftermath. I know I have a need to recognize and talk about losses again and again and again. I am grateful for a place where I can be heard and unburden myself and where I can be blessedly silent by choice.

Today, *moving on* is more about staying. Grief makes it very clear that the earliest influences that fed and profoundly shaped me, those which have come in through my navel before birth, are essentially and in large measure Christian.

Here, at Germantown, I can wrestle with and honor them.

Douglas Alderfer grew up in Harleysville, Pennsylvania. He moved to Philadelphia to attend Tyler School of Art and received a BFA in 1979. In 1989 he obtained a Master's of Education degree in Counseling Psychology from Temple University. Since 1990 he has been coordinator of HIV/AIDS Support Services and Gay and Lesbian Services for Jewish Family and Children's Service of Philadelphia. He attends Germantown Mennonite Church.

Part Two

Faith Stories of Those Who Love Them

Parents

32

Our Lovely Daughter

Anonymous

I can still remember when I first became aware that there were people who had sexual desires toward others of the same sex. I was married and had three children. While sitting in a doctor's waiting room I read a magazine article that told about two lesbian lovers. Naive and sheltered, I was shocked and horrified. Could there really be people who behave in such a way? Why would anyone choose to have a sexual relationship with someone of the same gender? How disgusting! Surely they must live in wicked cities and would never cross my path.

It is hard for me to believe now that I was ever so ignorant. My conservative Mennonite upbringing never included any mention at all of homosexuality, not even a warning against such behavior. It was as if such a thing did not exist.

I do not remember now if I discussed the magazine article with my husband. I certainly did not mention it to anyone else. Not even heterosexual sex was talked about, I would not have been so bold as to mention homosexuality to anyone. Furthermore, I was sure I would never meet such people, so I simply considered what I had learned as another example of the wickedness of the world and put it out of my mind.

But not quite. I was curious. So when I came across other information about gay people from time to time I read it all, wondering why and how these people could find sexual satisfaction together. I began to realize what kind of attitude society had toward homosexuals: derision, scorn, even hate was evident. They were called names: queer, faggot, fairy, and worse. One thing I was sure of, homosexual people were sinners of the worst kind. They were utterly perverted. Even God thought that of them. Did not God say so in Romans and 1 Corinthians?

Our firstborn was a little daughter, Jeannie,[1] lively and very bright. How proud her father and I were of her! She was a beautiful child who attracted smiles from all who noticed her. From her earliest moments she was interested in everything around her. I remember that a nurse told me in the hospital that the baby, only a day or so old, seemed to enjoy the walk from the nursery to my room! It was a joy to watch her grow and develop, especially when she began to make choices and express opinions of her own. She was creative and imaginative and very much her own person. I noticed that she did not enjoy playing with her dolls very much, nor did she like frilly clothes. Jeans were her preference and I recall a statement she made one time that "God would like it much better if everyone wore jeans to church instead of trying to outdo one another with fancy clothes."

Jeannie accepted Christ and was baptized at age 12 , and as a teen became quite involved in church activities, serving as Youth Group president for quite a few years. Our church had a Bible Quiz team in which she participated for several years, becoming a champion quizzer. This required her to memorize large portions of Scripture.

Jeannie dated occasionally but not a lot. There was one boy, a son of friends of ours, whose relationship with her we hoped would become serious and permanent. She lived at home during her college years, attending a local state university, but immediately after graduation with a degree in art she moved into an apartment.

Things started to change at this point. We began to realize that Jeannie no longer attended church. As time went by she became somewhat withdrawn from us, not always attending family gatherings. She talked about friends, but even though I suggested she bring them home with her to see us, we rarely met them.

---

[1] Jeannie's name has been changed.

By that time my husband and I were aware that the daughter of some good friends was a lesbian. I recall how, when Jeannie and I talked about it, I told her how disgusting I thought it was and how sad I felt for the girl's parents.

I continued to learn all I could about the issues of homosexuality. The feeling that it was perverted and sinful still prevailed in my thinking. It is hard for me to remember just when the idea that Jeannie might be gay began to cross my mind. I very clearly recall my sense of horror about the possibility. Not our beautiful daughter, surely not! I was still convinced at that point that homosexuality was a choice and could not possibly imagine that she would make such a choice.

Nevertheless, as time went on I became more and more convinced that this was indeed the case, our daughter was a lesbian. Occasionally her father and I discussed it. I said I wished if it were true she could feel it was safe to tell us. There needed to be honesty between us. Maybe then we could help her!

I worried a lot about what our friends would think **if** our daughter was in fact a homosexual. What would they think of us as parents? What awful things had we done that would cause her to choose such a lifestyle? With such a disgrace on our family would they even want to associate with us any more? I was sure that everyone in our circle of friends thought the same as I, homosexuality was sinful and disgusting and such people were outside the reach of God's grace unless they repented and changed their behavior. Sometimes I thought of asking Jeannie about her sexual orientation. But if it was not true what would she think of me, her mother, accusing her of such an awful thing? I wondered, too, how her father and I would deal with it, if indeed Jeannie told us she was a lesbian.

I will never forget the time when Jeannie did finally tell us that she is gay. She invited us to a small local restaurant for breakfast. As we finished eating she said she had something she would like us to know about herself, maybe we had already guessed. She told us she is gay and she is very happy being who she is. She assured us that it had nothing to do with how we raised her. She knew she was born a lesbian. She told us to feel free to ask questions and invited us to talk to her minister or the therapist she was seeing if it would be helpful for us. She told us she had found a church, the Metropolitan Community Church, that she was very much involved in and that she loved. I remember that her Dad assured her we loved her and that there was nothing she could ever say or do that would make us love her less.

I went from that breakfast somewhat stunned by the impact her telling us had on me. Thinking she might be gay and actually hearing her say the words were quite different things. Now we would have to face up to the fact that we did indeed have a lesbian daughter. Now we needed to decide how to react to what she had told us. What should we say to her? Should we witness to her about what God says on this matter? How ought we deal with our sense of failure to teach our daughter correctly? Should we share this information with our friends or family? Or would it be better if we kept it hidden as something too shameful to have known? Jeannie said she did not care who we told as long as we were comfortable with doing so. My mind spun in circles as we tried to find satisfactory answers to these questions. Why did this happen in our family? Why *our* daughter? It really was difficult, much more so than I had thought it would be, to know for sure that our daughter is a lesbian. The pain I felt went very deep. Especially hurtful was the conviction that Jeannie was living in sin. We were beginning to accept the possibility that perhaps homosexuality was not something one chose, and that maybe Jeannie could not change that tendency. We did believe, though, that she chose her behavior, and that choosing to be homosexually active was sin.

Our lives had always been deeply immersed in our church. We believed the church, representing Christ here on earth, had the last word. If the church interpreted the Bible as saying homosexual behavior was wrong, then it was, as simple as that. Our beloved Mennonite Church, while making big changes on other issues, adamantly declared homosexuality, under any circumstances, including committed relationships, to be gross sin. Even those who claimed not to be sexually active were strongly suspect and considered aberrant. We agreed with the church's viewpoint.

Somehow we managed to make a very wise decision early on in the new relationship with Jeannie. We decided that an attempt to change her was not going to be a part of our agenda, we would have no such expectations for her. We would accept her just where she was and hoped she could do the same for us. This lifted quite a burden off our shoulders. We did not wonder what to say or how to bring about the right circumstances to help our daughter see the error of her ways. We even refused to get involved with an organization recommended to us to help Jeannie to change. This group told us, "We will pray with you that your daughter will repent of her sin and change and we will stand with you to never stop believing that it will happen." I am so glad now that in those early days of groping for help we had the wisdom to steer clear of such a group.

We shared our problem with very few people. It was a risky thing to do. What would they say about our daughter? Even though we thought she was wrong, it hurt to hear others say so. Sometimes I felt anger toward God for letting such a thing happen. We had known other family pain and this seemed to be the last straw, just too much to bear. I wondered at times if Jeannie had waited so long to tell us because she did not want to add to the load of pain we already carried. My heart ached for her as I imagined what it must have been like for her to grow up in a church and a family where she could not share this part of herself. What must it have been like to come to realize the truth about her sexuality and know the attitude most of the people in her life would hold toward her?

It was difficult, though, to deal with the fact that Jeannie was choosing what we saw as deliberate sin. How could she believe that what she was doing was right? How had she gone so far astray? I found comfort in remembering that she had memorized a lot of Scripture while on the Quiz Team. Surely God would use it in some way to speak to her.

One thing we were sure of. Our daughter was certainly not the despicable person that much of society and the church would consider her to be. She was a warm, loving, responsible person and we began to realize that she was also a fine Christian who was very much involved in her church.

She started to occasionally bring her friends home to meet her family. They, too, were fine people. We were impressed, confused, but nevertheless impressed. I think it was the testimony of her and her friends' lives that planted the first doubts in our minds about whether what we had always believed about homosexual people could be right.

Then we attended a weekend conference for parents and families of gay and lesbian people. We met many wonderful people there, including same sex couples. Many shared stories of pain and joy, doubts and growth. We listened in amazement as the group worshipped and praised God together. These were Christians! These were people who came from the same background we did, heard the same teaching concerning this issue we had and yet they had been able to get a new picture of the grace of God. These were homosexual people who had agonized for years about their sexual orientation. They longed to serve the church and be fully included, they sought and received blessing from God and yet they were gay! We were astounded! Was it possible the church's teaching as we knew it, had been wrong? There was no doubt in our minds that these people were in touch with God, and devoted to seeking God's guidance in their lives. That weekend was the beginning of a wonderful journey for us as we allowed our minds and hearts to be opened by the Spirit of God, and witness firsthand God's work among those of the gay community, not a work of change, but of acceptance and inclusion.

We returned home from that weekend having been delivered from a great burden. We felt closer to God than we had ever been. We had just witnessed a new dimension of God's greatness. My husband said to me on the way home that perhaps we need to begin to tell others what we were learning. Sadly, though, he died soon after, so the journey has been mine alone.

What a lot I have learned! What wonderful people I have met and can claim as friends! As a Christian, I have been so blessed to see firsthand that God's grace is extended to all. My change came gradually. I could not lay aside the beliefs of many years without some doubts and hesitation. I wondered if I might be only trying to look for justification for my daughter. One time

I mentioned this concern to a wise friend who said, "Don't worry about whether or not you are trying to find approval for Jeannie, just be open to what God wants to teach you. Thank God that you have been given this opportunity to grow."

Some of the gay people I know have suffered deeply at the hands of family, church, friends, and society because of the homophobia that continues to be far too prevalent. I, too, have learned in a small way what it feels like to experience homophobia. For many years my husband and I had been part of a small group of people who met on a regular basis for Bible study, prayer, and sharing. We looked to each other for strength and advice through hard times, shared our joys, and were close friends. Our many long discussions about Scripture and about life's issues were challenging and invigorating. That is, until the subject of homosexuality was mentioned. My husband and I together told this group about Jeannie's sexual orientation. Our friends applauded our then held belief that she was living in sin and assured us they would pray for her to change. It became clear, though, that any mention of Jeannie and her friends in even a casual way made this group very uncomfortable.

Some time after my husband's death I decided to share with the group the story of my journey toward acceptance. The evening I did so was the last time we were together as a Bible study group. A couple of members decided that it was not possible to be in such a setting with someone who had thoughts and ideas as sinful as mine. There was some doubt among the group about whether I should even be attending the church where I had been a member for 31 years. I was shocked and very deeply hurt. It had seemed right to me to be open with this group who had shared so personally together for many years. I had assured them I was not expecting them to change their minds, I simply wanted them to know where I stood. Why could they not deal with this particular matter? Why were they so threatened by it that my very presence seemed sinful to them? I could not believe that friendships as strong as ours could crumble so easily. I grieved the loss of the group for a long time.

Most painful of all has been the influence of a couple from this group who persuaded the parents of my grandchildren that it is dangerous for the children to be in the presence of their Aunt Jeannie and her partner. They say that some evil influence from these two who are living such "sinful" lives might overtake the children and endanger their souls. They might even decide to become gay themselves! So now my family, already broken by several divorces, is even more broken and divided. I am very sad, but also shocked and angered by the homophobia of those who were once my friends.

Nevertheless, as painful as it continues to be, this experience is a valuable lesson for me. "So this is how it feels to be discriminated against, to be excluded. This is what it is like to be shunned for who you are, for what you believe!" I have been able to empathize in a greater way with my gay friends since I, too, have felt the scorn of others because of my stand on homosexuality.

I have made a U-turn on my journey. Now I travel in the opposite direction from which I started many years ago when I read that magazine article about two lesbian lovers. Incredibly, two such people are my daughter and her partner, beautiful, wonderful persons, whom I love very much.

I had the great joy of taking part in the Holy Union ceremony of Jeannie and her partner, Anne[1]. The Holy Union of my daughter was a special day for me. How different from my dreams of my little girl's wedding day, the beautiful gown, the handsome husband, grandchildren later on. At one point during the ceremony I realized with a shock, this is my daughter's wedding, there she stands with the one she is marrying, but, instead of the handsome man, there is another woman! Two woman, pledging their lives to each other, how could I possibly understand? But I saw the joy on Jeannie and Anne's faces, heard the love in their voices, recognized that the total Holy Union service was one of praise to their Creator for bringing them to this time in their lives, and I, too, thanked God for them and their ceremony that day. How I wished it could be considered legal.

Jeannie's partner, Anne, is a minister in the Metropolitan Community Church. I enjoy visiting their church and hearing

---

[1] Anne's name has been changed.

her preach. I have become a token Mom to the group. Some of those who attend are not yet out to their families, others have families who are not accepting of them. I hurt so much for them. How glad I am that I have been able to travel down the road from exclusion and rejection to total acceptance and know the joy and blessings that have come to me as a result. I humbly thank God for it all and for God's hand in guidance on me. I pray that my skeptical, rejecting friends may have the joy of learning to know personally someone who is gay so that perhaps they, too, can travel with me on this joyful journey.

The author lives in the same Pennsylvania county in which she grew up. Her present job as an assistant manager of an international crafts shop is one she loves. She continues to attend a Mennonite church, not the one, however, where she and her husband had been members for many years. The congregation where she now worships is a much more accepting one, consisting of great diversity. In this church she can worship God along with her gay and lesbian brothers and sisters. The relationship between her daughter, daughter's partner, and the author is a close one. This mother continues to pray for healing for those relationships among her family and friends which are broken because of the homosexual issue.

33

Overcoming Prejudice

Jack Keenan

Ten years ago I was a flaming homophobe but I did not even know the word. I was convinced that the homosexual community was attempting to introduce their lifestyle as an acceptable alternative through the use of the media. I would avoid films and change channels if homosexuality was being shown in a tolerant way. This to me was another liberal effort to accept any and all alternatives. I was convinced homosexuality was a choice, a poor choice, for those who were intimidated, feared, or could not be comfortable with the opposite sex. I was never abusive or confrontational but certainly participated in laughing at gay people and used derisive terms.

Six years ago, following my wife's death, I had a considerable problem with my grief. I am Catholic and was attending daily mass seeking solace. Our parish priest and I became friends and I joined a Scripture discussion group. This was the beginning of my more serious spiritual journey; I truly began to look for and see Christ in other people.

I met Verda at an Elderhostel and after the program we corresponded by telephone and letters and began a wonderful relationship. When I visited Verda in California, we realized the depth of our feelings for each other. However, she explained to me that to continue she had to be satisfied I could accept her lesbian daughter whom she loved dearly. Verda also actively pursued justice for the gay community. My new spirituality was being put to a test. We had a long discussion and fortunately I had an opportunity to attend a meeting of Parents, Families, and Friends of Lesbians and Gays (PFLAG). My mind was open and I listened to parents and members of the gay community. I heard and saw their love for one another, the pain of rejection by society, parents, and church. I began to see the Christ in all these people, and feel the spirit of God's presence.

Now I am at every PFLAG meeting. I am now firmly convinced that homosexuality is not a choice but a condition of birth. I am convinced the gay community's spirituality is valid and in need of support. I also have a beautiful, loving, lesbian step-daughter whose love and affirmation have helped me through some difficult moments.

I am convinced prejudice is formed by considering differences with suspicion and fear rather than love. I think if we can face our prejudices with an open mind, whether they be religious, racial, sexual, color, or language, seeing the individual, focusing on the spirit of God within, we can rid ourselves of our prejudices and open ourselves to love.

John H. "Jack" Keenan was born in Hazelton, Pennsylvania. He was an army veteran of World War II and a member of St. Nicolas Catholic Church in Berlinsville, Pennsylvania. A 1948 graduate of Lehigh University, he was an active member of its Alumni Association. He was assistant chief engineer for the Rockefeller Center Management Corporation in New York for 15 years, retiring in 1986. He was the father of three daughters, one son, three step-daughters, and one step-son. He had six grandchildren and four step-grandchildren.

After the death of his first wife in 1990, Jack traveled west where he met Verda M. Lindberg. They were married in 1992 and lived half time in Saratoga, California, and half time in Allentown, Pennsylvania.

Jack joined Verda as active members of Parents, Families, and Friends of Lesbians and Gays (PFLAG). He was a member of the NAACP and volunteered for the Literacy Council of Allentown. During their time on the west coast, he was a regular participant in the activities of Ladera Community United Church of Christ in Portola Valley.

Editor's Note: Jack died of cancer December 19, 1997. He is greatly missed by his family and his friends at PFLAG. He was a strong advocate for gay and lesbian rights and an inspiration to many of us who knew him.

34

Who Needs To Change?

Paul and Martha Snyder

We are the parents of three sons and a daughter. Our oldest child, Roger, was born in 1959. He was a delightful child, an excellent student, a very kind and compassionate man. He was baptized into our church, Bloomingdale (Ontario) Mennonite, when he was 15 years old.

We are proud of our first-born son. He did not choose to be gay any more than we chose to be straight. He lives his life with courage, dignity, and good humor, in a faithful relationship that makes many heterosexual relationships seem sleazy by comparison. He is loved and respected by his three younger siblings, six nieces and nephews, and a large extended family. If you met him you would say, "What a fine young man," and you would be right. We would not have had the courage to choose to parent a gay child, but we have come to feel that it has been a privilege.

When Roger was 18 years old, he dropped the bombshell one evening when he told us that he was gay. When we were a newly married couple we heard of a young man who was gay. The person who told us that information said that it was no wonder he was gay, his mother was a battle-ax and his father was a wimp. Can you imagine how we felt when we heard the news that our wonderful son was gay? We assumed it was all our fault.

We called the doctor the next day and set up an appointment for Roger. He asked Roger all kinds of questions. One was, had he ever had a liaison with another fellow, Roger said no he had not. The doctor called us the next day and said that Roger was not a homosexual, he was just a late bloomer, whatever that meant. That surely relieved us! The doctor suggested that Roger go for counseling, so he set up an appointment at the Inter-Faith Counseling Services in Kitchener.

Roger had many struggles with his sexual identity (which we did not even know about) in his younger teenage years. How we wish now we could have been there for him through those years when he prayed desperately night after night for deliverance! He did not want to be gay. He had heard enough over the years to associate homosexuality with sin and degradation and he did not want that!

We were desperately hoping that the counseling would change Roger and we could put this nightmare behind us. He continued the counseling for several months and the complete opposite happened. Roger started to have a much better attitude about himself. He came to realize that he was the person that he was meant to be and no one was at fault. That was not the answer for which we were hoping! We had prayed desperately that God would change Roger — and quickly before anyone found out! Roger kept telling us it was not our fault that he was gay, but we were still dealing with feelings of guilt and isolation. We were not free to go to anyone for several years to unload our deep burden. Anything we heard in church on this subject was all so negative that we did not dare mention it there! (Now we wish we, too, would have gone for counseling and told our pastors sooner.)

Part of our church experience had always been that the church was a safe place where people were close and where you could share your inner struggles. That security seemed to be denied us on this issue.

Roger attended Conrad Grebel College and then went to Los Angeles on a two year Voluntary Service (VS) assignment. We were somewhat relieved because we did not have to deal with this secret for two whole years! We even hoped that he would meet a nice California girl and get this out of his system. How unknowledgeable and naive we were at that time!

When Roger returned from Los Angeles, he lived at home with us and we first shared our anguish with our pastor. How we wish we had done it sooner! During that time period our feelings started to change. We were still hoping for change in Roger, and change did come, but it was not in Roger, it was in us and in our selfish attitudes! Our attitudes had been too much concern for what people would think of us and our nice family, and not enough of how we could, in Christian love, help our son in his struggles. We still had not told anyone other than our pastor, but Roger had shared his sexual orientation with several people in the church.

In the spring of 1985, a woman from our church told us that many people at church were beginning to talk about Roger because he was bringing a male friend to the services. She thought we should know about this gossip. We immediately asked our pastors to come to our home that day and we asked them what we should do about what the lady had told us. They suggested that we did not need to do anything. Our struggles were tremendous during that time. Going to church and not knowing who knew and who did not, made it very difficult to attend church and be as involved in its programs as we both were — and still are. We heard jokes and unkind remarks about homosexuals that were just not true, but we did not even challenge them! Gays are not the only ones in the closet.

Later that spring, we shared at our church retreat the pain we were having because we had a homosexual son. What a relief, it was finally out! The group at the retreat came and prayed over us and surrounded us with their concerns and their prayers and gave us many hugs. It was better going to church and knowing that everyone knew, but it is so surprising to us how few people are willing to really walk with you on such a journey. The initial affirmation from some of the people vanished when they realized we were accepting of our son's gayness and not sending him to a change ministry. We thank God for the few people who were supportive of us.

Roger moved to London, Ontario, where he works as a travel agent. He started attending a Mennonite church where he sang many solos, sang in the choir, and was involved in many ways. When they found out that he was gay, he was told that he could no longer sing solos, but he could remain in the choir. It would take them at least two years to decide if he could become a member. He knew that they did not really want him there. So he left and started attending a United Church where he was accepted as a Christian young man who happens to be gay. He was not judged as a sinner just because he was a homosexual. He became a member of that church in 1992 along with Kevin, his partner since 1988. It is painful for us as parents to know that they felt they had to leave the Mennonite church to find a safe place to continue their spiritual journey.

Roger and Kevin had a covenanting service of affirmation and celebration at the United Church where they are members. They publicly pledged their commitment and love for each other and asked for the support of family and friends and the blessing of God. It was a lovely service attended by 120 family members and friends. Understandably, some persons were very upset about this event and chose not to attend. For those of us who did, it was an opportunity to see the goodness and love of another couple dedicated to God and to each other.

Our pain is no longer that of having a gay son, it is a deep disappointment over the church's attitude toward our gay sons and lesbian daughters. Some siblings of gay men and lesbians are leaving the church because of the harsh attitudes directed against their gay brothers and sisters. Some parents are also leaving because they do not feel the support of their fellow Christians in their churches. Many pastors are supportive in a quiet but not a public way. Too many Christians are listening to television evangelists from the religious right and believing the misinformation and judgmental attitudes that they promote.

At the 1987 General Assembly, meeting in Purdue, Illinois, the Mennonite Church adopted a statement that said, "sexual relationships outside of heterosexual marriage constitute sinfulness." But the statement also called for dialogue and discussion within our churches. A number of churches have taken that seriously and have had a long and intensive time of searching the Scripture and scientific data. Through deep discussions with gay and lesbian Christians and much prayer, some of these churches have come to a different understanding than the Purdue statement. Because of this, they have been reprimanded and given associate status, sometimes even totally expelled from conference for doing the very thing they were told to do. In our churches and homes we teach our children to be honest, to share, and to be open with their feelings. But when they are honest about their sexual orientation, we tell them they should not have shared *that*. We would rather not know. We ostracize them for doing the very thing we taught them to do in the first place!

Our lives have changed so much since the first years of our struggles. At first we felt sorry for gay people, then we enjoyed getting to know them, now we see the face of God in them. We know that God loves them unconditionally as God loves us all. We have had the privilege three times of spending a weekend with the Brethren/Mennonite Council for Lesbian and Gay Concerns (BMC) at their convention. We were impressed with the dedication of those attending the convention to follow Christ and their desire to remain part of the church. We expected to see and hear anger because of the rejection they have felt from the church. Instead we saw a group of people with a dream and a hope that they too will someday be welcome as brothers and sisters in the church that they love.

Our journey has led us into a deeper understanding of our faith. We have also come to realize that it is our Christian duty to help in some small way to dispel the ignorance in churches. We have had the privilege of sharing our story in over 25 Mennonite Church settings in the past number of years. This has been a rewarding experience for us and thought-provoking for many people attending. Another area where there is an unmet need is support for parents of gays and lesbians. We started meeting with one couple about ten years ago and now our support group has grown to about ten couples. We meet every six to eight weeks for support, sharing, prayer, and fellowship.

We want our gay sons and lesbian daughters to find a refuge where they are not rejected or alienated just because some people in the church are afraid of those who are different. Ignorance, no matter how much Scripture is quoted, is still ignorance. Rather than fearing the alienation among us, we have learned to fear each other. We hope and pray for the day when our Mennonite Church will be a safe place for our gay and lesbian sons and daughters.

Paul and Martha Snyder moved to the city of Kitchener in 1997 after farming for well over 40 years, and they love every minute of it. They are members of Bloomingdale Mennonite Church in Ontario where they are both involved in the church council, missions, community outreach, and teaching activities of the congregation. Their work with the parents' support groups of gays, lesbian, and bisexual persons continues to refresh and motivate them to become more actively involved. They work faithfully to help bring better understanding and knowledge among pastors and church members about the issue of homosexuality. The couple accepts speaking engagements, sends letters, makes phone calls, and shares brochure handouts wherever they have opportunity. Their continued prayer is that through love and changed attitudes marginalized persons may find the acceptance and understanding they so desperately need within the church!

35

My Son John

Helen Rawson Early

The tuxedo still fit. John's father had been right when ten years before, at the time of John's high school prom, he had said, "Don't rent, buy one, there will be other times to wear it." And there were — a couple of dances with girls in private schools, and his own junior and senior proms. Now he was wearing it to an AIDS benefit.

He had gone to the junior and senior proms with a lovely girl but it seemed strange that between proms they did not see much of each other. I told myself they were bright kids, busy with school. Then we were invited to go sailing with them. I thought, "Do you invite your parents on a date?" We went and enjoyed the day, but it became apparent that the two had a lot in common and liked each other as friends, nothing more.

So it was more a relief than a surprise when John, home on vacation from college, said, "I am sure I am gay." Relief, because we had known something was very wrong — his grades had plummeted, and even when we did reach him on the phone, we felt shut out. Now at least we knew what he had been going through. Still, the finality of that "I am gay" hit hard. All I could think of was that there would be no grandchildren at the lake. When I voiced this, John and I both started to cry. I have loved the lake since I was a child, staying there in a one room cabin without electricity. Now we had a house there that John had a large hand in building. He loved the place as much as we did, and he, too, would have liked to teach a child to swim and sail up there.

But at least now the wall was broken and we talked. He had already told two of his friends from high school. The one who was straight was supportive, the other revealed that he too was gay. "I've known since I was sixteen," he said. However, they had never talked to each other about it until that college vacation.

John talked about meeting his first boy friend at college. (Why is it that "girl friend" is a neutral term, but "boy friend" is not?) The relationship had not lasted because the other boy wanted to see if he could be straight. It did not work!

John has always seemed mature for his age. At nine we sent him to a YMCA day camp and had no indication that he felt out of place until the day he came home and said, "I've found someone to eat lunch with! He knows about Einstein too!"

Later, I began to hear about a man who had graduated several years before who eventually became John's partner. They have been together eight years now. They had a home built and later built on a deck themselves. I donated some sweet gum seedlings that are growing into respectable trees. All the furnishings were selected with great care and whenever I am there, I think how nice everything looks — even if two day's worth of mail **is** piled on the breakfast nook table.

My relatives see them as a couple and as part of our family. When John is invited, they both are invited. I am sometimes consulted by either one on "marital" problems. I remember assuring John once that I was sure his father found me equally aggravating at times. He replied, "You just don't want to lose him as a son-in-law!" And it is true.

Helen Rawson Early grew up in Scranton, Pennsylvania, as a hard to manage only child whose father talked of sending her to military school to learn some discipline. She graduated from Syracuse University summa cum laude, and went on to medical school at Syracuse. After a pediatric residency at Children's Hospital of Philadelphia, she opened her practice in Lansdale, Pennsylvania. After she married Martin Luther

Early she continued to practice under her maiden name, Helen H. Rawson, M.D. Her husband died in 1991. They have two children, John, in Whitehall, Pennsylvania, and Elaine, who lives at home with her mother.

During 35 years of pediatric practice, she knew of only one gay patient. Now several former patients, knowing that she is openly the mother of a gay son, have talked to her about the true cause of their headaches and stomach aches and need for gym excuses. The doctor's partners continue her practice and now they have pink triangle magnets on doorways, hoping that gay and lesbian patients will no longer be afraid to discuss their concerns.

36

Our Journey to Understanding

Hilary and Gladys Bertsche

As we try to think back to our earliest memories of what homosexuality meant to us, our memory of anyone talking about or discussing it with us is very unclear. Even within our church, we do not recall it being discussed. We do remember vaguely hearing that it was sinful.

We do not remember knowing anyone who was openly gay or lesbian. Probably to survive, especially in the rural conservative area in which we grew up, it was necessary to stay in the closet. When Hilary was in Chicago for a Mennonite youth retreat, he and some friends attended a concert in Grant Park. He remembers being told to be careful of the homosexual men hanging out in the park. Later, when he was in a Voluntary Service (VS) program of our church, he worked in a mental hospital. He heard about the problem of a patient trying to deal with her gay husband.

Hilary served his 1-W assignment in a hospital in Chicago. (The 1-W classification was given by the U.S. draft board in 1945 to men who are opposed to war because of religious conviction. It permitted them to serve in community service in lieu of military service.) There were some gay men on the staff and Hilary was rather fearful of them. Because of this fear, he never really learned to know them.

After VS and 1-W, we returned to the farm and our local Mennonite congregation. We took foster children into our home and adopted two young boys. Seven years later our first daughter, Laurie, was born to us. She was the delight of our life, as was her sister who was born sixteen months later. Our entire family was busy and active in the local congregation, youth organizations, and school activities. Laurie was the one who always loved to be playing sports with her brothers, cooking with her mother, or helping her dad on the farm.

She did not date much in her high school years, but usually would do things together with a group of boys and girls. Laurie, her sister, and two girlfriends spent two weeks in a Mennonite Voluntary Service work camp in Seattle, Washington. That experience really opened her eyes to the needs of others. It seemed as though she was much more attuned to God's love for peace and justice and God's caring for those who are vulnerable and in need.

While in college, Laurie dated a man for a couple of years, but it never developed into a serious romantic relationship. After college she worked for a Mennonite institution and seemed to be more involved with women friends.

We always had a close relationship and as she grew older we were able to share more of our personal feelings with her. We discussed faith issues and what it meant to be a Christian. Because of this closeness, Laurie felt more free to share her feelings with us when the issue of homosexuality began to be discussed in the church. Her sharing helped us to believe that God does accept people with homosexual orientation.

Then one day when Laurie and her dad were on a walk at a family retreat, she said to him, "Dad, I need to tell you that I am a lesbian." It was difficult to express his feelings at that point, except to say that he loved her for who she was and it did not make any difference what her sexual orientation was. A couple days later she told her mother and she too, was able to accept the information and continue to express love for Laurie. She was still the wonderful daughter that we had always known.

The one problem that we were sad about was the prejudice that she would have to face, especially in the church. Laurie had always been active in the Mennonite Church, in Mennonite Youth Fellowship, and as a youth leader. Now that she was honest about who she was, the church would reject her.

Laurie helped us by recommending material and books that would help us to better understand her in our role as parents.

Probably the best suggestion that she gave us was to get involved in the Connecting Families group. This is a group of parents and families of gays and lesbians, mostly Mennonite and Brethren. We gather once a year for a weekend retreat of sharing and learning together. The group has been such a blessing to us! We have learned to know many people who are involved in the church and who have family members who are gay or lesbian. It has been a special blessing to us to learn to know wonderful gay and lesbian brothers and sisters who are committed to Christ and his teachings.

We are now trying to share with others where we are in our journey. There are times when we wish we would have spoken out more in support of our lesbian sisters and gay brothers. But we keep trying, and hopefully we are growing in our understanding and ability to speak up on this as a justice issue. We have been sharing with some of our family members, some members of our church, and other friends as we feel comfortable. We endeavor to help our congregation to understand what it means to be inclusive and to welcome all people. We appreciate the wonderful support our pastors have given to us.

The video, *Body of Dissent*,[1] is an excellent tool to stimulate discussion. We invite small groups of people into our home to look at the video and hear these faith stories of gay and lesbian Christians. Afterwards we provide a time for discussion.

Laurie is now in a committed relationship with a partner. We have some wonderful times together and with her partner's parents whom we have learned to know also.

Our prayer is that we can all work together to include **all** people in the fellowship of Christ's church. We can all worship God, love each other, and accept each other even though we may not be at the same place in our journey.

Hilary and Gladys Bertsche are retired farmers, living in Central Illinois. They are members of the General Conference Mennonite Church.

---

[1] The video, *Body of Dissent: Lesbian and Gay Mennonites Continue the Journey,* is available from BMC, Box 6300, Minneapolis, MN   55406. Phone: (612) 722-6906. E-mail: BMCouncil@aol.com

37

No Barriers?

Michael and Patricia Glasgow

In recent months, our congregation has become increasingly active in our commitment to eliminate architectural barriers to those with disabilities. Our slogan, stated in fliers and worn on lapel tags, is "No Barriers to God's Love." We share that goal and look forward to a time when anyone will be able to enter any part of the church building, regardless of their handicap.

Another barrier exists in our church however, a nonphysical one that bars many of our loved ones from taking their rightful places at God's table. How many families, in this church alone, have a member who is homosexual? We know we are not alone. Many of us must feel the pain of having someone we love and respect judged to be unfit for ministry because the image of God, as it has been created in them, is not acceptable to some Christians.

Even the idea that a homosexual is created in the image of God seems foreign to many people. We have been taught that homosexuals are distant, perverse people, who have no place in a decent family, much less a church family. Furthermore, this position has been strengthened by archaic misinterpretations of a few biblical passages which appear to address homosexual behavior, but more clearly condemn the sinfulness of any relationship in which one person is subjugated to the selfish interests of another.

Our son, David, is gay. If you were part of our congregation during his youth, you would probably know him. You might have watched him grow up, active and involved in the church, full of energy and enthusiasm, and sure of God's love. You might have known him as an adolescent on youth work retreats, or tormenting his younger sister, or singing in church. You might also have been at his Senior Concert, near the end of his college years, when he shared his music and his heart in the process of coming out. David still feels called to work in the church, and he follows that calling by directing youth choirs and conducting a weekly contemporary worship service in the church he joined while in college. Yet if he wanted to serve in an ordained capacity, he would be barred from doing so because of his sexual orientation.

Like many people his age, David wants a close and stable relationship on earth to support the one he has with God, a source of support in a difficult world. In fact, he and his companion, Mark, have been providing this support to one another for more than three years. Yet that anniversary remains significant only in their own minds, for there is no legal ceremony and no ceremony within our church to support their faithfulness and devotion, nor the faithfulness of any same-sex couple. We often bemoan the scarcity of young people who choose to become religious leaders, and we also are saddened by the frequency of broken marriages that leave children to experience their developmental years without loving adult guidance. Even in the face of these concerns, our prejudice prevents us from supporting some of those among us who seek to serve God professionally or to establish family relationships of integrity and commitment, simply because of the sexual orientation God has given them.

Our religious history includes a time when people with physical handicaps were believed to be suffering the wrath of God because of sins committed by them or their parents. Now, thank God, we are less ignorant on that issue, and we realize that people with physical challenges also are created in the image of God. We have begun to realize a magnificence in creation that far exceeds our capacity to describe the diversity it encompasses. While once we perceived anyone different from ourselves as suspect, dangerous, frightening, or even hideous, we now know that our heritage as children of God is far greater and more important than the differences we perceive. Yet we still support the barriers we have constructed between our brothers, sisters, children, and friends of different sexual orientations and the goals they long to achieve. We can, we should, and we must tear down those barriers too!

We are members of a national organization called Parents, Friends, and Families of Lesbians and Gays (PFLAG). In this group we support one another in our journey and work together to find ways to correct injustice and erroneous beliefs about homosexuals and to advocate for their full acceptance by the church and society. Please see the Resources section in the back of this book for more information about how to contact a PFLAG chapter near you, if you would like to join in the ministry to make a safe place for all people regardless of race, creed, color, or sexual orientation.

In Part One, **David Glasgow**, Patricia and Michael's son, shares his story. See page 111, Chapter 21.

Patricia Glasgow is a science and math teacher at Gleneig High School in Maryland, where she is faculty sponsor of the Rainbow Youth Alliance, a new organization established to meet the needs of young people as they struggle with their own sexual identities and those of their friends. Patty also is active in strategic planning and Bible study at Glen Mar United Methodist Church.

Dr. Michael Glasgow is a physiologist and college professor at Anne Arundel Community College near Annapolis, Maryland, where he is a faculty advocate for Lambda Pioneers. Mike is active in Bible study, Stephen Ministry, and the Men's Vocal Ensemble at Glen Mar United Methodist Church.

38

We Three and More!

Mary K. and Roy Gascho

Let us tell you about our family and how we learned that we have a gay son. We have three daughters: Judy, Sandra, and Evelyn, and one son, Robert. After 13 granddaughters, Robert was the first boy born in his generation in the Gascho family.

Robert had come out to his sisters about his sexual orientation and the four siblings discussed what would be the best way to break the news to us. Judy, the oldest, talked to our family doctor and our pastor with the hope of finding a base of support for us. Our pastor suggested that Robert write a letter to break the news and diffuse the immediate emotional impact.

Judy asked us if we could have a family meeting and we arranged a time to suit everyone's schedule. We had no idea what the meeting was about. Robert was in town for the weekend, but stayed at the home of friends. He was not at the first meeting because the children felt it best if the sisters would do the initial telling of the story. They agreed that Judy should read the letter to us. I want to share excerpts of that letter:

I need to tell you something very important. It is not something that will be easy for you to hear, as it is not easy for me to tell you. Writing you a letter was actually a suggestion of our pastor, though I thought that I should speak to you in person, initially. As I thought about it and deliberated over what would be the best time and place, I decided that this would be a good idea.

What I want to tell you has to do with my sexuality. Most of my life I have struggled with this aspect of myself. After a long period of denial, rejection, and non-acceptance, I have finally come to terms with the fact that my sexual orientation is homosexual. I realize that this must seem like a bolt out of the blue, and it changes many of the assumptions and ideas you may have had about me. Finally having been able to admit this about myself and to have accepted it has been a great relief and a freeing experience for me. It also has many ramifications for what I will do in the future, and these I am working at.

There must be many questions and feelings for you to deal with. I do not want to start throwing too many things at you right now, but one thing I want to be clear on from the start. Why people develop the sexual orientations that they do is not fully understood. Only a few basic things are generally agreed on. One is that orientation is established very early in life, at the latest, before the age of five. Parents do not cause or create their children's sexual orientation. There is nothing that either of you did or did not do that significantly affected the development of any of our orientations.

I need to know when (and if) you want to talk with me. I will leave the initiative for that with you, so you can contact me when you are ready.

Finally, I should mention why I am telling you this now. It is because I thought you deserved to hear it from me, and not second-hand.

I do not remember ever having said this to you, and I do not know why, maybe it is because we have never been a very expressive family, or maybe it is because I had to grow up first, but I want to say that I love you both. I hope that you can continue to love and accept me.

Robert

After Judy read this letter, our reactions were shock, hurt, disbelief, and a lot of crying. But we did want to see our son again and talk to him face to face. So on Sunday he came home and we spent the morning talking together before he needed to leave town again to continue his summer job.

As soon as possible we consulted with our family doctor. His advice was that we should not try to change Robert or "bring on the dancing girls." About a month after Robert broke the news to us, he brought a boyfriend home for a family gathering. We accepted our son and his choice of friends and do not regret it.

When it became public knowledge, we had some negative response from some relatives, but also a positive phone call from a neighbor. Some church friends also responded positively with cards. Some women from First Mennonite had an afternoon support group, which was a very positive and caring experience.

Robert was interviewed by a local newspaper reporter. The headline was *Gay's Gift a Church Dilemma*. Excerpts from that article reveal some of Robert's faith journey:

"For me to take back a gift from God and exchange it, is, somehow, blasphemy. Gay people and the whole church always need to be involved in the search for the appropriate use of God's gifts. This [homosexuality] is just one of the many gifts.

"I know that my orientation was not of my own choosing. I chose at one point *not* to be gay, but it did not work."

Delegates to the 100,000 member church's general assembly agreed last August [1987] that homosexuals could belong to the church as long as they remained celibate.

The young University of Waterloo history graduate, who agreed to talk publicly of his sexual orientation, even though he knew it would come as a surprise to some at First Mennonite, has not been asked to leave his congregation (though he was asked to stop leading singing).

Despite the fact that his own pastors and board have been supportive (though not fully in agreement with him on this issue) he believes the church's stand on homosexuality is inconsistent.

"I have decided to be open about it because it is necessary for me to have integrity in my own relationship with the church, also, because it is an important issue."

As a historian and a Mennonite, Gascho is inclined to be patient. The Mennonite Church seems to have two speeds, he says, "slow and reverse," and he accepts that.

Today Gascho looks back on the days when he was involved in conference-wide youth work [Rockway Mennonite Collegiate] and First Mennonite as "Golden Years." . . .

The "scary" prospect of telling his parents he was homosexual was overcome by their support. He decided to talk to his congregational leaders when he was invited to speak at a seminar on sexuality at Conrad Grebel College.

To be able to express God's gift of his sexuality is a matter of justice for this Mennonite. Many letters to the editor in Mennonite publications denounce homosexuals in such strong language the sense of Mennonite justice seems absent to him.

But Gascho looks also to the Mennonite Hymnal with its more inclusive attitude demonstrated in these words:

> There's a wideness in God's mercy,
> Like the wideness of the sea:
> There's a kindness in God's justice,
> Which is more than liberty.

Our church received many phone calls, and many responses were sent to our local newspaper. This was a very trying time for our family because many of the people at First Mennonite were unhappy about the article. But our church bulletin included the following announcement:

> This month has been a difficult one for the Gascho family. Let us exercise much compassion for all of them, and pray for them. Remember Robert, too, his search for a job continues.

Some time after this, Robert began to attend Waterloo North Mennonite Church. Waterloo North began a series of discussions about homosexuality and the Christian faith. Robert invited us to hear him speak there on a Sunday afternoon, and that gave us a bit more insight into his struggle. We heard him describe how he had been aware of his feelings back in seventh and eighth grades, how these feelings did not fade in high school, and how he finally dealt with reality in college. He attended the General Assembly in Ames, Iowa, in 1985, where he met people from the Brethren/Mennonite Council for Lesbian and Gay Concerns (BMC) at some workshops. He talked about having been in a position of privilege as a white, university-educated, middle-class male, and how it was a shock to find himself suddenly in the minority. He talked about the need for gay and lesbian people to value themselves, and how that is easier when other people help.

We have also found other people to help. In Ontario we have a group of five or six sets of parents of gay and lesbian Mennonite children. We get together about every six weeks, talk on the phone, and send each other cards. Our pastor first helped us to find another couple with a gay son and our parents' group has grown from there. We try to invite other parents we know who are struggling with the issue. Sometimes we take a few steps backwards and sometimes a few steps forward.

Today Robert works for the AIDS committee in our city. We have hopes and fears. We hope our son can be accepted as a participating member in the church as he used to be. We fear the rejection he may face in society. We fear for his safety, and we fear AIDS.

Our observation of gay people is that many of them are sensitive, intelligent, and talented. The world and the church lose out in denying them their rightful place in our society.

Roy Gascho is a retired truck driver, working part-time at a local Ford dealership. **Mary K. Gascho** has retired from working in a gift and card store and works part-time at a

Kitchener bowling alley. Roy's hobbies include woodworking and Mary does oil painting. They are both natives of Waterloo County and members of First Mennonite Church in Kitchener, Ontario.

39

Faith Journey:
A Mother's Perspective

Sid Flickinger

We were a family of seven growing up together in a normal setting. We lived, loved, worked, and vacationed together in Kansas, Minnesota, Costa Rica, Colombia, and Arizona. We had many good times together discussing, analyzing, joking, and teasing. Every morning we read Bible stories, had devotions, and prayed. We cherished our Christian heritage and our connectedness with our extended families. We were active in the Mennonite Church and Conference. We trusted in Christ's promise of salvation and divine inspiration for our daily activities.

Did we suddenly one day, in April 1983, under the shade trees on the Campus of Fresno Pacific College become an abnormal family? My husband, Cal, and I had driven with friends all night from Phoenix, Arizona, to take part in the Mennonite Central Committee Auction and Men's Chorus. Our son, John, had come from San Francisco and when we met, he asked if we could have lunch together. We went to pick up our traditional Mennonite lunch of verenike, sausage, zwieback, and drink and walked to the farthest end of the grassy picnic area. As we sat around the picnic table away from the crowd, we caught up with what was going on in our lives.

John told us about a friend who was Director of the Mennonite Church Voluntary Service units for the western region. This friend had been asked to leave this position because word had come to the conference board that he was gay. "By the way," John said, "I am also gay."

From our past experience working with people of different races and cultures, Cal and I knew that John had not chosen to be gay, and that he could not change his sexual orientation. My concern was that it was difficult for gays to live in a homophobic society. The fear was that he would not be accepted by many in the church and in the community. How could he feel good about himself? I suggested that John seek out a professional counselor and get some help. John's response to our concerns was, "I think I am handling being gay very nicely." He had thought about the gay issue for several years. He understood it much better than we, his parents, did.

The ride back to Phoenix was long. We did not share our newfound knowledge with our friends. Back home we asked each other, "What does it mean to be gay?" We checked out books from the public library and sent for literature offered by organizations dealing with the issue of homosexuality. I shared with the counselor at my work place. One of the emergency room doctors at this time was giving lectures to a group of nurses on the subject of homosexuality. The counselor gave me a copy of his lectures. His main points were:

1. Homosexuality is not a mental illness.
2. Homosexuality is not sin.
3. Homosexuality is a normal variance like being left-handed.

He explained that it would take much scientific study to determine why a certain percentage of the population is gay or lesbian.

For three years we silently continued our study of what it meant to be parents of a gay son. We had to deal with the passages in the Bible that refer to homosexuality as sin. We knew that John's desire was to follow Christ's teaching in the context of the Mennonite Church. The fact that Jesus went out of his way to help the outcasts of society brought comfort and hope. Jesus said, "Whosoever will may come." The mother of Jesus lived with Jewish leaders who must have given her much heartache. They opposed her son's teaching. Mary's love followed her son as he went about doing good. She went with him all the way to the cross.

Our understanding of the description of the homosexuals in the Bible did not fit the homosexuals we knew. Rather than the negative aspect of rape and prostitution that the Bible emphasizes, the homosexuals we know are those who do not want to hurt or take advantage of others. They are promoting loving relationships and service-oriented lives. Meeting our sons' and daughter's friends was helpful in understanding this. We also became connected with other parents who had gay, lesbian, and bisexual children, which broadened our understanding of the scope of the issue. It was a time of growing spiritually and learning to know God better.

In 1986, our son, Dan, attended the General Conference sessions in Saskatoon, Saskatchewan. It was at this conference where the resolution on homosexuality was discussed and voted on by the conference members. To Dan it was clear that the members at this conference had experienced little contact with openly gay and lesbian people and did not understand them. After the conference Dan called from his home in San Francisco to tell us that he was coming home for the weekend. We wondered why he chose to come home at this time when he was so busy, but we always welcomed visits from our children.

In the evening, after picking him up at the airport, we were sitting comfortably in the living room listening to his report of the conference. Suddenly Dan announced, "I came home to tell you that I am gay and have written a letter to be published in *The Mennonite* to explain my sexual orientation."

Wait a minute, not Dan! Gay men were not supposed to be tall, have a deep bass voice, and be outgoing with a pleasant sense of humor. Did Creator God make a mistake? We were again struggling with our stereotypes about what gay and lesbian people were like.

On our way back to the airport, Dan wanted our consent to send the letter to our church publication. He was also getting approval from his brothers and sisters. We suggested he should do what he felt was right for him. He explained that it would affect all of us. Little did we know how prophetic his warning was.

After Dan's article appeared, we had several letters from friends and relatives who were understanding and supportive. A good friend called and questioned, "Is that how you brought him up?" However, another good friend's advice was to accept him, love him, and enjoy him.

At this point we knew that Ron, our oldest, and Lois, our youngest, were heterosexual. We knew that Dan and John were gay. Approximately one week after Dan's visit, I called our oldest daughter, Su. The conversation was about the reason for Dan's visit. "What are you, Su?" I asked her. The answer was that she had wanted to tell us for some time but wanted to wait until she came home and could talk about it in person, not over the telephone. "Yes," she said, "I am a lesbian." Now we had another word to add to our vocabulary. What is a lesbian? Trying to understand this term was a new challenge. Soon, however, we realized that Su had not changed. We now knew her a little better. We were at peace with our children's sexuality.

For several years we lived and interacted with opposing forces in our church and continued to worship our Maker and Redeemer. Not much was said about homosexuality. However, in June of 1991, a number of churches in Phoenix were trying to get a proposition on the November ballot that would deny equal rights to gays and lesbians in the work place. Two members from our church's deacon board attended the meeting and came back wanting our church to participate in this venture.

At the next deacons' meeting, one of those who had attended the city meeting confronted another deaconess about her relationship with the woman with whom she was living. The deaconess acknowledged that she was in a lesbian relationship. What followed were many intense discussions at the deacon and church council meetings for several months. Some unkind words were spoken and the church became divided over the issue of homosexuality. The lesbian couple stopped attending church hoping that it would take care of the problem. There were those of us who felt the lesbian couple had not been treated fairly.

The church council decided to enlist the assistance of a mediator. In February of 1992, the mediator facilitated a congregational meeting to resolve the issue of whether the lesbian couple could serve in leadership positions within the church. After much discussion, the lesbian couple was persuaded to come to the meeting in hopes of telling their side of the story. Many members in the church had not been a part of the council discussions and were uninformed about homosexuality. The mediator gave all members the opportunity to express their opinions. After some unkind words had been spoken, the lesbian couple asked if they would be allowed to continue actively serving in the church where they had been active members for fifteen years.

Finally, the congregation was given the opportunity to vote on two questions. The first, "Is homosexuality sin?" The second, "Should gays and lesbians be allowed in leadership positions in the church?" Two-thirds of the members voted "yes" on the first question, and approximately fifty percent voted that gays and lesbians should not be leaders in the church. When the results of the vote were read, the lesbian couple got up and walked out of the church. After a prayer by the pastor, the meeting ended.

Cal and I were surprised, confused, and frustrated. Did our friends at church not hear us or understand us when we told them about our gay sons and lesbian daughter? Did they not understand that gays and lesbians do not choose to be so? Or were most of the church members undecided because the pastor said, "The Bible clearly teaches that homosexuality is sin. The problem is then, what to do with our members who openly declare that they are gay and lesbian."

Those of us from the church who did not think the couple had been treated justly looked for ways to support them. They were deeply hurt, both spiritually and emotionally. Several of us met together on Sunday evenings to talk about our feelings and encourage each other. During this time we thought the pastor and church council would realize that talented and hardworking members were leaving the church. Attempts at reconciliation with the rest of the church at this point were unproductive.

Those of us meeting on Sunday evenings started looking for a place to worship as a newly organized fellowship. Approximately a year later, Cal and I withdrew our membership from

First Mennonite church. It was painful to leave the church where we had worshiped for 30 years, but God gave us strength.

Feeling the need for more support and looking for opportunities to help other parents accept their gay and lesbian children, we joined the Parents, Families and Friends of Lesbians and Gays (PFLAG). Listening to the stories of others with gay and lesbian family members has helped us to realize how fortunate we are. We are united in our effort to make our own family and others more accepting and loving. We realize that there is much work to be done before gays and lesbians will have equal rights in our society and in the Mennonite Church. However, attitudes are changing. We have hope that the Brethren/Mennonite Council for Lesbian and Gay Concerns (BMC), Connecting Families, and the Supportive Congregations Network will help to hasten the change.

In Part One, **John Flickinger**, Sid's son, shares his story about his coming out and faith journey. See page 102, Chapter 19.

Sid Flickinger was born on a farm near the small Mennonite Community of Mountain Lake, Minnesota. She is a graduate of the former Bethel Deaconess Hospital School of Nursing and earned her Bachelor of Science in Nursing degree at Bethel College, North Newton, Kansas. Sid and her husband, Calvin, were with the General Conference Mission Board when they served in Cachipay, Colombia, and Kykotsmovi, Arizona. In 1963 the family moved to Phoenix, Arizona, where Sid continued nursing until her retirement. Sid and Cal are now living in an apartment in the Glencroft Retirement Community, Glendale, Arizona.

40

Unmentionables, Hermeneutics, and Idolatry

Earl Loganbill

Institutional churches are in an uproar about an *unmentionable* subject! Some individuals are sharpening their skills in biblical interpretation and trying to discern the conceptual characteristics of idolatry and thereby avoid the worship of a false God.

As a parent of two *unmentionable* children who is interested in the proper understanding of scripture and the worship of the true God, it is a formidable task to give my story. I am affected because I love my *unmentionable* children. I would be helpful to others whenever possible, but I can give only a part of my story.

The love of my *unmentionable* children has caused me to deal with mystery. It has activated me. It has stirred my curiosity and nudged my soul. It has caused me to search for answers. It has led to a deeper faith and a better understanding of history, culture, and human relationships. I have achieved a more wholesome understanding of theology and gained an enhanced desire to become more humane.

I was on the listening committee of the joint General Conference Mennonite (GC) and Mennonite (MC) churches in the early 1990's. At that time I remember telling the other members of the listening committee that we were assigned the wrong subject. Instead of dealing with homosexuality (the *unmentionable* subject) we should be talking about the sin of the church and its tenacious adherence to the enculturated fear of people who are different. What devastation has been wrought by this sin!

This sin is a form of idolatry! Christianity is not a religion of the book with "proof texting" quotations. Instead, the starting point for Christian theology and authority is God as revealed in Jesus who is called the Christ. The hermeneutical key in the Bible is a story climaxing in the Incarnation. It is the fundamental point of orientation for the community of faith.

On October 1, 1997 the *Wichita Eagle* newspaper carried a story, "Bishops urge parents to support homosexual children." In a ground breaking pastoral letter, the Roman Catholic bishops of the United States said homosexual orientation is not freely chosen and parents must not reject their gay and lesbian children in a society full of rejection and discrimination. God does not love someone any less simply because he or she is gay. The document also encourages priests to welcome homosexuals into parishes, to help establish or promote support groups for parents of gay children, and to let people know from the pulpit and elsewhere that they are willing to talk about homosexuality issues.

Gay men and lesbians are an oppressed people, even though they constitute a significant percentage of the world population. The church must bear the blame for its part of this injustice. Christians often lack sensitivity toward people who are different. Many gay people have been consecrated as infants and later rejected by the church and parents when the child's distinctive difference was discovered in adolescence.

The oppression of homosexuals has become institutionalized in both church polity and laws of America. Some political bigots are even advocating more drastic laws while church conference leadership moves to oust some congregations who are accepting gays into their fellowship. The church should become a leader in gay liberation, not an instrument of oppression and pain!

My understanding of the Gospel includes the imperative to welcome the stranger, promote justice for the oppressed, and to love your neighbor as yourself. Remember the parable of the Good Samaritan? Are homosexuals my neighbors? Yes, indeed!

I believe gay and lesbian people in our fear-ridden society experience intense pain, at the deepest level of human relationships. The taboo against homosexuality does not allow them to openly express their emotional commitment to the people they love. In many cases they are coerced into a life of great deception. Among gay people there is a rising tide of resistance to leading a double life and we, who love the church, should welcome that resistance.

I am inspired by a renowned clergyman who said, "Homosexual people are victims *not* of religions, and *not* of the church, but of people who use religion as a way to devalue and deform those who they can neither ignore nor convert."[1] This same clergyman argues against the zealous interpretative impulse that manifests itself in the sins he calls "bibliolatry" and "literalism." "To make the Bible the object of veneration is to ascribe to it a glory that should be reserved for God. To worship the literal text of the scripture is to make the letter superior to the Spirit — and this error leads the literalist to apply God's Word in a mechanistic, unreflective manner." He advocates a holistic approach that looks beyond the Bible to the larger truths of the Christian faith — religious principles that transcend both the historical context of the original writers and the prejudices of contemporary interpreters.

Can we be Christ-like enough to welcome, listen to, befriend, and confer with our gay and lesbian brothers and sisters, and allow the power of the Holy Spirit to transform the polity of the church, to accept them for who they really are as whole persons and call them by their real names?

Earl Loganbill is a seventy-six-year-old retired community newspaper publisher. He is the straight father of a gay son and a lesbian daughter. A member of Faith Mennonite Church in Newton, Kansas, Earl's interests include theology, human

---

[1] The Rev. Peter J. Gomes, minister of Memorial Church, Harvard University, and Plummer Professor of Christian Morals. He is author of *The Good Book*. The source of the quotes here is an article published in *The New Yorker*, November 11, 1996, "God and Harvard," written by Robert S. Boynton.

sexuality, conflict resolution, political issues, international relations, ecology, social justice, and peacemaking.

41

My Hope for the Church

T.O.D.

Living my younger life on a farm in a small community, I was always told that people were different, but all are God's children. This meant homeless, handicapped, homosexual, all different races — everyone! Unless it was a person who was lawless and dangerous, you should treat all with respect.

After moving to the city my thoughts have not changed. As I try to be a Christian, freeing myself of sinful ways and living for a better peaceful place ahead, I want to accept all people. When I hear others say this same statement and add "*but,*" my response is, "All are sinners and can only get to heaven by the Grace of God."

I am 77 years old. I have tried to be a good Christian in the Church of the Brethren. My hope and prayer is that people of the church will change their way of thinking and remember that in God's eyes all are loved equally.

When I was young, the church taught this statement of belief: "I will approach all people and all situations good or evil with a Christian attitude of sympathy, understanding, appreciation, and positive helpfulness."

I have two daughters. One is heterosexual, the other is homosexual. I love my homosexual daughter just as much as my other daughter. I am an older, handicapped widow. I believe that respect for all persons is the Christian way to live. Everyone has a handicap, even if they do not realize it. This in no way causes me to see persons who are different as someone I can not love.

To justify heterosexuality as the only Godly way of living, one can say, "God said go and multiply and fill the earth." But God also says to each of us, "I give you a gift to use to spread the good news that Jesus is Lord." Therefore if everyone, no matter who we are, works for the glory of God, by using the gifts we have been given, then we are doing our part.

Loving God with all our hearts and loving our neighbor is a great way of saying, "All can be loved!" This is true even though we do not know who our neighbor might be.

I am uncomfortable when gifted people such as singers or teachers, are rejected and shamed by the church just because they are homosexuals. The church loses many blessings because of this discrimination.

I feel deep concern for my daughters and the hardships they face in the world. This is why I pray that the church and the world will change. I hope these words help some people to understand the pain of those who are discriminated against and will help those who are hurting to be strong!

The author began life on a farm in West Virginia. She had four sisters, so they did many jobs on the farm that were considered man's work. She also worked in the community as a mother's helper and during the fall season, worked at a cider mill making apple cider and apple butter. When she was 18, she moved to Baltimore, Maryland where she worked in the BVD underwear and shirt factory and later in the Airplane Plant during the Second World War.

After the war she married and in the years ahead two daughters were born to them. At age 32 she became the victim of polio and was hospitalized for over a year trying to survive. Although handicapped from the polio, she raised her daughters and watched them grow into responsible adults. Throughout her life she has used the talents given her by God to serve her family, church, and community. She lost her husband to heart disease eighteen years ago. At age 77, she continues to live in her own home, surviving one day at a time by the grace of God.

Families and Friends

42

Lost in the Midst of Conflict

Anonymous

I sat on the couch with a blanket wrapped around me staring at the pictures of our two daughters on the wall. I was shivering all over. It was only early September, Labor Day to be exact, but I could not stop the shaking. My husband of 11 years had for the past three hours been trying to tell me what had been weighing so heavily on him the past summer. Through sobs and tears he tried to tell me. In my heart I knew, but did not dare whisper the words I did not want to hear. I prayed to myself, "Please let it not be that. Anything but that."

Finally it was past midnight and I suggested he write it down and I could read it. He did and I unfolded the paper. On it were words that would mean life from that point on would no longer be the same. They were words that would shatter forever what we had hoped for in our marriage and family. My husband in those moments finally told me of his 26-year struggle with his sexual orientation. He is gay.

Now I was the one sobbing. His first fear, as I sat on that couch, was that I would kick him out of the house. I knew I could not. As we sat there together in each other's arms, mixing tears, my mind was already racing ahead. We can deal with this, I thought. We can deal with it and no one ever has to know. We will still be the family we wanted, we will just have to make some adjustments and be more open with each other about what we need.

I walked through the next months in a fog. The next day when we got up it was as if nothing had really changed, yet everything had changed. I remember sitting and staring at the bathroom rug, admiring how its colors matched the floor, and deciding I would never move it. It would stay just as it was. I needed to keep everything as it was. I could not accept the massive changes that were about to come into my life.

The bathroom rug would stay the same, but nearly everything around it would change. I did not kick him out, but in that moment of disclosure he started to leave me. He did not do it physically at first. But within the next months he began to be gone overnight more and more often. At first he was still home more than away, then it was about even. Then he was gone more than he was at home. Finally, only two months after he opened up to me, he decided to move out. I was devastated.

I had always blamed our problems on myself. Now I found out it was not all me. However, that was little consolation. I had two children and a third on the way. How would I survive? How would I ever get through this?

This is the part of my story where the blame usually creeps in. If only my husband had not. . . . It is all his fault. The two sides of the homosexuality issue become even more polarized. People, upon hearing, want to be supportive of me, so they berate him. This is anything but helpful. I found that when others put him down, I felt put down. After all, this is the man with whom I had become one. When someone condemned him I found myself feeling that I wanted to defend him. Some people could not understand how I could do this and I felt even more alone and isolated.

When I first heard the news that my husband was gay, it put me into internal conflict. I knew that it was a difficult issue, mainly because the church has for centuries condemned it as sin. This was not my first encounter with someone who was gay. Throughout the years I have witnessed the struggle of friends and family who came out. More recently there has been conflicting evidence on the causes and origin of human sexuality. Yet on the other hand the person telling me he is gay was not a statistic. He was not a neutral face in a crowd. He was not even just someone I knew. This person was the man I had pledged to support and love for life. This was the man whose well-being I sought out as diligently as my own.

I saw what keeping his secret was doing to him. He is only still alive today because he was able somehow to fight off the impulse to end the pain by ending his life. I could see in his tears and hear in his voice that this was not something he had chosen to do because he thought it would bring him a more exciting life.

The moment he began to pull away from me, he also began to grieve for what he was leaving behind. He was leaving all the things that were considered normal — a wife, children, a home, a church — in exchange for a life of discrimination, scorn, and isolation. But staying in his present situation was killing him and moving on seemed to offer an identity he felt he had denied since coming into adolescence.

So how do I continue to live up to my vow to seek out his well-being and at the same time let go of my marriage? Last week these words appeared on a bulletin insert, "Whatever path you follow, let it reflect the Love of Christ." That has been my approach from the beginning of this painful journey. Each time I struggled with how to relate to my husband, I came back to the desire to show him God's love. I believe this is what he needs more than anything. In a world where there is anything but love for gay and lesbian people, I felt I could offer that.

Not that it was easy. Loving someone who hurt me so deeply took resources beyond my own human capacity. I am confident that God was and still is loving him through me. I know for many this sounds too much like I am condoning his choices. Friends, family, and counselors have urged me to get angry. Though some may find it helpful to get angry, it would not be the way that feels right to me.

In any case, the struggle has been exhausting. I had to come to the decision to let him go with his choices. I could not make him stay in a marriage that seemed to deny who he was. At the same time, he continued to express his love and concern for me.

It took me several months before I could share publicly what was going on in my marriage. One writer describes the coming out of the closet for a gay spouse as the other spouse entering a closet. From the beginning I did not feel that it was safe to let anyone know my secret. Whom can you tell? I felt that I was unique in this situation. Who would understand? Will they stereotype me and label me as they do my gay spouse? Would I be asked to give up my church positions if they knew? Would I lose my career? Would it be awkward for others to know what to say to me, so they would gradually begin to avoid me? Would I become just a novelty for others to gossip about and pity?

Trying to keep our secret was even more difficult. Living as if life was just fine and that the marriage and family were in good shape felt like a sham. I felt that I was walking around with a huge pack on my back that I could barely carry, but that no one else could see. To others I looked just fine. I gradually told a few family members and friends from church. Surprisingly, they offered support.

Now, even though I have told my entire congregation the bigger story and word is spreading through the grapevine, I still do not feel safe to disclose my name in this story. Not only do I fear for myself, but for my husband who would be the target of discrimination he does not deserve.

When the debates about homosexuality heat up in print or in conversations, rarely is consideration given to those who are the silent victims of its pain. Parents, siblings, relatives, and friends struggle with how to love someone who is seen as controversial and who is condemned by many as immoral and unnatural. We are the people who get lost in the conflict. We are the people who get caught between the two sides who wish to make their views heard. We are the people who are afraid to mention that we have a gay or lesbian son or daughter or sibling or grandchild or friend or even a spouse. What will people say? Will we be blamed?

I need to say to those caught in the conflict that you are not alone. I have been overwhelmed since my husband's revelation with how many others there are. My hope is that someday the church can be a place where people are not shamed for who they are, but where all who desire God's grace are loved and welcomed. There are no easy answers. There are no clear solutions. For some of us, more than you might think, there is only the pain and silence of the closet.

The author of this article is a pastor in a Mennonite Church. She is the mother of three beautiful children, two daughters and one son. She and her husband divorced in 1997, but remain friends and co-parents of their children. Changes and adjustments continue in their lives, but God is faithful and walks with them.

43

My Predominantly Lesbian Wife

Anonymous

About three years ago, after letting guilt bury the truth for decades, my wife came to the realization that she is bisexual. Teenage memories came flooding back to her — memories of being attracted to and aroused by other women, memories of an incident of caressing and kissing — long repressed by intense guilt. It took her almost another year to decide to tell me. We were very close, deeply in love, and she wanted the marriage to continue. However, I suppose she had to prepare herself for the possibility that I would turn my back and walk away.

I pondered my options . . . for about two seconds. She was still the same woman I had married and been with all these years, and still loved deeply, and she still loved me. I suppose I could have felt betrayed, but I do not think that is what happened, she merely made a shocking discovery. I made the decision to stay with our marriage and I have no regrets. Her honesty has brought us even closer, in spite of the fact that in exploring her true sexuality, she has become much more attracted to women than men, closer to lesbian than bisexual. Obviously, I consider it a blessing that she is still attracted to me.

Together, we have read much literature on the subject, the biblical and nonbiblical arguments on both sides. We have covered all the views from "Romans and Corinthians mean exactly what the translated words say, that homosexuality is an abomination to God," to "Paul was stating currently held views which he later refuted in those same epistles," and everything in between, such as "The word 'homosexual' as Paul used it referred to boy slaves," and "The sin of Sodom (Genesis 19:1-11) was not homosexuality, but gang rape and, as God says, 'haughtiness and preying on the weak' (Ezekiel 16:49-52)."

I have come to the conclusion that it is impossible to understand exactly what someone was saying 2,000 years ago in a different language and a different culture. Contrary to what many believe, this subject is very cloudy in the Bible. Let's face it, if we are going to take these passages as perfectly translated dogma, then effeminate men — and I would assume conversely masculine women — are also going to hell along with homosexuals. So, at this theological impasse I can only turn to God for an answer. What I have learned is the same thing as Peter in Acts 10:1-48, no meat is unclean, the Holy Spirit fell on the gentiles also. This went directly against Peter's understanding of scripture, but he was forced to say, "I am not going to argue with what the Holy Spirit is doing." Neither am I. I personally know homosexuals — including my wife — who are committed Christians. They follow Jesus and call him Lord. They bear the fruit of the Holy Spirit and my spirit bears witness with theirs that they belong to Christ. They are my friends. Some of them are in a committed relationship with a same-sex partner. When they tell me they are praying for me, I say, "Thank you," because I know their prayers are equally valid. They are not freaks. They are not degenerates. They are a minority.

I would like to get somewhat candid in this section. It seems Puritanism and other well-meaning belief systems have robbed Christians of one of God's most wonderful gifts: sexual intimacy. We think sex is dirty and ugly, when it was created clean and beautiful, as the writer of Song of Solomon so clearly portrays.

Since my wife decided to stay with me and remain faithful to me, to forego any relations with a woman in order to satisfy her sexual needs, I asked God to help me satisfy them as best I could. Having a fairly strong drive, I could imagine how strong her desires to be with a woman must be, since those desires had been buried and pressed down for so many years. It could be overwhelming to let them surface.

God honored my request, and I will very briefly share part of our intimacy pilgrimage over the past two years. We basically took two steps. However, before I begin, let me say that none of this has made me feel less of a man, incredibly, just the opposite has occurred.

First, I supported and encouraged her need to fantasize about being with a woman without guilt or shame (fantasy is not lust, is not sin). I described for her as vividly as I could what all the various aspects of sexual intimacy with a woman felt like (tactile, olfactory, oral). Solomon would portray it as, "enjoying the bountiful fruits of a woman's body" (Song of Solomon).

Initially she fantasized alone, later, I lay quietly beside her while she pretended. It was wonderful for both of us for her to be able to express this part of her sexuality with me present. It was not something to hide from me, I could participate in fulfilling her needs.

The second step was to include a fantasy woman in our own lovemaking. This has opened a door to a vast plateau of fulfillment for my wife, and again, nothing has been taken from me. She still enjoys me, and always knows I am right there, part and parcel of what she is experiencing. To help her fantasize, I touch her in ways that help her fantasy seem almost real.

I hope this was not too explicit, but I firmly believe God has helped me bring homosexual satisfaction to my wife. While I can not be a woman for her, I can be a fairly good substitute when she needs it, and I am still nonetheless a man to her. She says she feels incredibly lucky to be so sexually fulfilled, to have these homosexual needs to a large extent met, without being unfaithful to me. She never expected to experience that fulfillment in this life.

My wife and I feel nothing but acceptance from the triune God. We have peace in our hearts. Our sexual relationship is nothing less than a spiritual experience, which is what we believe it was intended to be all along, for all married couples.

So, my word of encouragement would be, if you are in a situation similar to mine, perhaps God can help. I feel fortunate in that my wife is still sexually attracted to me. You may be in a different situation. But who is to say that my willingness to experiment along with my wife was not a factor in her continued attraction to me? I can only speculate.

If your wife (as a lesbian or bisexual) wants to continue to honor the marriage, and you do also, it would be unfair to expect her to deny her sexual needs. Let her take the first step I mentioned earlier, by herself, without guilt or shame (remember, fantasy is not lust, is not sin). If she wants to include you at some point, give it a try. Ask her what she would like you to do. You might be in for a blessing.

As of now, I can only say that God has honored my willingness and desire to be what my wife needs, as much as I can be. To see her truly enjoying her sexuality was even liberating for me, her inner beauty has only been enhanced. And I am still a man, a very happy man.

44

My Painful Journey

Anonymous

We had been married 15 years. On the way to a counseling appointment, my husband revealed to me that he felt he was homosexual. He had promised our counselor he would share this information with me before our next appointment. My husband admitted that he was scared to share this information with me and kept putting it off until he had to. I arrived at the appointment numb. My body could hardly move — I was in such shock.

I had grown up with the belief that being homosexual was a choice, a moral issue. Being homosexual was a sin and persons could change if they wanted to. Long before our congregation had an intentional study on homosexuality I was questioning this belief. I started reading books and sometimes talked with other persons about their views on homosexuality. Over a very gradual period I was coming to the belief that persons did not choose to become homosexual — that they were actually born with homosexual or heterosexual orientations.

I felt as if my secure world and what I thought was a good marriage was falling apart. I had so many emotions all at the same time. I was hurt, angry, scared for my marriage, and also so concerned for this man I loved very much.

Our counselor felt that my husband's homosexuality was because he had been sexually abused by another male when he was 10 years old. He put us in contact with an organization that works with men to change their orientation. I also attended meetings of their spouses' support group. This organization believes that if you pray enough God can change your orientation, but they really did a lot of damage to my husband. He was already confused enough and in the meetings they preached that God could change you. However, when he shared with the men after the meetings, God did not seem to be taking away any same sex desires for the men who were a part of this group. They still struggled and many were tempted or went to gay bars to find someone with whom to have sex. Were our faith and prayers not good enough to enable my husband to change his thoughts as well? Gradually we came to realize that this was not for us. My husband's orientation was something that could not be changed and the counseling we were getting was doing more damage to both of us than being helpful.

I had learned enough in my life to know that keeping secrets inside of you was harmful and trying to go it alone without God and supportive people was not helpful. I knew that I could not keep this secret inside of me. I asked my husband who he would be comfortable with my telling what was happening. Gradually we told a number of persons in our congregation, a few friends outside the congregation, and most of my siblings and their spouses what was going on in our marriage. Most of this telling we did together. It helped us to be closer and feel that we were a team.

What I wanted for my husband was that he could just accept himself the way he was and still be committed to our marriage. Even though I felt closer to my husband because he had shared this intimate part of his life, I had many fears as well. I wanted him to find supportive people or groups because I knew how much I had been blessed over the years with supportive groups, but I was scared! I did not want him to go to gay support meetings. I feared that he would want to end our marriage. He kept telling me that he was committed to our marriage. However, as we told our story to other people I continued to be bothered when he would say he was gay. I wanted him to say he was bisexual because we still had a sexual relationship. His saying he was gay seemed to negate our marriage. We struggled with this for several years. Even though my husband is attracted to me, I now know that saying he is gay is much more authentic for him because his erotic thoughts are with men, not with women. I often wonder why we have to struggle with language as well as many other pains.

There are very few success stories out there about marriages that work out after one spouse comes out. We continue to struggle with our need to find role models of other couples who are in mixed orientation marriages that work. It is hard not to project a dim future for us when most couples split up.

My husband has always struggled with depression. I now know that much of this is because he is gay and has received negative messages throughout his life. Because of his depression, we have developed patterns where I continue to be the strong spouse who needs to hold our family together. We have been seeing a new counselor in the last year to help us work on some of the patterns we have that may need changing in order for our marriage to survive. We feel more positive because this counselor has worked with other couples who have mixed orientation marriages. But the negative comments about homosexuality, both in the world and in our larger church community, continue to aggravate my husband's depression and we revert back to old patterns again and again.

Recently a congregation within our denomination was disfellowshipped because they allow persons who are in committed same sex relationships to be members of their congregation. This action hurt us deeply and caused us to question our faith. Where was God in this unloving act? While there was a church in our denomination that openly welcomed gay and lesbian persons, we felt safe. We always knew, if for some reason we were not welcome in our church, there was a congregation in the denomination of our roots where we would be welcome.

When my husband came out to me a part of my life went in the closet. It does not feel safe to be open to all people about my journey. I have fears that people will be judgmental toward my husband without even getting to know him. What will they think of me as well for being in a mixed orientation marriage? It has not felt safe yet to tell my parents, our children, my husband's siblings, or the rest of our congregation. These are people that for the most part are very active in their church congregations and are very close to us and yet they do not know much of what we struggle with daily. This is very sad, but I am hopeful that someday we can tell more people.

Not all of my life is a struggle. I am grateful for many things. My spouse and I continue to find much joy in the midst of pain. I have learned so much in this journey and have learned to know many beautiful gay and lesbian people.

45

Strength of Love

Lora Nafziger

I found out that my mom is a lesbian when I was 13 years old, the summer before I entered high school. My life was changing and because of this so was my world. I did not know what to think or who I could talk to about this experience in my life. I was standing in the kitchen and my sister had just asked, "Mom, are you gay?" I was so startled I almost dropped a plate. When Mom answered the question, I ran out of the house as fast as I could, got on my bike and rode and rode and rode. I rode with a fierce intensity like I had never ridden before or since. I needed to get away — very far away!

I did not know that my mom is a lesbian until that moment, but I think I sensed that something was going on. I have always been a worrier. My mom says that no one else has to worry because I will do it for them. In the years preceding my mother's coming out and the subsequent separation of my parents, I often had nightmares — nothing that one could describe, but horrible nonetheless. I would wake up with my stomach in knots, sweating profusely. As I got older and these dreams became more frequent I would stay in my bed and read or go to the bathroom and pray. I was afraid that something was wrong with me, so I never told anyone about the frequency of these dreams. Occasionally when they became too much for me to handle, I would go to my parents' bed. They would comfort me and I would spend part of the night there. When my parents separated, my nightmares stopped.

I went to summer camp the week after I found out that my mom was a lesbian. It was a week-long Christian camp. Every day they had a time when the campers sang, did crafts, and played group games. That week we also wrote in our journals about forgiveness and love. We wrote about people we needed to forgive — people with whom we were angry. We talked about how we are forgiven and even though people hurt us, we need to love and forgive them because they are hurting too. That week I wrote about my mom. At the end of the week we all put our journals into a Jesus box, a box with a crown of thorns and gloves attached to the sides with nails through them. That night around the campfire we burned the box and watched all the ashes float away. All the problems in that box were given to God, because we did not need them anymore. I wept.

School started in the fall and my mom moved out October 1. I told my friends my parents were separating, but I did not tell them why. It was too hard for me to confront the reason my mom had moved out. For me, my mom's being a lesbian was a betrayal of trust. I felt there should be a few things a child could rely on. One of those things was that parents who are married are heterosexual. I believed that because, if they were homosexual, why would they even marry? It felt like betrayal of one of the most fundamental things a child ever learns or believes. I also did not want to tell my friends because I did not know anyone else who was homosexual and I did not want them to make judgments on me. A number of my close friends asked a lot of questions and could not understand why my parents were still friends but could not live together. Sometimes I wished my mother had just died because that would have made the grief more understandable and explainable.

The church I grew up in was birthed by a few families, including mine. When my mom came out to my sister and me, she was only out to a few people in the church. They tried to be supportive of my sisters and me, yet they did not agree with my mother's life choices. When my dad announced in church that he and my mom were separating, people comforted me and told me that what my mom had done was not my fault. Later people offered to pray with me against generational sin. It really bothered me that this was a church in which my mother had long been involved. She had been among the first members, yet people were telling me that my mother was not welcome. I was still active in the youth group and that year there was a new youth pastor. He found out that my mom was lesbian, so he talked to me, loved, and accepted me. He told me it was all right for me to love my mom and that I did not have to condemn her to hell. I did not even need to take a stand on the issue if I was not ready. Some of my friends who attended that church were not allowed to sleep over at our home. A number of my sisters' friends were not even allowed to come and visit at my mom's house. I saw people who had been my mom's friends turn away and no longer associate with her. They hurt me by hurting her.

Through this whole time my father found support and comfort within the church. They helped him with his grief and he made new friends from the church. The hardest thing I ever saw my dad do was to let my mother go. He wanted to do everything he could to make their marriage work, even though at that point that was impossible. I saw my dad cry and it made me angry at my mom. I felt that she was being selfish. By making her life more comfortable she was making the rest of us miserable. She told me that she had to take care of herself too. I did not know how I could take care of *myself* though. I felt as if I no longer had anyone to take care of me. I felt I needed to take care of my father and let him know that he was an amazing person. I also wanted to take care of my mother and protect her from all the mean things that people said or felt. My younger sisters, too, needed care. I wanted to make sure they still knew they had someone to take care of them. I did not want them to feel as deserted as I did.

A woman moved in with my mom after Christmas of that year. I was angry. My mom had asked my opinion about someone moving in and I told her, "No!" Bonnie moved in anyway. I felt as if my opinions were not respected. I wondered why my mom even bothered to ask. The anger that I felt toward my mom was directed at Bonnie — really more at their relationship. When Bonnie moved in, it made real the fact that my mom was a lesbian. It was the proof that had not been there before — the final evidence. I vowed that I would not visit my mom, though I always did. After Bonnie moved in and had "made" my mom a lesbian, I slowly began telling my friends. By doing so I found acceptance and love within my peer group.

My sister told people more quickly than I did, and she was often teased because of it. I wanted to save her from the teasing, but I felt she needed to be more secretive about our home life. Lisa, though, would never live something she felt to be false. The situation for her became worse when one of the people at my dad's church asked Lisa if my mom was "still living with **that** woman." Lisa did not feel any support from that congregation.

Through the next year I continued as an active member in the church youth group where I felt fairly well accepted. Lisa was too young to be part of the group. During this time I confronted one of the youth sponsors about the pain she had caused my mom and, consequently, the pain she had caused me also. She would not let her children visit at my mom's house, even though her daughter was my youngest sister's best friend. I told her that it was unfair for a child in third grade to be faced with friends who could not visit because of my mom. Sometime after that, my mom and the youth sponsor went on a picnic to the beach with their children. Their relationship was better after that.

My mom started attending another Mennonite congregation with Bonnie, a very small congregation. Now that church needed to face the issue of homosexuality. Lisa and I became active participants in their small, but very close youth group. I was attending a small Mennonite high school. By the end of tenth grade, most of the people in my class knew my mom or knew about Bonnie.

In the late spring of tenth grade I began dating a guy in my class. This relationship helped me to trust people and myself. It enabled me to deal with questions of my own sexuality that were presented because of my mom. We dated for two and a half years and became best friends.

Bonnie and my mother continued living together and eventually bought a house. My parents shared custody and the new house gave my sisters and me a place to call home with my mom. We met Bonnie's children and grandchildren. They became a second family even though for me, deep down, I still felt resentment towards Bonnie. In the summer of 1994, when I was sixteen, Bonnie was diagnosed with cancer. She fought it and the cancer went into remission.

During the summer of 1995 I decided that I wanted to be baptized. This was an important decision for me, one that I felt quite strongly about. A problem arose when I was faced with the question of church membership. Being baptized in the Mennonite church goes hand-in-hand with membership. I was an active participant in two congregations and did not want to be baptized in either one. I was fearful that people from the other church would not attend or believe I was making a terrible mistake. The choice of membership was also very difficult because for me it was choosing between my parents, and I could not do that. The politics of the whole situation became overwhelming. Because I was working at camp on the weekend, I used my dad as the go-between. I was baptized in September at the summer camp to which I had always gone. A pastor from each of the two churches participated in the ceremony. Though I had arranged the joint baptism to suit my own agenda, it was a learning and growing experience for both congregations. People from both churches realized that people from the other church were not monsters, nor were they uncompassionate people. It was a very emotional time for me and many others also. I am now an associate member at both churches.

Bonnie was then diagnosed again with cancer and she became very sick. In school we were performing *The Sound of Music* and she really wanted to see it. Because of her desire, a group of my friends and I went to the hospital and sang choir songs and pieces from *The Sound of Music* for her. In April, 1996, she died, I was on a choir trip when I received the call. After I turned away from the phone, my friends gathered around me and cried. About a dozen of us joined in a circle in the home where we were staying and held hands, cried, and prayed together. That circle is a symbol for me of very deep and true friendship. My dad came to pick up some of my friends and me and we drove home for the funeral. Bonnie had been sick a long time. During the last month, I was able to come to terms with my anger at her and settle it within myself. I was also able to tell her that I loved her, because I realized that she had become a very important person in my life.

The summer of 1996 my mom met Liw and they started dating. I decided that I was not going to make the same mistakes with Liw that I had with Bonnie, so I made an effort to learn to know her. I graduated from high school in 1997, and that summer Liw and my mom had a service of commitment. I was proud and honored to be a part of it. At the end of the summer I moved to Albany, Oregon, to begin a term of voluntary service. Both of my churches have been very supportive of me and my venture. I am learning a lot and trusting God to continue to lead me.

In Part One, **Gloria Nafziger**, Lora's mother, shares poetry and journal entries about her faith journey and coming out. See page 68, Chapter 12.

Lora Nafziger is 19 years old. She is completing a one-year voluntary service term in Albany, Oregon, through Mennonite Board of Missions. Next year she plans to move back to Canada and attend University in Kingston, Ontario.

46

Roses and Thorns

Keith Kratz

As the nephew of a lesbian aunt, the church's traditional stance of non-acceptance of homosexuality has had a significant impact on my personal faith journey in many different ways. If the Christian church were a rose bed, this issue is like a prickly thorn, inhibiting much of my desire to pick and smell the roses' sweet fragrance. Other smaller thorns exist on the stems of these plants, such as the view that non-Christians are going to hell, that women should not be in leadership, or that Christians should not get angry, but the homosexuality thorn is definitely the sharpest and biggest.

Like most people growing up in my generation, the one dubbed *Generation X*, my views of homosexuality were shaped by the prevailing view of society. This view was expressed in the form of one student derisively calling another a faggot or accusing him of being gay. With a parental vacuum on the morality of homosexuality, my view developed from these school yard statements. Thus, homosexuality was viewed to be something debased and abnormal, practiced by only a disturbed fringe of society.

This view changed in my high school years when I got to know the warm, funny, and humane personality of my father's gay sister. Developing a relationship with my aunt and other homosexuals soon made it clear to me that all the messages implanted in my head as a child were just plain inaccurate, if not cruel and cowardly. Thus, heading into my college years, it seemed as obvious and indisputable as the existence of the sun that a minority of society had a homosexual orientation. This had no relationship to whether they were functioning, responsible, healthy, caring, or anything else.

In my college years I began to explore the sweet fragrance of God's grace through the usual things a searching college student does: attending various churches, joining different religious groups on campus, and reading selected pieces of literature. As my involvement with a Christian group on campus deepened, some of the church's thorns began to emerge, revealing themselves in sometimes subtle and sometimes conspicuous ways.

The homosexuality thorn arose in full focus in my college campus group with the ignorant statement, "AIDS may have been given to gays as punishment for sin," and with crass insults through words such as "flamer" or "fairy." Initially, the prickly irritation I felt was not enough to keep me from staying near the roses. I liked the people and I needed a place to explore my spirituality so, what are a few little drops of blood? As time went by, "the Jews are going to hell" thorn arose, as did the "evolution is wrong" thorn. The homosexuality thorn drew major blood with an article in the school newspaper written by a fundamentalist professor likening homosexuals to "pigs at the trough." This article was endorsed in another article by nine students in the Christian group I attended. Suddenly, this flower bed had become a major health hazard. I did not break off completely from the group, but my energies and priorities certainly shifted to other areas of my life.

Much of the aroma that sustained my spiritual life in college involved participation with social service organizations, such as Habitat for Humanity. With this background, I began exploring another flower bed resting nearby, one that is heavily involved with social service and justice, the Unitarian/Universalist Church. Here, there is no homosexuality thorn (at least by official church declaration). During my stay in the Unitarian Church for three and one-half years, gays and lesbians were my pastors, my friends, my fellow church members, my fellow employees, and, in a spiritual sense, my brothers and sisters. The notion that they are more debased, vile, immoral, or disturbed than heterosexuals was now not only relegated to the fringe of the flower bed, but was escorted completely out of the garden.

Throughout these years, while my hands remained far less poked and pricked, I found the aroma of the Unitarian flower bed could not match the sweetness of those roses I had known in my Christian past. I thus began the journey back into the fields, looking for smooth, clean stems, stems of acceptance of all God's people. Fortunately, I have found a rose, Perkasie Mennonite Church in Pennsylvania, that is very smooth and has just a small thorn — that of majority acceptance of homosexual persons, but with no official declaration. Unfortunately, it is linked to a large bush of thorny roses, the denominational conference, that is almost consumed by these thorns, making it nearly impossible for Perkasie to remove its thorn without being cut from the bush.

The real tragedy of these thorns in all denominations is, of course, the injury it causes to gays and lesbians. They are kept from the sweet fragrance of Christ's church and choose other flower beds to experience their spirituality. Meanwhile, not only do gays and lesbians suffer, but this sweet rose garden continues to produce these menacing thorns, speckled with the blood of innocent seekers.

Keith Kratz lives in Telford, Pennsylvania, and presently attends Perkasie Mennonite Church. He works as a tutor for a tutoring service and a group facilitator for a traumatic brain injury rehabilitation organization.

47

Are You Gay? No? Then Why . . . ?

Grace A. Black

Recently a lesbian friend asked me if I were gay, and if not, why I would work for gay rights. I was telling her enthusiastically about my vacation at which I had attended a conference of celebration sponsored by the Brethren/Mennonite Council for Lesbian and Gay Concerns (BMC) and Supporting Congregations Network (SCN). My answer to my friend's questions was, "No, I just love a lot of gay people."

As I thought about writing a story of support for my gay and lesbian friends, I wondered how I could encourage people to an attitude of sensitivity and love toward gay people. My life as a gay advocate has not included much drama and pathos.

Although I was raised as a fundamentalist Christian (Methodist) and am heterosexual, I never hated, feared, or condemned gay people. I was raised in a family who identified more with the loving and accepting Scriptures than with any which might be judgmental or condemning of homosexuals. We believed in "Judge not, that ye be not judged" (Matthew 7:1, King James Version). When I first became aware that there were some aspects of sexuality other than heterosexual, they just seemed part of the interesting diversity in the world. My parents were always concerned about civil rights and were involved in social justice issues. Following their example, I have always believed that love and inclusion are a vital part of being Christian.

The first time I became aware that these differences could be considered a problem was during high school when one of my teachers disappeared. I do not recall that any explanation was given to the student body as to why he had been replaced. When I asked my mother why the teacher was gone, she told me truthfully that he had been asked to leave because he had taken two of the teenage boys to the movies and afterwards asked them to touch him on his private parts. They had told their parents and the parents talked to the principal. Mom did not rant and rave or attack him. She said some people did such things and it was a kind of sickness. It did not seem fair to me that he could not just get treatment for his sickness and come back, but the people in authority had decided his departure should be permanent.

Although I have learned since of other people that I knew in my youth who are homosexual, I was pretty much oblivious to this aspect of life until I entered nursing school. My classmates and I were clued in by our medical student friends to *The Encyclopedia of Sex Knowledge*. It was then I discovered the areas of sexuality that were omitted by my mother in the liberal sex education she provided.

The next step in my education about the gay/lesbian community came during my psychiatric affiliation. Our teachers scheduled individual conferences with us. The most memorable one was with a teacher whom we speculated was lesbian. During her conferences with me and also with my most frequent companion, she seemed to be trying to find out if we were lesbians. We compared notes and treated it as a joke, but both read and discussed, *The Well of Loneliness* by Radclyffe Hall, a classic about a lesbian heroine which the teacher recommended. I sympathized with the heroine, but knew that I had no such feelings. Although my friend joked about it, she came out as a lesbian years later. Having had this close personal friendship, as well as getting to know some of our patients who were homosexual, reinforced my feeling that gays and lesbians are good people.

Over the next three decades I heard about Parents, Families, and Friends of Lesbians and Gays (PFLAG) and other support groups and applauded families who were accepting and supporting of their loved ones. However, I did not really need to confront my own attitude toward homosexuality often. When

I did, I found myself being more and more supportive of homosexuals. Several times along the way I reviewed the Scriptures supposedly dealing with homosexuality and they seemed irrelevant. All the men of Sodom, "both old and young" (Genesis 19) were probably not of homosexual orientation. It is clear to me that the intent of these heterosexual men was to gang rape the angels. Since age nine, when I gave my life to Christ, I have been open to God's leading for my life. Early on I learned from an outstanding Bible teacher that two of the elements of interpreting Scripture are to invite the Holy Spirit to be present to guide me during Bible study and to check my interpretation to see if it is consistent with the Christ I know. If the interpretation is not in the spirit of Christ it cannot be correct.

For many years of my adult life I was a Southern Baptist. In this church I was able to grow spiritually and enjoy many loving Christian friendships. However, after about 20 years, I sensed that the church was becoming less inclusive. An example of this was their support of Anita Bryant in her crusade against gays and her efforts to exclude them from teaching positions in Dade County, Florida. This implied that gay teachers might recruit children to their way of life. When the Southern Baptist Pastors' Conference invited Ms. Bryant to be their keynote speaker at their annual conference, I wrote a letter of protest to the *Maryland Baptist*. Surprisingly, one of the two letters in response criticized me for daring to criticize the Pastors' Conference, but said nothing about my attitude toward homosexuality. I also received a late night, low-voiced call from a young man I scarcely knew, thanking me for writing the letter.

After a few more years as a Baptist, we moved from Essex to Dundalk, Maryland, about five miles away. Since I was disgruntled with my church, I planned to visit each of the five Baptist churches and change my membership to one of them. This was a time of change and anxiety in my life, as my husband's health was deteriorating. Whether or not it was a conscious effort, I was looking for more security, serenity, and love in my church life. When it came time to choose a new church I decided not to visit any of the Baptist churches. I had been to Dundalk Church of the Brethren for several secular activities and had been warmly welcomed. Finally, I realized that I wanted to go there. It was a very liberating experience to realize I was not obligated to choose one of the Baptist churches. Although I joined a new members' class in the Church of the Brethren, it was without a commitment to join. I soon felt very accepted although I had previously been divorced, was a pro-choice advocate, and believed in inclusion of all outsiders into the church. They also did not insist on my being rebaptized. When the class was completed, I was ready to join. Because of my husband's health he did not attend church regularly but encouraged me to do what felt right to me. The pastors and members of the Church of the Brethren ministered to him during his illness although he maintained his Baptist membership.

Sometime after my husband's death, my interactions with gays took a more personal turn. In 1984, I rented a room to a young man from a nearby college. When he first came I thought he might be gay, but reasoned that, if he was, he might be less trouble than a heterosexual young man sneaking girls into his room. After I met a strange young man coming out of the bathroom in the middle of the night, my suspicions were strengthened. My renter still struggled to keep his homosexuality a secret, while his relationship with his "best friend" was deteriorating into an abusive one. He was such a dear person that I had become quite fond of him and sympathized with him. I felt I would know better how to help him deal with his pain if I could talk about his orientation. So, I asked him and he told me that he was gay. His next question was, "Do I have to move out?" I reassured him that I thought he was gay when I accepted him into my home and I had come to love him. From then on he told me many stories of discrimination he and others had experienced. Also, when his parents visited us I could see their love for him was struggling with their discomfort because he is gay — even though there are other gays in their extended family and their close friendship circle. Some family members love him unconditionally, while others love with reservations. The young man became part of my family about the time that the Human Sexuality paper was accepted by the Church of the Brethren. Also, about that time I went to the annual conference for the first time as one of the delegates of Dundalk Church of the Brethren. Wanting to experience everything at the conference, I visited the Dialogue Room to give support to gay people's right to be themselves. I wanted to learn more about them and how straight persons might help to promote better relationships. At that time the room was sparsely staffed by a few brave people who were very patient with an inquisitive old lady and her many questions. One of the young men told me that if our church wanted to learn more about homosexuality he would help us. Later, he was invited to do this. That week at conference was really my first exposure to the fact that there is hostility in the broader Church of the Brethren against gays. I had not experienced that kind of hostility in Dundalk Church of the Brethren.

A closeted lesbian pastor of our Dundalk Church of the Brethren resigned while going through the struggle of coming out to herself. Only a few intimate friends knew she was lesbian. Although she had homosexual feelings for years, she could not accept herself as a lesbian because her Brethren upbringing led her to believe homosexuality is wrong. As she finally came out with the help of therapy, I became closer to her and acted as her mother surrogate at the Connecting Families weekend. The pastor who succeeded her, other church members, and I supported her as she went through the heartbreak of losing her ordination. Although she had provided much leadership in the larger church and in the gay and lesbian group, she was vilified by some other Brethren leaders. For a while she could scarcely earn a living because of persecution within the Brethren Church. This was still evident at the 1997 annual conference. She has survived and moved on to become a very effective pastor at the Metropolitan Community Church of the Spirit in Harrisburg, Pennsylvania.

Over the years I have become more personally and emotionally involved with other gay and lesbian people and have come to love them also. The part of my life that is best known to my denomination (COB) consists of speaking whenever God leads me to an opportunity to speak out, whether in a group dialogue session or with individuals I happen to meet. God has made it possible for me to speak out on the floor of the annual conference several times and in numerous human sexuality sessions.

I had an opportunity to share my views at the infamous Greenmount meeting,[1] and in friendlier gatherings at Lake Junaluska and at Connecting Families weekends at Laurelville, Pennsylvania. My church and my workplace have also provided moments for dialogue. It has been a great blessing to me to see the quality of the lives of gay and lesbian Christians I know. They feel God's sustaining love even while being mistreated by people who claim to be Christian. It is a joy to me to share in the growth of the BMC and to see how this organization provides fellowship for gays, lesbians, bisexuals, and those who support them. It is very gratifying to see the joy of young people and their parents as they experience BMC events as a graced and safe space. As I have become more aware of and involved in the gay world, I have become more certain that loving inclusion of gays, lesbians, and bisexuals in the life of the church is God's will. I believe that friendship and advocacy is what God wants from me. Whenever I ask if this is still what God wants me to do, each time the answer has been, "Yes." I am grateful for this affirmation because of the many cherished friends I have learned to know who bring much joy to my life.

For over a decade I have shared my life and my home with young gay friends. Life has not always been serene. Supporting a gay adult who is like a son to me through the ups and downs of his life is as painful as seeing a natural-born child go through heartbreak. Whenever I feel that at my age I should be able to live a more leisurely life, I recall my belief that whenever you love, you run the risk of getting hurt. I have not yet reached the point where the joy of loving and the exhilaration of sharing the lives and the dreams of thoughtful, caring young people is outweighed by the trauma of seeing them hurt, either by the world or by their loves. I have also had opportunities to relate in positive ways to children of my gay friends.

As friends of gays and all of us who have gay relatives work together for the understanding and inclusion of our dear ones, the friendships we have made with them and with each other strengthen us on our journey. The day will come when we will

---

[1] A controversial meeting called by some Virginia churches to protest actions of several Church of the Brethren leaders who had acted in support of the inclusion of gays and lesbians in church life.

enter together into the Kingdom of Heaven where there will be no more divisions, only God's inclusive love. Until then, I want to be faithful in living out the reality of the Kingdom of God on earth as I join with the persons who welcome **all** of God's children to God's bountiful table.

Grace A. Black was born in Baltimore and grew up in Prince George's County, Maryland, where she lived until after completing secretarial school, several government jobs, and part of her nursing school program. Nursing proved such a good fit as a career that she went on to complete a Master of Science in Nursing and is still working. Most of her career has been in pediatrics or community health. In private life she had a great marriage to James Black who died in 1983. She has one daughter, five grandchildren, and 14 great-grandchildren.

48

Guess Which Sister Is?

Sylvia Eagan

I grew up in the shadow of my sister, Dottie. I suppose you could say I grew up in the shadows of all three of my older siblings. They were all bright and capable. They were popular and good looking. Maybe I was, too, but it was hard to notice that while living in their shadow. Still, I did not mind being the youngest. It had its advantages. I had all that accumulated wisdom at my fingertips. They went down the road of life ahead of me, and if they survived, I probably could, too.

I do not remember being jealous of my siblings. According to my dad, the oldest, Glenda, was a real sweetheart. To me she was the caretaker, a companion in horseback riding, milking cows, and other outdoor farm chores, and my best pal. Dottie preferred to do more domestic indoor activities. My brother was usually off working with our Dad. Mom seemed to hold my brother in a special place in her heart. Maybe it is because he was her only son, maybe to make up for the fact that my father made such a big deal of loving little girls. His daughters all sat on a high pedestal in his eyes. Dottie had a special bond with Dad through music. While we all learned to read music, Dottie learned to play the piano and Dad taught her all he knew. She was good, and she was rewarded for her efforts, but that all seemed fair to me, I guess. I was the baby, and as such my place was secure.

Glenda was seven years older than I, and when she left home for college, I lost my pal. Living in a very rural community in Southwestern Nebraska did not give lots of options for playmates. So Dottie was the logical choice. Not that we never played together when Glenda was still at home, we did, but much of the time we argued about what to play. Once Glenda was out of the nest, we were forced to develop our relationship. We played great imaginary games. There was "Aunt Mary" and "Finger-Nail Eater" and a whole host of games we played with paper dolls cut and dressed from the Sears Roebuck catalog. I agreed to a certain amount of paper doll playing in exchange for a horseback riding companion.

I was the tomboy. Dottie was the domestic. She loved fingernail polish and make-up. She was pretty and feminine, smart and funny. I was the dirty ragamuffin who hated to clean fingernails much less polish them. Wearing a dress was a necessary evil that was forced upon me. Dottie begged me to let her paint my fingernails and sometimes I let her. Then when they were just dry enough, but not too dry, I would carefully peel the polish off. She got very angry with me and I must confess that is partly why I did it!

High school introduced a new phase to our relationship. Dottie was popular with both boys and girls. I had a lot of friends, but never dated. I just did not have the feminine charm necessary. She was on Student Council, president of her class, pianist for the choir, and her grade average was at the top of her class. She was president of the Church District Youth Cabinet. Everybody liked Dottie. I was definitely in her shadow, but that was fine with me. I was proud of her, and it kept me out of the limelight. I did not like being the center of attention. We were becoming friends. Good friends!

Her high school boyfriend, John, was like a big brother to me. I loved it, and made great plans for them. It was a stormy relationship and I went through all the emotional ups and downs along with Dottie. Selfishly, I wanted things to work out so I would not lose my new brother. But when he showed up at camp one summer with a new girlfriend on his arm, I knew it was over.

That was the first of several emotional involvements with Dottie's male friends over the next ten years, including her first husband. I kept assuming that it was safe, because this one would surely last. By the second husband, I was beginning to realize that it did not pay for me to grow to love the men Dottie brought into my life. I ended up losing friends and brothers, and it was just too painful. I resolved to keep my distance.

The big announcement came one holiday season after her second husband left her. I do not remember the exact words she used, but she told me she had fallen in love with a woman. She realized that she was a lesbian. I am not sure what kind of reaction she was expecting. Since I had not shared my private resolve with Dottie, she assumed my rather cool response to her big news was because she was talking about a woman. She could have been in love with a Martian for all I cared. I was interested in what she was telling me, because she is my sister and I love her. If she had found happiness with another woman, that was fine with me, but I had no intention of getting close to another of Dottie's companions, male or female. It was a losing proposition for me.

Another thing Dottie did not know was that I had done some profound growing in my attitudes about homosexuality. I honestly do not recall whether we had ever talked about it. I assume I grew up with the usual cultural biases: it is not natural, it is not biblical, people like that are strange and maybe even freakish. I say, "I assume," because the subject was never discussed at home or in church or even with my peers. I had simply not given it any conscious thought. I became aware of my prejudices when I read a book as part of my exploration of feminist issues during my early post-college years. It was called *Sappho Was a Right On Woman*,[1] written by two lesbian women. The chapter that smacked me between the eyes was the discussion of how painful it was to be a lesbian in school and have to laugh at jokes disparaging homosexual people lest someone suspect the truth. How painful it was to experience the "Do not wear green on Thursday" custom, because wearing green on Thursday means you were *queer*! I had been raised to believe that the paramount Christian virtues were love and compassion. To willfully, or even unintentionally, participate in something that caused human suffering was unthinkable, a sin. My father was in many ways a biblical literalist, and one of the

---

[1] *Sappho Was a Right On Woman: A Liberated View of Lesbianism*. Sidney Abbott and Barbara Love. New York, NY: Stein and Day, 1972 and 1985.

things he took quite literally was that God is Love. Therefore, as children of God, we are to love one another, not hurt each other. To be Christlike is to show compassion even for those we perceive as enemies. In reading *Sappho Was a Right On Woman* I realized that I had participated in activities that had surely resulted in the pain and suffering of some of my school mates. My behavior had been far from Christ-like and I was appalled.

From then on, it did not matter to me whether I understood human sexuality. What mattered was that I learn to accept people whatever their human condition and to love all kinds of people because God made and loves us all.

Once we clarified the meaning of my failure to express unadulterated joy in her newfound relationship, Dottie and I talked freely about her self-discovery. Dottie seemed happier in her relationship with Ivy than I had known her to be for years. My resolve to keep a distance from her partner weakened as the relationship outlasted any thus far. I grew to love Ivy as a sister. As an only child, joining Dottie and her two sisters and their flocks of noisy children for holiday gatherings was sometimes an intimidating experience for Ivy, but she grew to love us, too.

Ivy conceived of and coordinated the organization of a March On Sacramento one year in opposition to a political issue. Our sister Glenda, Dottie, and I decided it would be fun to march together carrying a sign that said, "Guess Which Sister Is?" Most people were hesitant to guess and Glenda and I both got more votes than our more feminine looking sister. We proved our point: you just can not tell by looking!

Ivy visited our elderly parents with Dottie several times, but it was nine years before Dottie took the risk of coming out to them. I am sure they were not thrilled, and Mom went through the wondering what she had done wrong questions with me, but Dottie is their daughter. I am quite certain that rejection of her never entered their minds. Members of the extended family had various reactions when Dottie came out to everyone at a family reunion which Ivy also attended. Our brother and his wife just do not talk about it, but Dottie has formed a relationship with grown nephews in that family who seem to accept who she is just fine. Some aunts, uncles, and cousins have expressed a genuine desire to understand and accept.

Others worry about the destination of her soul and some are sure she just has not met the right man yet. When I was asked by some what I thought they should do, I urged them to pray that Dottie would find her way to a renewed relationship with God. I figured they would pray anyway, I might as well tell them what to pray for. Their prayers must have been powerful because in recent years, Dottie has indeed found a renewed spiritual life after many years of absence from the church.

When Dottie's relationship with Ivy ended painfully 13 years after it began, I once again lost a significant relationship, and once again I resolved to resist growing to love Dottie's significant others. Then after eight years of estrangement, Dottie and Ivy reestablished a friendship and Ivy has reconnected with the family. I have regained a sister!

In many ways having a lesbian sister is no different from having a straight sister. They are both my friends. They both have strengths and weaknesses. We have all grown closer over the years as the painful rivalries and conflicts of earlier life are resolved and left behind. We celebrate each other's joys and successes and bear each others burdens. However, because Dottie is a lesbian, my world is a bigger place. I am more attuned to the beauty of diversity, and also to the pain of people whose difference is perceived as an abomination.

Perhaps the greatest blessing of all is the built-in model she has been for my children and our nieces and nephews. My daughter fails to see why some of her friends have such a big problem with homosexuality. It is not a problem for her, she says, because she knows Dottie and Ivy and they are great people and wonderful aunts. So what is the big deal? Her generation and the next generation of children in the family need not grow up with blinders or blatant prejudices because they have a delightful aunt who just happens to be a lesbian. What greater gift could a sister give?

Sylvia Eagan is a clergywoman ordained in the Church of the Brethren and recently approved for standing in the United

Church of Christ. She is currently serving as an interim pastor at Bethel Congregational Church in White Salmon, Washington. Following graduation from Pacific School of Religion in 1986, she served as pastor of Peace Church of the Brethren in Portland, Oregon through 1995. The thing she finds most fulfilling in her ministry is walking alongside those who have been wounded by the church, or who have never experienced a relationship with a loving God. In addition to her ministry, she loves being a grandma, playing in her garden, reading great or even not-so-great novels, visiting with friends and family, and her cats.

49

Personal Sharing With My Church Family

Roberta Showalter Kreider

(This is a message I shared with my church family during an intensive study on homosexuality beginning in the fall of 1996 and ending in the spring of 1997. I had written the following article, "Fifteen Reasons Why I Have Changed My Mind," in May of 1995, but had not yet shared it with all of our church family.)

The journey to where I am today has not been an easy one. In my growing-up-years, I do not remember that much was said about homosexuality, but somehow I knew it was that terrible, awful sin that made me shudder to think about it.

As I read my Bible I *knew* that what Paul was talking about in chapter one of Romans was exceedingly sinful and obnoxious to God. I had never known anyone like that and did not really want to.

I had three older brothers and I very much wanted a sister. When I was three years old, my parents told me that we were going to have a baby in our home. I very emphatically exclaimed, "Well, if it is a boy, I am going to take him out and bury him!"

My favorite story at that time was about Baby Ray to whom the tree gave an apple, the cow gave milk, etc. I think my father had a good reason for reading that story to me a lot as we waited for the birth of the new baby.

I remember sitting on the side of my mother's hospital bed, holding my brand new baby brother and my parents told me I could name him. Of course, the name I chose was "Baby Ray," which I am sure was the name my parents had in mind all along because it followed their naming pattern. So we became the "Five R's." And, what about my threat to bury the baby if I did not get a sister? Why, I forgot all about it in the joy of naming and claiming my baby brother. He was so special to me and I felt very responsible for him.

We grew up as siblings, playmates, and friends. Soon after Harold and I moved to Kansas City, Missouri, to help my uncle and aunt at the Mennonite Gospel Center, Ray was one of the first volunteers for the Voluntary Service (VS) unit that was just beginning. He came to live with us until the unit house was ready and worked as a hospital orderly. I remember wondering how he came to choose that job since the sight of blood nauseated him. When I welcomed him home each night, he did not want to talk until he could shower and change into other clothing "to get the hospital smell off of him."

After Ray completed VS he followed us to northeastern Missouri, where we had moved to be partners with Harold's parents on their farm near Palmyra. Ray worked as a hospital orderly in Hannibal. When he decided that his calling was to be a nurse, he went back to Kansas City and took his training at General Hospital, where he had worked in VS.

On his wedding day several years later, we were alone with Ray in his apartment a while before the ceremony. He said to me, "Oh, Roberta, I am so scared, so scared!" I had no idea why he was so scared and of course, he did not dare tell me.

Ray excelled in his profession. He and his wife were missionaries in Puerto Rico for one term. Later he had a large part in setting up the nursing program at Hesston College. After employment by the State of Kansas as Executive Administrator of the State Board of Nursing, he accepted a position as Associate Executive Director of the National Council of State Boards of Nursing and they moved to Oak Park, a suburb of Chicago.

In the spring of 1984, Ray entered the hospital for tests. He was hospitalized for several months. Though I talked to him almost every Saturday, I never could find out the diagnosis or prognosis of his disease. But one Saturday when I called, I knew that he wanted us to come. So the following weekend Harold and I met my brother Russell and his wife at Ray and Ann's apartment and Ann drove the four of us to the hospital.

As we entered the hospital room, it was a shock to see the emaciated physique of my brother. After we all hugged him and sat down, there was an uncomfortable silence. Then a childhood memory, that had surfaced as we drove through the mountains of Pennsylvania, came to my mind again. So I said, "Ray, as we drove through the mountains of Pennsylvania yesterday, the clouds were so beautiful and fluffy and reminded me of how you and I used to climb up on the chicken house roof and watch the clouds. Do you remember the time we saw a cloud that we thought looked like Jesus and his disciples in a little boat and we talked about that maybe they were coming to take us to Heaven?"

He answered, "Oh, Roberta, I have been thinking about that a lot," and then he was ready to tell us his story. It was one of the most traumatic experiences of my life to hear the words, "I have a sad story to tell you. I have AIDS and I have nobody to blame but myself." He also added very wistfully, as if he really wished we would understand, but doubted that we could, "Since childhood, my sexual fantasies have all been with men."

Our greatest concerns for him at that time were that he would know that we still loved him and that he was ready to meet God. He assured Harold and me, when we were alone with him the next day, that he had made his peace with God. We needed to start home that day. That was the last time I was with my brother. Two weeks later he died.

I have searched my own heart though the years trying to figure out what happened to influence my brother to have such a strong homosexual desire that he risked his family, his career, and his life to fulfill it! I have cried out many times since his death, "Oh, Ray, Ray, how could you do it?"

I do not ask that question anymore and I would like to tell you why. I began to search, to read, to question people, and to try to determine what *changed* my brother so drastically from the sibling with whom I *thought* I grew up. Everything I read reinforced the judgment that homosexuality is a learned experience — a chosen one. So, even though it was my brother, whom I loved, I came out stronger and stronger against all homosexuality. I remember being quite disturbed at one of the men from our church when he taught the class on human sexuality a few years ago. He seemed to come out strongly on the side of making room for homosexuality in the church. After that class session, I asked myself and others, "Does the teacher really believe that we should allow non-celibate homosexuals to be members of our church, or was he just trying to get us to argue against it?" Well, he got the argument from me!

As the years went on and more and more rumblings were heard, I began to be terribly fearful of the time when this issue would come before the church. I was afraid that my church would decide to accept practicing homosexuals as members and then what would *I* do? I even worried that my husband would go with the majority and I would have to make a different decision. Then what would *we* do? To be true to God, would I have to go to another church? Would Harold and I grow apart?

We had some uncomfortable times discussing theology together those days. However, we kept searching and asking God to lead us, and finally, I became more willing to look at views other than my own.

Then the time I feared arrived! Harold came home from conference with the news that, in the next session, the issue of Germantown would be coming before the conference body, because they have members who are living in same-sex relationships. *Suddenly,* we knew that we could no longer avoid the issue! Because he is a minister, Harold was one of the delegates who needed to vote. The destiny of a whole congregation was hanging in the balance! We both agreed *instantly* that we did not feel it fair to vote about other people's lives when we had never listened to them and heard their stories.

So we began to diligently seek out resources that presented the other side. It is too long a story to tell of all the ways we felt God's Spirit pushing us on. There were times I became very fearful and started to draw back, but each time, as I cried out to God for affirmation, for guidance, and the assurance that I was not going astray or leading others astray, I received the assurance I needed, sometimes in some very unexpected ways.

One evening, in our home, one of the men from our congregation said to me, "Roberta, I would like to know why you have changed your mind." I tried, as best I could, to tell him my reasons, but I felt I did a very inadequate job. Sometime later after the Germantown congregation was demoted to "associate member" status (April 1995), I was awakened at three in the morning with the words, "Fourteen reasons, fourteen reasons," running through my mind. I became wide awake and asked, "Lord, do I really have fourteen reasons?" The reasons began to come fast and I knew there would be no more sleep for me that night until I got up and wrote them down.

The next morning I looked at the reasons, but did not feel like putting flesh on them. However, a few days later, it became like "fire in my bones." I am not much of a writer, but when I worked on that paper, the words flowed out quite easily. The fourteen reasons became fifteen and I entitled my article, "Fifteen Reasons Why I Have Changed My Mind."

Some questions I have needed to ask myself are: "What if it were my daughter, my son, my grandson, my granddaughter, or someone else dear to me? If it were me who was born with this sexual orientation, how differently would I view this issue?" At this point, it surely does not seem as if any of my children or their spouses are gay, but even if it is not someone related to me now, it could be my grandchildren's spouses someday.

My brother was in our family for 55 years and we never knew he was a gay man until he was on his deathbed. We have met a Mennonite missionary couple who have five children. Three of them are homosexual. On my mother's side I have two cousins who are gay, on my father's side a first cousin's son is gay and another's daughter is lesbian. One of the young men at Germantown is the son of my second cousin. So, you see this issue very deeply affects my life.

I feel caught in the middle! I very deeply love and care for each of you and do not want to hurt you in any way. It has been very comfortable to walk along together, affirming and encouraging one another without many major conflicts. Truly it is good when God's people dwell together in peace! But when I am about ready to say, "Let us just keep it that way," then immediately, I see the faces of our many gay and lesbian friends and their parents. I remember their heart-breaking stories and their long wait to be invited to God's table and I cannot turn them away.

I have made myself vulnerable with this personal story. I hope that you can still love me and know that I truly am seeking to follow God in the way Jesus modeled for me. I want those who differ with me, because of their own religious convictions, to know that I feel that they also are sincerely seeking to follow God. I hope we can keep seeking together and trusting that God will guide us.

Adapted from a booklet that contains this article and the one following. The booklet is produced and distributed by Lehigh Valley PFLAG (Allentown/Bethlehem, PA). It can be ordered from Ray L. Moyer, 216 N. Centre St., Apt. 5, Pottsville, PA   17901-2538 (rlm@pottsville.infi.net). Cost including postage: 1-9 copies, $1.00 each; 10-99 copies, $0.50 each; and 100 or more, $0.25 each.

50

Fifteen Reasons Why I Have Changed My Mind

Roberta Showalter Kreider

In August of 1984, my youngest brother, who had been my childhood playmate, died with AIDS. Just two weeks earlier, while visiting him in the hospital, he told my husband and me his lifelong secret. He was gay and had always been gay.

I have wished many times since that brief encounter with the person he really was that we could have been granted more time so that he could help me understand this complex reality. But for some reason (possibly my own pious and judgmental attitude that kept him from sharing this secret with me) our time of unmasked openness with each other was limited to a few short hours. Yet it was freeing for both of us to realize that when the secret was out in the open, we loved each other more deeply than ever before.

Because this issue touched me so personally, I began to search and try to understand the gay/lesbian issue. It has only been within the last two or three years that I began to see that the beliefs I had held all my life might not be absolutely correct. I want to share with you the reasons why I have changed my mind.

1. The testimony of my brother's wife

My sister-in-law did not allow the tragic death of her husband to make her bitter. Nor did she shrink into oblivion and live as a recluse. She had only a few months to adjust to the truth about who her husband really was. That time became a time of new openness, understanding, and compassion between them. After his death she sought out his gay friends and learned to know them. She sat by the bedsides of persons dying with AIDS and ministered to them. She became director of pastoral care of an organization that promotes understanding and caring for these afflicted people. She began to share her story and became an advocate for gay and lesbian people. Families with homosexual members began to come to her for understanding and counsel. She has touched the lives of many people throughout the United States and Canada because of her compassionate understanding. Today she serves as associate pastor of a Mennonite Church in Denver, Colorado.[1] In our discussions together she has helped me to a new and deeper understanding of Scripture on this issue.

2. The testimony of my brother's life

My brother was an excellent nurse. We had not known about the special contributions he had made to the nursing profession until some of his colleagues shared this information during the memorial service. The Governor of Kansas sent a letter of condolence to his wife and children with appreciation for his services as Executive Administrator of the State Board of Nursing. When he died he was Associate Executive Director of the National Council of State Boards of Nursing.

He was a respected member of his church. When they learned his lifelong secret, they did not shun him, but made it possible for him to die at home through their round-the-clock care for him and his family.

3. The testimony of Peter to the Church at Jerusalem concerning fraternizing with Gentiles

Circumcision was at the heart of God's covenant with Abraham (Genesis 17:9-14). It was the sign of the everlasting covenant between God and God's people. The importance of this rite is emphasized in Genesis 17:14[2]: "Any uncircumcised male who is not circumcised shall be cut off from his people, he has broken my covenant." This became such an important

---

[1] This article was written in May 1995. Presently my sister-in-law is serving as an interim pastor at a Mennonite Church in Kansas.

[2] All Scripture is from The New Revised Standard Version.

doctrine of the Jewish faith that to eat or fellowship with an uncircumcised Gentile was unthinkable. So we can understand Peter's consternation with God's object lesson (repeated three times) that he was to do something contrary to what he had always taught and believed firmly to be right.

Peter was called to account for his actions by the circumcised believers in Jerusalem. Step by step, he told how God led him to act contrary to the tradition and teaching of the church when he went to the home of a Gentile. Then he said, "And as I began to speak, the Holy Spirit fell upon them just as it had upon us at the beginning. If then God gave them the same gift that he gave us when we believed in the Lord Jesus Christ, who was I that I could hinder God?" (Acts 11:15 and 17).

I thank God that Peter was willing to risk his reputation and position as a leader of the church to follow the truth to which God was leading him. If Peter had not obeyed, where would we Gentiles be today?

4. New insights in books and articles written by biblical scholars

As I looked to God to guide me, more and more resources were brought to my attention. You will find an up-dated list under Resources for Study of Homosexuality at the end of this book.

5. The testimony of an associate pastor of a church that provides a "safe haven" for all people

This friend and I worked together for several years in our conference offices. My husband and I went to visit the church at Germantown and had an interview with this pastor. When I asked her how she had come to believe that it was right to include homosexual people as members, she replied, "My parental home was always an open and welcoming home. So I learned to accept all people." Further dialogue with her helped us understand why this congregation had to risk the censure of the conference body in order to follow the way God was leading them.

6. Personal witness of Christian gays and lesbians

The video, *Body of Dissent,* prepared by the Brethren/Mennonite Council for Lesbian and Gay Concerns

(BMC), helped me get in touch with the personal struggle and pain of people who are born with homosexual orientation. I also read the book, *Stranger at the Gate: How to be Christian and Gay in America*, by Mel White.

The next step was to personally meet and know gays and lesbians. In all the years I wanted to learn to know these people so I could help them change, God brought only one to me and he did not need my help to change. Now that I have allowed God to change me I have many gay and lesbian friends. Their lives have greatly enriched mine. I continue to be challenged by their sincere desire to know and honor God.

7. Testimony of straight members of a safe haven church

The members we have talked to from the Germantown Mennonite Church, who are of heterosexual orientation, have assured us that they do indeed see evidence of the Holy Spirit's work in the lives of the gays and lesbians who worship with them. Because God has given the witness of God's Spirit within God's homosexual children, they can not refuse membership to them.

8. Testimony of parents of gays and lesbians

We are continuing to meet more and more parents of gay people. I never before realized how many children of this sexual orientation are born to families who are highly regarded as sound biblical families in our Mennonite Churches. Their sons and daughters are neither rebelling against God, their families, or the church. I have been much impressed by the quality of relationships among these family members. Most of the parents we know are very supportive of their children. My husband and I frequently attend the Connecting Families weekends. This is a group of families from Brethren and Mennonite Churches (other denominations are also represented) who meet together once a year to learn from and support one another. One couple we met had been members of a Mennonite Church, but when their lesbian daughter was not accepted, they supported her by going to a denomination that would welcome them all. How sad that such gifted persons needed to find fellowship elsewhere! I had the privilege of sitting in with a small group of mothers who have lesbian daughters. Each mother shared the *gift* that her daughter has been to her. The relationships expressed were, without exception, loving and warm.

9. Testimony of Christians throughout the broader church

Letters to "Readers Say" (*Gospel Herald*, now known as *the Mennonite*) and "Viewpoint" (*Mennonite Weekly Review*) have strengthened and added more insights to the truth I have been seeking. Especially meaningful to me have been the letters written by persons who at various times in my life have walked *the path* with me.

10. Loving, committed relationships of same sex monogamous partnerships

My husband and I have been blessed with the privilege of being a guest in one of these homes. There we also met other couples. We are inspired by their love and respect for each other.

11. Actual success rate of ex-gay ministries

I am certain that ministries designed to help gay people change do help some to change. People, who have much more knowledge on this subject than I, describe it as a continuum, where at one end are people completely heterosexual, at the other end, completely homosexual, with varying degrees toward the center. Those nearest the center are the ones who are able to change. Many people say, "But God can change all of them." Some of my gay friends have earnestly prayed for God to help them change, but they have finally found peace by accepting themselves as people created by God to honor God. In this acceptance they have come to a new realization of God's love for them.

12. Contributions to the Church and society by gay and lesbian people

King James I of England, who authorized the revered King James Version of the Bible, was homosexual. So also were artists, Michelangelo, who painted the frescoes on the ceiling of the Sistine Chapel in the Vatican, and Leonardo daVinci, painter of "The Lord's Supper." On the lesbian side are Willa Cather, a writer, and James Miranda Barry, the first British woman doctor, who passed as a man all her life to avoid the consequences of full disclosure.[3] There are many more!

13. The church has been wrong before

Yes, I know the church has voted and usually that settles it for me, but this time it does not. Years ago my father was denied church membership because, as a banker, he wrote insurance policies. (Some of the people who voted him out came to him for insurance.) Later when that no longer seemed to be "sin," the church leaders again considered if he might be a member. That time he did not want to take off his tie! So my family suffered the consequences of that decision. I am sure that many of you in my age group (65-75) can recall other instances where the church has been wrong.

In the days of slavery some church people used the Bible to prove that it was right to own slaves. Other church people laid their lives on the line to provide an underground railroad to freedom for many slaves. Today my husband and I feel God has called us to put our lives on the line in a different way.

We do not like conflict and feel much more comfortable when brothers and sisters live together in peace. But we cannot accept the kind of peace that shames our homosexual brothers and sisters for being who they are (using terms borrowed from Lewis B. Smedes in his book, *Shame and Grace*).

14. I know what it feels like to be judged a sinner

While I was suffering for years from a strange and puzzling illness, a beloved family member wrote several letters telling me that I could get well if I would "quit my sinning." My sins were sins of dress and hair style. I knew then (and still know) that I am accepted and loved by God, for God's own Spirit affirms that truth to me. But I know how frustrating it is to be told, "God cannot accept you because you do not live the way I interpret the Bible." I am sure I have done my share of making people feel rejected by God with my own narrow interpretations and for that, I am truly sorry. If I would have followed Jesus' new commandment to love others just as Jesus loves me (John

---

[3] Quoted from *Homosexuals in History* by A. L. Rowfe and *Lesbian Lives* by Barbara Grier and Coletta Reid in *Is the Homosexual My Neighbor?* (p. 30ff) by Letha Scanzoni and Virginia Ramey Mollenkott.

13:34) and if my church could have trusted God to do the judging, I believe my brother might be alive today.

After an intense day of debating this issue in our conference (April 1995) that ended with a majority vote to make the Germantown Congregation a "second class" congregation, we ate dinner at a local restaurant with one of our friends. As we shared feelings and experiences together, he said, "I always enjoy the peace of 'back roads' of the countryside, but today I will be glad to get back to Philadelphia *where I can feel safe again.*" Quite an indictment on a church meeting where we were urged to "hate the sin, but love the sinner."

15. The life and teachings of Jesus

Now I come to the most important reason of all. I see no condemnation for those of homosexual orientation in the words of Jesus, my Lord and model. I do see and hear condemnation for those who interpreted the Scriptures and formed their own human laws. But I see Jesus loving and identifying with all persons who were marginalized and shamed by others. In answer to a lawyer's question about which commandment in the law was the greatest, Jesus said, "'You shall love the Lord your God with all your heart, and with all your soul, and with all your mind.' This is the greatest and first commandment. And the second is like it: 'You shall love your neighbor as yourself.' On these two commandments hang all the law and the prophets" (Matthew 22:37-40).

I am sick and tired of the terms "heterosexual" and "homosexual" and I long for the day when we no longer label one another, but reach out in love and caring concern for each other, admitting that we do not have all the answers, but trusting God to show us how to listen to each other and accept each other with love, allowing each person to have the freedom that God gives to all of us.

I wonder what history will record about the decisions made by the church in 1995. I believe God is weeping for all God's children.

PS. *(added several months later)* **To All Who May Read This Article:** In sharing my experience I want to make it **very** clear that I am not advocating promiscuity of any kind. Nor am I making a case for partners in a "mixed" marriage (heterosexual and homosexual) to separate. But considering the pain and heartache that is usually a part of those marriages, I feel it would be much better if they were never entered into in the first place.

I am saying that God gives each of us freedom of choice and the Holy Spirit's guidance to make **good** choices. Therefore, in my opinion, the church should bless covenanted, same-sex, committed relationships between two persons who are sincerely seeking to do God's will.

Adapted from a booklet that contains this article and the preceding one. The booklet can be ordered from Ray L. Moyer, 216 Centre St., Apt. 5, Pottsville, PA   17901-2538 (rlm@pottsville.infi.net). Cost including postage: 1-9 copies, $1.00 each; 10-99 copies, $0.50 each; and 100 or more, $0.25 each.

51

Epilogue: My Song

Jim Helmuth

I have been given a song to sing. It is a song about who I am and what I feel and know inside. It is a beautiful song that is spontaneous and creative and flows from the core of my being.

Early in life I learned that it was very risky to sing my song. When I tried to sing my song, it was quickly rejected and corrected. The important adults and peers in my life all had songs prearranged for me to sing and they taught me how to sing them just right. I learned quickly and learned to appreciate singing their songs.

However, their songs were not my song. I was very unsure of my song because I knew it was different from other people's songs. I hid it and did not sing it except when I was alone. I was afraid to sing it. It had words and verses to it that I was told were bad, shameful, and sinful. I felt deep shame about my song and learned to hate it.

Sometimes, I sang parts of my song to others but held back singing it in full. In fact, I never really accepted my song until, in 1982, I had the courage to sing it out to myself on a lonely, desolate beach on Cape Cod. I sang every verse and every line. While it scared me, it sounded good to my ears and felt real. It had a beautiful but strange ring to it that was loving and happy. I cried tears of anger and joy. To my surprise, the ocean did not swallow me. Lightning did not strike me dead. I lived.

I was very afraid to sing it to others who had different songs. I was afraid of rejection and ridicule. I was afraid, so I just sang their songs, the ones they taught me to sing, the ones they expected to hear from me. Sometimes I sang their songs better than they did. However, their song was not my song.

Inside, I became restless and depressed. My song was wanting to burst forth but I held it in. I was in a prison of fear and loneliness. The tension grew and I could hardly contain it. If I sang my song it was out of harmony with others. In our family, singing off key was prohibited.

Then I began to find others who sang like me. I found a whole chorus of people who sang as I did. Their words and music were in harmony with mine. They liked my song and I liked theirs. We had a different beat, but it was in sync. I relaxed for the first time in my life. I let go of my fears and inhibitions. I danced with joy as I sang my song freely with theirs. I reveled in the delight of the God-given song with which I was born. Nevertheless, I only sang it freely with those who sang like me.

To the rest of the world, I sang their song most of the time and hid mine. Gradually, slowly, I began singing my song to others who did not sing like me. I looked to them for approval. When my song was accepted I was exhilarated. When it was rejected I was angry and depressed.

Most people did not understand my song. It was dissonant to their ears. Many were afraid for me and for themselves. My song seemed like heresy. It seemed dangerous and even revolting. Others only tolerated my song. Some thought I made it up just to be bad. Some people cried and pleaded with me to change my tune for them. Others accepted my song with open arms and understood.

However, I was letting others decide if my song was all right. I was allowing them to decide its value, but most of them had no idea where my song came from or what it really meant.

I became more afraid and confused. I wondered if I had better silence my song altogether. It seemed that if I could not sing my song, I did not want to sing any song. Life was not worth living if I could only sing other people's songs. I felt invalid. I was angry. Maybe they could play my song at my funeral. Then perhaps the world could hear it clearly. Maybe then they would feel the depth of my pain at having to hide my song and look beneath the surface. I wonder, though, if they could hear it even then.

I was perplexed. I was taught that Jesus wanted me to sing the song that others gave me. I was told that my song was selfish and hedonistic, that it was not love. I could sing it in my heart but not with anyone else.

I wondered if Jesus would recognize my song. In meditation, I sang it to Jesus. Deep within, from all that I had learned about Jesus, I sensed he understood. He knew what it was like to sing off key and be misunderstood. I felt his love. I sensed that he only asked that we sing our own song because that is who we are and how God made us.

Then, I began to sing it out, with less and less concern for others' approval. My song did not need to be validated by others. My song did not need anyone's approval. My song was the gift of my being, of who I was as a spiritual being. Who was I to question my song?

I sang my song through my body. I sang my song through my actions. I sang my song through all I did every day. I sang my song through my tears and my laughter. It became my life. It was an expression of the truth of my being. Then I knew I had come home. I had come home to myself with respect and dignity. I had come home to me with Love. I had to be who and what I was or die. I could then be a friend to myself and say: "Welcome home, Jim. Sing your song. Sing the one given you at birth. You have a right to sing your song. Sing the verse that was written with tears. Sing the one that was hammered out in anger and fear. Sing the one you once called shameful. Sing the one that Love sings as it passes through this earth. It is the Song that beats in every heart and body, for each one's song is only a variation of that One Song that brings us together as one."

Then I could reach down deep within and respond: "I will sing **my** song. I will sing it, friend. I will sing it, mom and dad. I will sing it, brother and sister. I will sing it, son and daughter. I will sing it, beloved wife. I will sing it, friend. I will sing it and live!"

Jim Helmuth is a licensed psychologist from Akron, Ohio. He has had a counseling and consulting practice there for 20 years. Prior to his coming out, he was married for 21 years and has two grown children. He now lives with his partner, Richard. They have been together eight years.

Resources for the Study of Homosexuality

Videos

Body of Dissent: Lesbian and Gay Mennonites and Brethren Continue the Journey. (39 min.) Toronto: Bridge Video Productions, 1994. Personal stories of lesbian and gay people from Mennonite and Brethren backgrounds. Available from BMC, P.O. Box 6300, Minneapolis, MN 55406-0300. (612)722-6906. E-mail: BMCouncil@aol.com

How Can I Be Sure God Loves Me Too? (23 min.), *The Rhetoric of Intolerance* (29 min.), and *The Trials of Jimmy Creech* (28 min.). Three messages by Mel White on one video. ($6.00) Available from Dubose McLane, 500 East Marilyn Avenue, Apartment E-75, State College, PA 16801-6267. Telephone: (814)231-8318. E-mail: foxdaler@juno.com

Marsha Stevens Live in Concert. (Part 1, 59 min. - Part 2, 36 min. - Total, 95 min.) Costa Mesa, CA: BALM Publishing, 1993. Marsha Stevens, who wrote and composed the song, "For Those Tears I Died," when she was 16 years old, presents 14 songs that were written by her and composed with the aid of others from the Universal Fellowship of Metropolitan Community Churches. She also shares anecdotes and her personal story of being a lesbian woman of faith. Available from BALM Publishing, P.O. Box 1981, Costa Mesa, CA 92628.

Straight From the Heart: A Journey to Understanding and Love. (24 min.) Woman Vision Productions, 1994. Stories of parents' journeys to a new understanding of their gay and lesbian children. Available from Motivational Media, c/o PFLAG Pittsburgh, P.O .Box 54, Verona, PA 15147. (412)363-8839.

Two Sides of a Christian View of Homosexuality. (50 min.) Tony and Peggy Campolo speaking in North Park College Chapel, Thursday, Feb. 29, 1996. ($10.00) Available from North Park University, 3225 West Foster, Chicago, IL 60625. Contact person: Bill Hartley. (773)244-5579.

Books and Periodicals

Aarons, Leroy. *Prayers for Bobby: A Mother's Coming to Terms with the Suicide of Her Gay Son.* San Francisco: Harper, 1995.

Barbo, Beverly. *The Walking Wounded: A Mother's True Story of Her Son's Homosexuality and His Eventual AIDS Related Death!* Lindsborg, KS: Carlsons, 1987.

Barnett, Walter. *Homosexuality and the Bible: An Interpretation.* Wallingford, PA: Pendle Hill Publications, Pamphlet #226, 1979.

Bess, Rev. Howard H. *Pastor, I Am Gay.* Palmer, Alaska: Palmer Publishing Co., 1995.

Blair, Dr. Ralph. *Homosexuality: Faith, Facts, and Fairy Tales.* New York: Evangelicals Concerned, 1991.
Contains two messages given to a United Methodist Church.

Borhek, Mary V. *Coming Out to Parents.* 1983; Cleveland, Ohio: The Pilgrim Press, revised and updated, 1993.

_____. *My Son Eric.* Cleveland, Ohio: The Pilgrim Press, 1979.

Boswell, John. *Christianity, Social Tolerance, and Homosexuality: Gay People in Western Europe from the Beginning of the Christian Era to the Fourteenth Century.* Chicago: The University of Chicago Press, 1980.

Buxton, Amity Pierce, Ph.D. *The Other Side of the Closet: The Coming Out Crisis for Straight Spouses.* Santa Monica, CA: IBS Press, Inc., 1991.
Not written from a Christian viewpoint.

Cantwell, Mary Ann. *Homosexuality: The Secret a Child Dare Not Tell.* San Rafael, CA: Rafael Press, 1996.

"Christians and Homosexuality: Dancing Toward the Light," special issue of *The Other Side* magazine, 300 W. Apsley, Philadelphia, PA, 1994.

Cole, Beverly. *Cleaning Closets: A Mother's Story.* St. Louis, MO: Chalice Press, 1995.

Cook, Ann Thompson. *And God Loves Each One.* Washington, D.C.: Task Force on Reconciliation, Dumbarton United Methodist Church, 1988, 1990.

England, Michael E. *The Bible and Homosexuality,* 5th ed. Gaithersburg, MD: Chi Rho Press, 1998.

Glaser, Chris. *Uncommon Calling: A Gay Christian's Struggle to Serve the Church.* Louisville, KY: Westminster John Knox Press, 1988.

_____. *Come Home! Reclaiming Spirituality and Community as Gay Men and Lesbians,* 2nd ed. Gaithersburg, MD: Chi Rho Press, 1998.

Helminiak, Daniel A., Ph.D. *What the Bible Really Says About Homosexuality.* San Francisco, CA: Alamo Square Press, 1994.

Hill, Leslie. *Marriage: A Spiritual Leading For Lesbian, Gay, and Straight Couples.* Wallingford, PA: Pendle Hill Publications, Pamphlet #308, 1993.

Marcus, Eric. *Is It a Choice? Answers to 300 of the Most Frequently Asked Questions About Gays and Lesbians.* San Francisco: Harper/San Francisco, 1993.

Morrison, Melanie. *The Grace of Coming Home: Spirituality, Sexuality, and the Struggle for Justice.* Cleveland, Ohio: The Pilgrim Press, 1995.

Piazza, Michael S. *Holy Homosexuals: The Truth About Being Gay or Lesbian and Christian.* 2nd ed. Dallas, TX: The Sources of Hope Publishing House, 1995.

Scanzoni, Letha and Virginia Ramey Mollenkott. *Is the Homosexual My Neighbor? Another Christian View.* San Francisco: Harper & Row, 1978, 1994.

Scroggs, Robin. *The New Testament and Homosexuality.* Philadelphia: Fortress Press, 1983.

Spahr, Jane Adams, et al, editors. *Called OUT! The Voices and Gifts of Lesbian, Gay, Bisexual, and Transgendered Presbyterians.* Gaithersburg, MD: Chi Rho Press, 1995.

Switzer, David K. *Coming Out As Parents.* Louisville, KY: Westminster John Knox Press, 1996.

Thorson-Smith, Sylvia. *Reconciling The Broken Silence: The Church in Dialogue on Gay and Lesbian Issues.* Louisville, KY: Published by the Christian Education Program Area of the Congregational Ministry Division, Presbyterian Church U.S.A., 1993.

White, Mel. *Stranger at the Gate: How to be Christian and Gay in America.* New York: Simon & Schuster, 1994.

Williams, Dorothy, Editor. *The Church Studies Homosexuality: A Study for United Methodist Groups.* Nashville, TN: Cokesbury Press, 1994.

Wink, Walter. *Homosexuality and the Bible.* A booklet of an earlier version of this article that appeared in the *Christian Century* magazine, Christian Century Foundation, 1979. Revised version, 1996 by Walter Wink.

Organizations

Brethren/Mennonite Council for Lesbian and Gay Concerns (BMC), Jim Sauder, Executive Director, P.O. Box 6300, Minneapolis, MN 55406-0300. (612)722-6906.
E-mail: BMCouncil@aol.com
Web site: http://www.webcom.com/bmc/

Connecting Families, Ruth Conrad Liechty, Contact Person, 1922 Cheryl Street, Goshen, IN 46526. (219)533-5837.
E-mail: rliechty@juno.com

Evangelicals Concerned, Inc., 311 East 72nd St., New York, NY 10021. (212)517-3161.
E-mail: ecincnyc@aol.com

Parents, Families, and Friends of Lesbians and Gays (PFLAG), 1012 Fourteenth Street, NW, # 700, Washington, D.C. 20005. (202)638-4200.
E-mail: pflagdc@aol.com

Universal Fellowship of Metropolitan Community Churches, 8704 Santa Monica Blvd., 2nd Floor, West Hollywood, CA 90069. (310)360-8640. Fax: (310)360-8680.
E-mail: UFMCCHQ@aol.com

About The Editor

Roberta Showalter Kreider was born during a huge snowstorm on April 3, 1926, in a farmhouse near the small town of Inman in McPherson County, Kansas. Her three older brothers remember that they were sent upstairs to play and when they came down they had a baby sister. Two young cousins took a team and wagon across the fields to meet the doctor and bring him the remainder of the way. Roberta arrived before the doctor did.

She attended a two-room country elementary school near Yoder, Kansas. Her father was president of the small town bank and her mother was a homemaker. In 1943, Roberta graduated from a Mennonite high school in Hesston, Kansas.

Her preacher brother, who later became a psychologist, often asked her to teach summer Bible school in several states, including Kansas, Oklahoma, Texas, Mississippi, and Alabama, beginning after she was a freshman in high school.

There was a shortage of teachers during World War II, and after one semester of college, Roberta was granted an emergency certificate to teach. She and a friend boarded with a local family and taught in a two-room country school near Meade, Kansas. The first year she taught grades one through four and the second year she moved to grades five through eight, so another friend could teach the lower grades. As the upper grade teacher, she also served as principal. Janitorial services were shared by both teachers.

In April 1946, Roberta married Harold Glenn Kreider, a farmer's son from Palmyra, Missouri. He was ordained to the Christian ministry in the Mennonite Church in 1950. Harold finished college and seminary when their children were in elementary and secondary schools. The couple served in pastorates at Palmyra and Hannibal in Missouri and Osceola and Goshen in Indiana. Harold served two terms as interim pastor in a team ministry at Perkasie Mennonite Church in Pennsylvania.

In 1983, they moved to rural Sellersville, Pennsylvania, where they remodeled an old stone house with their daughter Evelyn and son-in-law Nelson Martin. The Kreiders live in the first floor apartment and the Martins and their three children live in the two floors above.

Roberta has always enjoyed books. When Harold was in seminary she worked part-time in the seminary library and after they moved to Pennsylvania, she worked part-time in the Resource Center of Franconia Mennonite Conference for seven years. Homemaking has always been a top priority for her. The couple has three daughters, four grandsons, and one granddaughter.

In their retirement years, Roberta and Harold are involved in seeking justice for their lesbian, gay, bisexual, and transgendered friends and enjoy the many friends that God has brought into their lives.